SEA OF GREED

THE TRUE STORY OF THE INVESTIGATION AND PROSECUTION OF MANUEL ANTONIO NORIEGA

J. DOUGLAS McCULLOUGH
AND
LES PENDLETON

SEA OF GREED is published by:

Deer Hawk Publishing, an imprint of Deer Hawk Enterprises
www.deerhawkpublications.com

Copyright © 2014 by J. Douglas McCullough and Les Pendleton
www.seaofgreedbook.com
www.lespendleton.com

All rights reserved. Without limiting copyrights listed above, no part of this publication may be reproduced, stored in a retrieval system or transmitted in any form or by any means: electronic, mechanical, photocopying, recording or otherwise without prior written permission of the copyright owner and/or the publisher, except for excerpts quoted in the context of reviews.

The authors have tried to recreate events, locales and conversations from memories of them. In order to maintain their anonymity in some instances the names of some individuals and places have been changed as well as some identifying characteristics and details such as physical properties, occupations and places of residence.

Cover design by:
Ray Polizzi

Layout by:
Aurelia Sands

Library of Congress Control Number:
2014941297

Printed in the United States of America

To my wife Lucci, for without her encouragement and support, this book would not have been written.

Judge J. Douglas McCullough

On Dec 20, 1989, "Operation Just Cause" began in Panama. The United States, growing dissatisfied with Manuel Noriega's involvement in drug trafficking into the States, invaded the country and, in less than a week, secured the victory with minimal loss of life.

Manuel Noriega was indicted in Miami and Tampa and, after his conviction, was sentenced to forty years in prison. He completed that sentence as well as a short sentence in France where he had been convicted in absentia for money laundering. He is now in Panama under house arrest.

Even though many Americans are familiar with this period in history, most are not aware of the remarkable undercover investigation that led up to the invasion and war.

The following story is taken from the original FBI files, witness testimonies, U.S. Senate hearings and recollections of the principal FBI agents and U.S. Attorney's involved.

The story is told through dialogue even though exact words would be impossible to achieve. However, events, locales depicted and principals involved are all factual, and based on case files. Names have been changed to protect the lives of informants.

While some events may seem far-fetched, they are based on testimony of Stephen Kalish to the U.S. Senate, included in Appendix 2.

The story you are about to read is true...

- CHAPTER ONE -
ABANDONED LADY

Bobby M, ABANDONED SHIP
10:30 p.m. July 7, 1982 – Beaufort Inlet,
Beaufort, North Carolina

Beaufort Inlet, situated on the mid-Atlantic Coast, and known to boaters as part of The Graveyard of the Atlantic, could be nasty when it chose. One of only three all-weather inlets on North Carolina's coast, Beaufort provided entrée to high-traffic, commercial container ships and was a harbor of refuge for a myriad of fishing vessels, sailing yachts, and cabin cruisers. The nearly 300-year-old fishing village of Beaufort was a popular stop on the Intra-Coastal Waterway.

Patrolling the area, and often saving sailors in distress, the United States Coast Guard maintained a major station near the mouth of Beaufort Inlet at the Civil War redoubt known as Fort Macon.

Like every summer holiday, July 4, 1982 resulted in an extremely trying time for the men and women who kept watch on Beaufort Inlet--pleasure vessels ran aground, novice skippers tried out their new toys, and diesels stalled as 900-foot container ships bore down on them.

That year, Fort Macon's " Coasties" were counting the hours until the holiday weekend ended. The sun had been down for an hour and the 'day sailors' had called it a day, retiring to local bars in Beaufort and Morehead City while Coast Guard Bosun's Mate Second Class Frank Verheul and BM3 Richard Hall patrolled the waters.

Frank wiped sweat off his forehead with a weary hand. "Damn, I'm ready to drop."

"Yeah, I need to start taking vacations inland," Richard replied. "I think some mountain air might be refreshing about now."

Frank laughed and shoved Richard good-naturedly. "You know you'd suffocate without salt in the air. I figure you'd last about two days away from the ocean."

"Well, after this past weekend, I'm ready to try it. How many calls did we get? Something like two hundred?"

"Sounds about right, and at least half of them were just kids playing with the radio."

"I'd like to get my hands on those little bastards."

The two commiserated as they untied their 21-foot launch and prepared for a routine patrol of the inlet and the surrounding shoals at Shackleford Banks. Frank fired up the twin-100-horse Mercs, while Richard freed the dock lines and pushed the bow off the seawall out toward the channel.

As they got underway, Frank set the game plan. "Let's work the inlet for a while. The earlier shift said some sailboats were anchoring pretty close to the ship channel. The last thing we need is to have some Panamanian freighter making port with a grease spot on his bow that used to be a 40-foot sloop."

Richard snorted. "Yeah, they anchor in the middle of the ship channel, but it'd be our fault for not placing yellow dye in the water reading 'No Parking Zone'." Both men laughed.

They motored out through the wide inlet. Boat traffic was light that time of night, so the running lights they spotted on the far side of the channel caught Richard's eye.

"Hey Frank, we've got some running lights off to starboard. Looks like they're about to hit the shoals at Shackleford. They're definitely outside the channel."

The young officer grabbed rubber-shielded binoculars from the console to take a closer look.

"Actually, it's two vessels, a small one in the lead and a larger one close on his ass. Looks like a shrimper to me. Must be from the Gulf; no locals run that close to the banks."

Frank turned the launch to starboard and gave the throttle a little push. They picked up enough speed to gain on the two boats and generate a good amount of spray flying up over the bow to hit their faces; cold but invigorating. The evening air was still steamy and heavy with the remainder of the day's 95-degree heat as they came alongside the smaller vessel and hailed it.

"Do you need help negotiating the channel? You're headed into some very shallow water."

The boat's pilot shook his head and waved them off. There was an odd assortment of men on board, which raised some red flags for the Coast Guard. Frank decided to follow behind the open runabout.

As they fell in behind, the boat increased speed and turned into Taylor's Creek, the approach channel to Beaufort. Richard followed the smaller boat's movements with binoculars, not wanting to lose the craft among the fleet of sailboats anchored across from the picturesque waterfront village. They had both gotten a vibe from the whole situation. They were now on the hunt.

"Looks like a lot of guys for an open boat. Let's see if they've got enough jackets onboard. Bet you $10 they're two short, and don't have current flares. You in?"

"No way, I'd bet $50 you're right! Hit the light."

The rotating light on the launch lit up a large section of the waterfront as it played off the storefronts and windshields of sport fishing boats tied up at Beaufort Docks.

As they came alongside the open runabout, both officers were taken aback by what they saw. The incongruent contingent aboard the twenty-two-foot Cobia jumped out at them like a neon sign that said, "something is off here".

Five men, clad in street clothes, one wearing gold chains, an unbuttoned silk shirt, and a sport coat, stared at them with obvious concern.

Two men stepped off the boat onto the dock, and briskly marched toward Front Street. The three remaining crew had a briefcase, duffel bag, toolbox, and SCUBA tanks. The boat operator moved from the wheel toward the side of the boat and spoke first.

"Well, good evening boys. What can we help the Coast Guard with this evening?"

Frank had just opened his mouth to ask them the same question when he heard a distinct splash on the opposite side of the runabout. He cataloged that away in his mind for later investigation, but pretended not to notice for the moment.

"We're just fine, Sir. Can you show us your life jackets and flares please?"

"No problem, officer."

He reached under the console seat and started pulling out bright orange life jackets. Obviously two short, he looked under several other seats. It was apparent he didn't know where to look for safety equipment on the boat.

Meanwhile, the two Coast Guard officers surveyed the crew. They were definitely not fishing. There was only one small freshwater rod in the boat, and the cooler on the floor of the cockpit wouldn't hold more than a six-pack of beer.

"Damn, I can't believe this. We're two short. Got flares right here though." He handed the three flare casings to Frank.

"Sorry, Sir, but these are outdated. What were you doing out on the water this evening?"

"Fishing. Been over to the banks, just watching the sunset and putting out some rods, I mean *a* rod."

Frank had heard enough excuses over the years that he could tell the difference between embarrassed negligence and outright lying. This was lying, but in his experience, it rarely paid to confront the liar immediately. He played along with them.

"Did you have any luck?"

"Luck with what?"

"With your fishing."

"Oh, that—no, we didn't catch nothing."

While Frank talked with the would-be fishermen, his partner caught a glimpse of the larger shrimp boat that had been following them. It bypassed Taylor's Creek and headed straight into the commercial port area of Beaufort.

Frank continued with his questions.

"Any identification on you?"

The boat pilot searched through his pants pockets. "Damn, I must have left my wallet back at the dock." He smiled wryly, affecting an affable nature to try to win the Coast Guard over. "This sure isn't my day."

Frank wasn't fooled in the least, but he continued to play along, just to see what happened next. "And what dock would that be?"

"Uh, in Wilmington. Just borrowed the boat from a buddy and forgot to get his registration." The guy did his best to look chagrined. "You're not going to give me a ticket, are you?"

Frank got a mental picture of a shark in in a guppy suit. This guy was shady for sure. His subconscious was sending him all kinds of warnings. He knew better than to turn his back on these guys. "I'm going to let you fellows go, but you need to carry identification on you when you operate a boat, and you better get some more life jackets."

Frank made a note of the registration numbers on the boat. Richard caught his attention and motioned for him to expedite the proceedings so they could follow the larger boat into port before it disappeared from view. Frank gunned the throttle as they sped off into the main ship channel, while Richard kept eyes on them as long as possible.

"Still see them?"

Richard sighed, but didn't turn. "No. They probably killed the running lights and turned into port." It didn't matter that he couldn't see anything any more. Something about that group made him not want to turn his back to them just yet. "There's not that many places there to dock a smaller boat, just a bare seawall and the fueling area."

Frank jerked a thumb back over his shoulder. "What did you make of that group of thugs?"

"They sure as hell weren't fishing."

"Did you see them toss a package overboard as we came alongside? I heard a splash."

"Affirmative. And I also did a quick triangulation so we can go back and take a look at what's on the bottom there. If the current doesn't move it off too much, we'll see what scared them enough to shit-can it. See the shrimper yet?"

Frank indicated the darkness ahead of them, answering Richard's question wordlessly. Richard shined a high-intensity spotlight along the wharf area. It was very still that late in the evening with no one stirring on shore. It didn't take long.

"Got it! She's tied up next to the State Port docks."

Frank took a deep breath. He had a bad feeling about this, but they had a job to do. "Let's go have a look at her."

The two Coasties motored alongside the shrimp boat, noting the name on the stern, *Bobby M* from Wilmington, North Carolina.

She was a wooden, about 70-feet long, and appeared to be nothing special as far as shrimpers went. In fact, the only thing that really stood out was the fact that she was tied to the dock with a single bowline. No waterman would consider that proper docking.

Frank grabbed a bullhorn from the console and yelled.

"*Bobby M*, this is the United States Coast Guard launch off your stern. We'd like to come aboard for an inspection."

It was the time of year when the Coast Guard and wildlife officers routinely inspected commercial fishing vessels, since any shrimp on board were subject to fishery regulations, so there was nothing odd about the Coasties calling to board. However, there was no reason for any shrimp boat to run around at that time of night, either. A dark figure could be seen in the wheelhouse of the *Bobby M.* Frank repeated his call.

"Skipper, permission to come aboard. This is the United States Coast Guard."

From the cabin, a figure appeared and moved toward the Coast Guard launch.

"Sorry, fellas, didn't hear you. I was listening to a weather broadcast on the VHF. My crewman went to find some fuel. We're running pretty damned near empty. What can I help you with this evening?"

"We'd like to do a safety inspection, Skipper. Anything in the hold?"

"Nope, ain't the season for shrimping, boys, but you know that, don't you?"

"Yes, Sir, mind if we come aboard?"

Both Coasties knew it was the middle of shrimp season and every shrimper in the area expected to be boarded and checked for illegal catches. This captain's slip was a major red flag, and if his face were any indication, he had just realized that . Sweat started to pile up on the captain's brow. He switched his tone to friendly immediately.

"Well, of course you can come aboard. I've got to make a phone call myself, so you fellas just help yourself."

Frank jumped aboard as the *Bobby M*'s skipper stepped off to the seawall to make his call.

The officer entered the shrimp boat's pilothouse and found an unusual assortment of paraphernalia strewn about: A briefcase with red letters reading *Lady Mauricette,* an overkill in radio and navigation instrumentation for a shrimper, a custom gun case, night-vision goggles, and SCUBA tanks. It looked more like the conning tower of a destroyer than a simple shrimp trawler.

Frank stepped back out to the deck area and noticed that a heavy canvas cover nailed over the hatch shielded the boat's hold. He lifted a corner to look inside, but as he prepared to go below, he heard an unmistakable sound—the pump action of a shotgun just inside the hold. He immediately backed off and into the launch. Richard looked up in confusion from the cockpit as Frank nearly jumped on him.

"What's up? Not going to check it out?"

Frank's eyes were round and wide as adrenaline started pumping through his veins, making him a little breathless. There was nothing like the certainty that a gun was aimed at your back to get the blood pumping. "Let's get out of here for the time being. Somebody in the hold was loading his shotgun as I started to go below."

"No shit?" Richard's adrenaline started flowing also. "What on Earth is going on out here tonight?" Not waiting for or expecting an answer, he powered the throttle up, aiming for a normal looking, unrushed exit.

Once out of view of the shrimp trawler, Richard pulled into a slip at Radio Island Marina and Frank called the duty officer at Fort Macon for advice.

"Yes, Sir, this is Verheul. We've got a suspicious shrimp trawler down here at the Port Authority docks. I'm not sure what they're up to, but when I was getting ready to search their hold, somebody below was cocking a shotgun, getting ready to give me a personal welcome. No, Sir, I'm on a pay phone over at the marina. I was afraid to use the VHF. Didn't want them listening in. They had more than enough equipment to make it easy to do so. They've got to be smugglin' something. The whole thing just doesn't smell right to me and Hall. We figured we should check in with the brass." Frank listened intently. He would never admit it, but he was relieved when he heard he should expect reinforcements on the double. The whole thing was exciting and scary at the same time. He'd seen his fair share of action, mostly small-time smuggling bungled by amateurs. This, he sensed, was something else altogether. "Yes, Sir, we'll keep an eye on 'em till you get over here, but you need to get a move on."

Frank turned to Richard. "Okay, they're on the way. I hope this isn't a wild goose chase 'cause they're pretty pumped up about it at the station. They said they'd be here quick as they could get the cutter running."

Frank and Richard watched as the *Bobby M* backed slowly out of her slip at the port docks and eased down the waterfront with no running lights. They followed, keeping their distance but never losing sight of the trawler. It wasn't long before they were faced with a major decision.

Richard asked the question they were both thinking. "She's pulling into the Texaco docks. Should we hold them till the cutter gets here? What do you think?"

Frank thought a moment, mentally seeing his picture in the paper with the caption "major drug bust worked by two Coasties". His subconscious changed the caption to "in memory of", making his decision easy. "I say we just wait right here. I've got a bad feeling about this boat. How many shrimpers you know carry hunting rifles and night goggles around with them?"

Around 1:30 a.m. the 42-footer from the Fort Macon station pulled alongside the small Coast Guard launch. Bosun's Mate Third Class Chad Weatherby leaped onto the deck of the smaller boat.

"Where's the trawler?"

"Right up against the Texaco sign. Engine is still running, haven't seen anybody topside for the past half-hour."

Chad looked the two men over. He'd known them a while, but never worked with them in a situation like this before. "Got your service revolvers handy?"

"Damn right." Frank and Richard produced their firearms, safeties still engaged. Weatherby felt a lot better having them at his back seeing that.

"Okay, let's check her out."

The small launch moved in alongside the *Bobby M*. Richard quickly tied a figure eight on the starboard stern cleat and all three officers stepped up onto the trawler's deck. Richard shined a large hand-held spotlight at the wheelhouse. All three of them looked around apprehensively. After a few seconds Chad said, "Announce us, and spread out a little."

Frank yelled out for anyone on board. "*Bobby M* this is the United States Coast Guard. Captain, we have boarded your vessel and request you and your crew present yourselves on deck, now."

There was no response. Foremost in the minds of all three officers was the pump action Frank had heard earlier in the hold. Sweat poured from under their dark blue caps as they moved around the boat. Richard shined the spotlight in every corner and dark crevice until they were convinced nobody was topside. Frank went back to the hold, tightly covered with dark canvas.

"Well, they haven't taken anything out of here since I was on board. Still nailed up like a whiskey keg. Let's just take a look-see, shall we?"

Frank and Chad ripped the canvas from the hold while Richard held the spot to reveal a hold full of bales of marijuana.

"Oh my God!" Richard exclaimed. "How much grass are we looking at here? Must be 50 or more bales!" None of them had seen so much weed in one place before.

Frank lay down on the deck, and hung his upper body inside the hull, looking all around. When he came up, he was smiling from ear to ear. "No, I'd say the whole damn boat is full. We have struck the mother lode!"

Chad picked up his handheld VHF. No longer fearful of alerting the fleeing crew, he called for the 42-footer to pull in close.

The next call was back to Coast Guard Station Fort Macon headquarters. He'd just keyed the mike when he paused and handed it to Frank.

"Verheul, this belongs to you and Hall. You do the honors."

Frank tried not to grin as he called in.

"Yes, Sir. This is Verheul. Switch and answer Channel 22."

Both ends changed to a working channel free of dialogue from other vessels in the area.

"We've boarded the trawler *Bobby M* at the Texaco docks in Beaufort. Its hold is full of contraband. No, Sir, I'd say you're looking at several tons of the stuff." The reply came through loud and clear despite the static. Richard laughed. Frank was quick to make sure they understood. "Yes, Sir, tons. Yes, Sir, we'll stand by till you arrive." The three men leaned against the outside of the wheelhouse staring at the open hull until the first group arrived.

By 3 a.m., the entire port was crawling with agents from all branches of government, each eager for a part in the largest drug seizure in the region's history. As investigators searched the surrounding docks and warehouses, the *Bobby M* and its cargo were seized by the Coast Guard and towed to Fort Macon station.

- CHAPTER TWO -
FEDERAL EYES

9 a.m. July 8, 1982–New Bern, North Carolina, Federal Building

Assistant U.S. Attorney Doug McCullough walked briskly toward the main U.S. District courtroom, a stack of manila folders gripped tightly in his right hand and a carefully-balanced coffee cup in the other. A voice he instantly recognized hailed him from behind.

"Doug, you hear about the seizure in Beaufort last night?"

He turned to face FBI Special Agent Terry Peters. "What are you talking about, Terry? They find two more bales floating up behind Mrs. Willis's diner?"

Terry had been with the FBI as long as Doug had worked the Eastern District and they were good friends. Both of them were in their early thirties, had the fit look of young athletes, and spent almost as much time together socially as they did working. The only difference between the two was that Doug grew up on in Swansboro, the son of a Marine Officer, while Terry hailed from Chicago.

"Not this time. Would you believe—get ready now—29 thousand pounds of marijuana! And good stuff, I'm told. Probably Colombian."

"You've got to be kidding. Who's bringing it in?"

"Don't know yet, but they left enough gear on the trawler they were using to open up some decent leads. I'm heading that way in a few minutes. Interested?"

"Tell you what, give me ten minutes to drop off these files and I'll ride down with you. Going to Beaufort, right?"

"I'll know pretty quickly. Waiting to hear from the district what they want me to follow up on."

Doug relished the chance to drive out to the coast. As a local boy, raised on the water in Swansboro, North Carolina, the coast was in his veins. He was glad to be working so close to home after Justice Department stints in D.C. and Philadelphia. He'd worked on high-profile cases and had scored a win as a member of the Philadelphia Strike Force that had conducted a huge undercover operation to infiltrate organized crime in the city. After all that, he felt lucky to be working just down the highway from where he'd grown up. It gave him insight into local crime. He wasn't an outsider trying to figure out where the locals were coming from; he knew their ways.

After a quick walk to the courtroom, he dropped off his documents and joined Terry for the anticipated ride to the coast.

"Change of plans, Doug. One of the suspects caught a cab from the Jefferson Motel in Morehead City around 12:45 last night; just about the time our smugglers high-tailed it. The driver took him to the bus station in Jacksonville. Cabdriver said the guy told him his name was Brad and that he was in a hurry to get home to a sick child in Houston. The cabbie didn't believe any of the guy's story. He stopped to eat and make several long distance calls. Cabbie said he finally just asked to be dropped off at the bus station, but he didn't know if the guy actually boarded one. Our agents called around with his description, and he matched a passenger at the Piedmont Airlines terminal in Kinston."

Doug's prosecutor mind worked quickly. "He had to give his full name to buy a ticket, didn't he?"

"Yeah, B. Cook bought a ticket to Atlanta, not Houston. Agents are waiting for him there."

Just then, the police radio in Peter's car relayed this information: "Suspect is male, Caucasian, 42, wearing black t-shirt with Jack Daniels logo. Last seen in Atlanta. Presence and disembarking confirmed by airline prior to agent's arrival. Suspect was not apprehended and his location is not known."

"Damn it!" Terry cursed. "That had to be one of 'em. Let's head on down to Beaufort and see what else they've come up with. I know the State Crime Lab and our guys are going through the boat with a fine-toothed comb."

"Sounds good to me." Doug replied, fully engaged in this new mystery. Both men were now on the hunt, and they aimed to win.

They drove to the Coast Guard station at Fort Macon where the trawler was under round-the-clock guard. Terry flashed his FBI badge and got them waved through the gate with barely a pause. They followed the road down to the docks where the fishing vessel was moored between a Coast Guard frigate and the cutter. Once parked, Terry and Doug walked over to the shrimper.

"Fred, you fellas having any luck over here?"

Terry hailed his friend and coworker, Fred McKinney, a special agent in charge of acquiring evidence on the crime scene; in this case, the shrimp trawler.

"Well, Terry, there's a lot of very un-shrimp like gear on board. Found some prescription bottles with labels from Louisiana still on them. And check this out."

The crime lab technician handed Doug a coke bottle.

"What's so special about this? Prints?" he turned it over and over in his gloved hands, but found nothing obvious that would make it a great find.

Fred grinned. "Might be, but what's so interesting is where it was bottled. Venezuela. And how about bread wrappers from Santa Maria, Colombia?"

Terry wasn't surprised. "Well, Fred, you didn't think they raised over six hundred bales of marijuana in Snead's Ferry, did you?"

"Hell, wouldn't surprise me a bit. You heard what the state Attorney General said—if he busted everybody there that was running drugs, most of the women and kids in the city would be on welfare while their men did time."

"Yeah, but it takes a huge operation to put this whole scheme together. I don't think this is a local operation at all. What do you say, Doug?"

"You're dead on. Let's get off this tub. I swear, you can get high just breathing with this much grass on board. How do you stand it, Fred?"

"I'm doing flashbacks to a weekend many years ago with a sassy young miss I took to Woodstock. Ever hear of that?"

"Of course, McKinney! We're not that square."

Fred barked a laugh. "Sometimes I wonder about you G-Men, know what I mean?"

As the two agents stepped off the trawler, Doug noticed two flimsy pieces of Masonite on the dock with *Bobby M* lettered on them by an obviously amateur sign painter. He called back to Fred. "Why did you strip the name off the boat?"

"Check out the side of the bow. They were covering up the real name, the *Lady Mauricette*. Oh, and there's one other little tidbit of interest."

"What's that?" Terry asked.

"The hold of the boat is refrigerated." Fred slapped his thigh absent-mindedly with the gloves he'd just removed.

Doug interjected, "To keep the grass fresh on a trip from South America?"

"Wrong. To keep surveillance aircraft from picking up the heat given off by fermenting organic matter. These guys put a helluva lot of thought in this operation."

Terry and Doug both realized they were on the verge of understanding the full scope of a very significant operation, but at that moment only one word came to mind.

Doug said it for both of them.

"Damn."

- CHAPTER THREE -
THE THREE MEET

7:48 p.m. July 26, 1982–Detroit, Michigan

"Son of a bitch! Do you know how much we've lost here? And I won't hesitate to remind both of you that this operation was paid for with borrowed money. Can either of you afford to pay McGhee back? I sure as hell can't!"

Michael Vogel was furious. A street-wise Detroit dealer with a taste for easy money, Vogel was far more at ease in criminal endeavors than his two accomplices, Leigh Ritch and Stephen Kalish. They didn't trust him, and for good reason, but Vogel served a purpose, selling the product after they got it into the country; or rather, he would, if they could get it into the country without getting caught.

Stephen Kalish didn't mind running marijuana to support his penchant for the fast life. Hanging with the jet set was his chosen vocation and he had no other way to make it happen. So what? Everybody smoked dope at one time or another.

Leigh Ritch, son of a wealthy Cayman Island hotel owner, had been born well-connected. Handsome, polished and capable of hiding his illegally acquired wealth from his prominent pals, his connections had led to the Colombian drug lords who had supplied the grass now impounded by the Coast Guard in North Carolina. They each had their part to play, but now, it seemed the whole scheme was falling apart before it even got started.

Vogel continued his harangue.

"You guys don't know shit, I tell you. People die for welching on drug debts!"

Kalish responded with his typical overdose of confidence.

"Doc McGhee is not going to come after anyone. First, it's not even big money to the guy, and secondly, I know all about his indiscretions and the not-so-wholesome incentives he offers to the bands he manages. He won't want that to get out."

Vogel wasn't impressed. "Oh, yeah, like a bunch of cock-sucking, long-haired perverts are worried that somebody might find out they smoke dope. Get real, Kalish. Nobody would even give a rat's ass about them."

"I think you underestimate the profile of Bon Jovi and Motley Crue. They're getting to be hot items nationally, and the authorities are always interested in busting rock bands or stars that teenagers admire. It's like sending them a message." Kalish shrugged and turned to pour himself another drink.

Vogel, on the other hand, didn't think Kalish and Ritch had a clue how screwed they truly were. "I really don't give a shit. I want to know what happened and how we're going to fix it. You ain't said shit, Ritch. How do you see all this?"

"The only way McGhee is going to get his money back is to extend us a little more credit. The plan was working out to the letter and we just fucked up one detail. We shouldn't have made the run while shrimp season was underway. Practically every trawler gets checked weekly during the season to make sure they're not breaking the shrimp harvest laws. We'll know next time."

Vogel stared at Ritch incredulously. "Next time? You want to do it again? Right there?"

"Why start all over again? The plan was working. We were home free and the law didn't have the first clue what was going on. Two incredibly lucky Coast Guard morons stumbled onto our load. That's all that happened. They'd never think anybody would immediately try it again, not in the same spot."

Vogel was still cynical. To his way of thinking, Ritch and Kalish were just spoiled, over-confident children of privilege who lacked his nose for deals like this, and he knew they were going to screw up everything if they didn't listen to him. At the same time, without their connections, he would never be able to step up to the next position he had in mind. They had access to the product he needed to build an empire, and make all his dreams come true. He knew if he pushed them too hard, it would ruin everything. Until he got his hands on what he needed, he had to play along. However, that didn't mean he had to do so blindly.

"And you know all of this, how?"

Ritch handed his glass to Kalish for a refill of his tumbler before he answered. "The mayor of Atlantic Beach is part of the team I put together. He says there was nothing on the scanners or the radio, and no one within any branch of the law there had a clue what was going down. It really was just a fluke they ever intercepted the *Bobby M*. Just a friggin' bad break." Ritch settled back on the plush sofa again and casually crossed his legs "I'm telling you, we can still make this happen."

Vogel's mouth watered at the prospect of the riches Ritch was practically dangling before him. The risk was high, but the potential profits were impossible to ignore. "Okay, and if we go along with this and it doesn't work, you going to pay back the money to Doc?" Vogel wasn't about to be Doc McGhee's pincushion if this fell through.

"I could if I wanted to. Trust me, it'll work this time."

Before Vogel could demand something more concrete than a verbal contract, Kalish joined in. "When do you plan on doing this?"

"November. The season's over and there's very little activity from the Coast Guard or local watermen. Who wants to be out on the water when it's cold? Our boat will go in totally undetected."

A phone ringing outside the room interrupted them. Vogel let it ring six times before answering. He had expected the call. His voice took on a harder quality as he spoke.

"Shine, you son of a bitch. Where are you? I hope you ain't got a tail on you. You lead the Feds to me and you're a dead man."

Shine was Vogel's demeaning name for Clinton Anderson, a hired hand and a middle echelon huckster who was actually smarter than anyone knew. After all, he'd convinced this "brain trust" to spend a huge amount of money on his "loyalty machine", a briefcase containing control knobs he'd attach to prospective employees of the smuggling operation.

The device supposedly read their anxiety level when asked questions. It was, for all practical purposes, a lie detector; but being a good self-promoter, Shine billed his machine as far more than a normal lie detector. He'd convinced the three smugglers that he could, using his wizardry, tell with complete confidence if they were being honest.

Whether they believed it or not was questionable, but they thought it was a great idea to keep associates convinced they could tell if someone was lying. If Shine said the crews were clean, they were— trustworthy, all honest crooks.

Shine was making a lot of money and getting first-hand information on a huge drug operation that stood to pay him a fortune if they could just make a successful run. He would do whatever he could to make it happen, and also to conceal from Kalish and Ritch that he was doing a little sideline venture with Vogel.

He withheld the news that he and Tony Reo had been detained by authorities at Charlotte airport, asked for identification, and had their luggage searched. Shine's stress evaluator had raised some eyebrows during that search. Reo didn't have his ID on him, but said he was a partner in Shine's Detroit auto dealership. They were not held and both went on to Detroit without incident.

However, Shine knew there had to be some reason they were picked out of the passenger list on the plane. It could have been the guy at the Avis car rental agency. Shine had chatted him up for two hours, before paying him two grand in cash. He wondered if there was anything he had said that might have raised their suspicions? He had mentioned that he was renting a trailer on Atlantic Beach for a couple months, but how could that have brought up any questions? Well, he was home and had more pressing issues now. Staying cool in front of his employers was Number One on his list.

"Hey, my trail is clean and cold. I know how the Feds think. I'm the last guy on the planet they'll find if I don't want them to. Me and Tony got back with no problems and I don't think none of our crew blew the whistle on the operation."

Vogel was constantly crude to Clinton. He wanted him to fully understand just who his superior really was.

"How about shutting the hell up, Shine! We need to talk in person about buying and selling cars. Don't want anybody eavesdropping on how we do business, you savvy?"

"Yeah, I'll swing by there tomorrow."

Ritch and Kalish thought it best that Shine meet with them all together to discuss the problems with their recent project. When things needed to be said on their behalf, Ritch always spoke up.

"Shine, what do you say you come on over now? Kalish and I want to talk shop with you, too."

"No can do, Mr. Ritch. Got a couple of fires I need to put out at home. I'll tell Mike everything I know later this week. There's very little I can say right now anyhow, at least till I've talked with all our salespeople. Then Mike can update you and Mr Kalish."

That wasn't what Ritch or Kalish wanted to hear. There wasn't much trust between them and Vogel, and the fact that Shine wanted to speak with Vogel by himself wasn't reassuring.

Sensing the unease in the room, Vogel tried to defuse the moment.

"Shine's our guy. He's as dependable as they come. We certainly don't need to be worrying about what he's up to. You know, Hoffa used him as a bomber. He made Jimmy's enemies think twice every time they started a car. Crazy muthafucker, but he's good for what I--we--need him for."

Ritch and Kalish didn't say it, but they both thought the same thing: It wasn't Shine they were worried about. Vogel was a sleaze bag, and they had both known he was untrustworthy when they crawled into bed with him. The trick, in their minds, would be to maintain dominance in the arrangement. Ritch struck his don't-fuck-with-me pose.

"Okay, Vogel. You go ahead and debrief Shine. Let us know if there's any problem we need to hear about. Just remember, my friends in Colombia are just that, my friends. I don't want to burn that bridge. They don't like dealing with fuck-ups and I'm afraid that one more episode like this past week and that's just what they'll see us as: Fuck-ups. Now, my vote is to do this same run one more time. We use the same people, the same plan, right down to the smallest detail."

Kalish always sided with Ritch. He certainly didn't want to partner up with Vogel. At least Ritch was civil and had an air of intellect and honesty about him. Vogel was as far in the other direction as one could get.

"I'm with him. I say we go right back to our original plan. Give it a couple of months for shrimp season to end and we'll do it one more time."

Vogel, always cynical, and trading heavily on his image as the street-wise member of the trio, offered in reply, "Okay, if that's what you both want to do. Just remember, if this all turns to shit, who it was that said he didn't think it was a very smart idea. Who was it that said if a man don't learn nothing from the past, he's doomed to fuck up again? I forget, but it was somebody real smart."

- CHAPTER FOUR -
EARLY CONFIDENCE AND EASY MONEY

August 15, 1982 – U.S. Attorney's Office-New Bern, North Carolina

After two days poring over all the police reports and forensic evidence gathered by FBI, DEA, Coast Guard and state and local police from the abandoned trawler at Beaufort Docks and surrounding area, Doug McCullough and Terry Peters felt confident that enough evidence had been gathered to tie someone to the crime. But who?

"The trawler is registered in Louisiana," Doug said. "A guy named Ellender, Carl Ellender, is the owner of record. He's already documented as a serious smuggling suspect in that state. He swears that the boat, the *Lady Mauricette*, was legally leased to another company for the purpose of shrimping the East Coast and that he hasn't had any contact with them since February. Of course, we believe this about like we believe J. Edgar Hoover was a ladies' man, but he does have a properly-executed lease and cancelled checks to back him up."

Terry Peters had seen all this before. He had been a journalist at the *Chicago-Tribune* until his investigative prowess led him to the FBI.

"Sure, everybody's a good guy. I'll guarantee you one thing: If he takes a piss, we'll know what color his boxers are. He and his son, Steve, are both under around-the-clock surveillance until further notice. His wife has been monitored on a pay phone talking to the old man. We got the number. Guess where that number's located?"

"Beaufort?"

"Morehead. Same thing. Yeah, he's in this up to his molars. We'll be interviewing him a lot in the next week. His story better be airtight. What did you find out on the registration for the small boat?"

"The Cobia was sold to a Don Nelson for cash about a month before the run. Paid four grand with a certified check purchased at the bank. Guy told the boat dealer he was working in Morehead for a couple of months and wanted to get in some fishing.

"And get this, when he came looking to buy the boat, he apparently had the same group of guys with him who were on the boat the night they were stopped. Apparently, it's a real family oriented company. You know, work together, fish together, run drugs together. Oh, a diver from Beaufort Police Department found what they threw overboard when the Coast Guard approached them."

Terry snorted, "Package of condoms? Afraid we'd know they were screwing around?"

"Close, a Diver's Certificate issued to a Mike Reichey, a Selective Service Registration Card for a Michael Reichey, a notice of classification from those same folks for Mr. Reichey. He is 4A, by the way. His Social Security card, and oh yeah, a Colt 357 Magnum, box of bullets for same and a beautiful leather holster. All this in a nicely bundled plastic bag. Turned all of it over to Ed Hinchman down at DEA."

"So, you figure the guy was worried about getting drafted, right?"

"Maybe so. We'll just have to ask Mr. Reichey when we locate him. Of course, I'm sure he'll say he was just fishing and accidentally dropped his stuff overboard when the Coast Guard startled him."

Terry cracked a smile, "I don't know, Doug. Sometimes you seem just a little too cynical for me. So what's the next step?"

"We've got agents chasing down some folks that took long cab rides away from Beaufort the night the bust was made. Several car rental agencies are coming up with some real interesting collections of customers. They gave fake names, paid in cash, told some bad lies, and then left the cars in airports. A couple of them were stopped in Charlotte as they boarded planes. They're getting looked at right now. My personal goal in all this investigating..." Doug paused.

"Is?" Terry encouraged him to continue.

Doug ran his hand over his hair and sighed. "I'd like to think that we could get some real Cajun cooking out of this in the next couple of days. I'd sure like to talk to Mr. Carl Ellender and Junior. I bet they could tell us a few things that would crack all this wide open."

"I'm sure you're right."

*****

August 20, Seven Mile Beach, Cayman Island

Leigh Ritch dined in a fancy oceanfront restaurant with a beautiful woman. Her bearing reflected the confidence derived from years in the limelight upholding her celebrity status. Her long, blond hair and laser-bright smile sparked an almost audible buzz in the restaurant as more ordinary folks pointed and whispered. She was unfazed and obviously used to such reaction.

Ritch, new to such attention, basked in the glow. In his mind, he'd finally arrived. Just to be in her company was a noteworthy accomplishment.

He was the son of indulgent parents who ran a prosperous tourist business on the island and most folks said he'd never amount to much. He felt that he was proving them wrong and that if they only knew the full scope of his plans, they'd be astounded. He stared into the eyes of his companion, known to all who watched television in the States.

"So, Beautiful, how do you like my little island?

"It's all yours, is it?" She smiled coyly, gently shaking her hair over her shoulders. Little did she know, flirting was unnecessary. Ritch cared about her celebrity status over her looks.

Ritch, for his part, reveled in the certainty that every eye in the place was on them. "Some is now, the rest will be soon. I have wonderful ideas for this place. An island of this much beauty begs to be filled with beautiful people, and I intend to bring them here."

"Am I one?"

"You are truly the most beautiful of all. To have you here with me on this island I love so dearly is the highlight of everything I have ever done." He leaned forward and grabbed her hand. "You know how much I think of you. Why don't you just stay here with me? I assure you that you would be the happiest woman on the planet."

It wasn't the first time she had received such an invitation, and she was fully prepared to let him down easy. She gently pulled her hand back and spoke to him quietly. "Leigh, you are truly the proverbial silver-tongued devil. You make it all sound so easy and wonderful. But, I have to tell you, I've heard just about every promise a man can make a woman and it makes me a little jaded. I love places like this, and I appreciate a caring, handsome man such as yourself, but I've just come to the point that I believe the person I can count on the most is me. I don't want to depend on anyone else to take care of me. I think I can make it on my own just fine. Not that your offer is anything less than spectacular. And for that matter, so are you. Don't think for a moment that I don't want to spend a lot of time with you. I certainly do. I just don't want a permanent man in my life. I hope that doesn't sound too pushy."

"You certainly are a confident woman. I like that. I don't want anything in my life to be acquired easily. I don't think you can ever appreciate something you didn't work for. If I have to sweat and work a great deal to convince you that I'm the man you've been looking for all your life, then so be it. It just makes me want you that much more."

They clinked crystal wine goblets as their eyes danced in celebration of their new, warm relationship. It took Ritch's majordomo several moments to get his attention.

"Mr. Ritch, I'm very sorry to interrupt you, Sir."

"That's all right, Bertley. What's the problem?"

"Someone is trying to reach you from the States. He's called you twice already."

"Do you have a name?"

"Mr. McGhee, Sir."

Ritch frowned, grew serious. Why would McGhee be contacting him instead of Vogel? "That's fine, Bertley. I'll take the call in the restaurant office. Tell him I'll be right there."

Ritch walked around the table, put his arm on her shoulder, and kissed her gently on the lips. "Can you forgive me for leaving you? I'll be back in just seconds, I promise."

Her smiled dazzled as she teased him. "If Doc McGhee is willing to spend the money to call you three times, it must be important. What are you two plotting? I didn't know you were interested in music."

"I'm thinking of investing in a few of his bands." The lie came easily.

"Bon Jovi's going to be huge. You could make some money putting them on top."

"I'll certainly consider your opinion when I start to make my selections. I'll be right back, Love."

As he walked through the wait-station and kitchen, the staff nodded and smiled in deference to the "big man" on the island. A dark-skinned local smiled as he held out the phone.

"It's for you, Mr. Ritch."

"Thanks. Please ask the kitchen staff to hold it down for a moment. This call is important." Taking an imperceptible breath to steady himself, Ritch put the phone up to his ear and prepared to do business.

"Doc, you old bastard. How are things in show biz? That band Bon Jovi, they going to make you rich?"

Doc McGhee was not smiling in Atlanta. He had been trying to get hold of Ritch for several days. He sat alone in his office, decorated with pictures of bands and gold records on the wall to show how well connected he was in the music business.

"It'll take a huge band to offset the losses you and your associates are throwing at me. How do you plan on handling this unfortunate turn of events? A hundred grand is a lot of money to me. A lot. You understand?"

Ritch remained calm and confident in his reply.

"Your money and your trust in us, especially me, is very important, Doc. You'll find it was well placed. The plan was bulletproof. What happened bordered on the bizarre. The Coast Guard just had an unbelievable break. They had no clue what was going on. It wouldn't happen again in a million years. Next time, you'll see. We'll make a fucking fortune."

"Next time? How is there going to be a next time? You said you were broke before. You spend my money and God only knows how much other money, and get no return. Where is the next time money coming from? I haven't got any more risk cash to play with."

Ritch knew that wasn't true, but he also realized Vogel obviously failed to convince Doc McGhee to pony up more cash. If he did step up to the plate and convince him to pay to let them try again, they were dead in the water. There was no way he'd let that happen. "Doc, this is the only way anybody is going to come out on this. I swear, you put up a hundred one more time and if we don't make a killing I'll work as a roadie for you for the rest of my life."

"I'm not a mobster type, Leigh, but if this thing screws up again, you might not have a very long rest of your life. Get my drift? "

"I know what's on the line, Doc. This will work. I'm betting everything I have on it."

"You're betting everything a lot of us have on it. When do you plan on making this trip?"

"November, end of shrimp season. It'll be dead on the Carolina coast then. Like taking a cruise ship into port. Nothing but good times."

"Well, Leigh. I guess I don't have much choice. You know what I'm expecting out of this?"

"You'll get your two hundred back plus a third one for your troubles. In four months, it'll be back in your pocket."

"The same crew is working with you again?"

"Yeah, Kalish and Vogel are in this all the way."

"I like the kid, but Vogel, you're crazy if you trust him."

"Doc, you and me are the only two people I trust."

"Yeah, right. When do you need the money?"

"I'll be in the States in a couple of weeks. I'll drop by and show you a good evening. You can let me hear some of the bands you're plugging."

"I need to spend my money on them. There's just as much dope involved, but at least they get paid when they play. See you in two weeks."

Ritch cradled the phone with sweaty palms, felt sweat bead his forehead. He was involved in a dangerous game and the other players couldn't be counted on to be loyal to the end. He would have to watch his back constantly. He needed to talk to Kalish.

Of the whole crew, Kalish was the only one he truly trusted.

He took a deep breath and walked back to the table where his impatient date waited, wine glass in hand, her smile gone. She was used to being attended to without interruption.

Ritch forced a relaxed smile, kissed the top of her head, and sat down beside her.

"Sorry, Beautiful. Doc wants me to put up some money to promote this other band he's representing. I don't think I'm that interested in the music business."

"Don't disregard the opportunity too quickly. There's a ton of money in rock music if your band makes it big."

"I already have a ton of money. And the company of the most beautiful woman I've ever seen." That brought back her smile.

"You're good, Leigh Ritch, real good."

- CHAPTER FIVE -
SECOND SWING

August 28, 1982 – Tampa, Florida-Stephen Kalish's House

Steve Kalish and Leigh Ritch kicked back on the couch in the living room of the small, framed house Kalish called home. Close in age and attitude, they felt far more comfortable with each other than with their other partner, Michael Vogel.

Kalish and Ritch had long made money selling what they'd both used for years with no harm, none they could detect, anyway. Kalish had been selling weed since he was 15, and eventually dropped out of college to pursue an easy route to fast cash, furnishing what other students wanted and bought with their parents' bucks. So, who was getting hurt? Nobody, in his mind. And the money was good, a lot more than any other job paid. Since high school. Kalish had relied on a network of buddies who helped move his product. As time went on, every deal grew bigger. Now, if he could just pull this one off, he'd officially be in the big leagues.

"Man, I know we can make this work. We were so damned close. It'll happen this time, just like we planned. I mean, c'mon, man, we haven't left a stone unturned. Don't you agree?"

Ritch rubbed the back of his neck, trying to ease the tension he had been hiding from everyone. "The fact I'm here tells you how I feel. And, fact is, it's got to work. I don't want to wind up on the beach running drinks and fetching towels for bored New York wives at my family's hotel. I'd just as soon they found my body floating in Pamlico Sound."

"Shit, Man! Don't even talk like that. Nobody's dying here. We're just going to be careful, plan every detail and watch our backs. Tell you the truth; I'm more concerned about Vogel than I am the Feds. I know what they're trying to do. I don't know what he's up to. I don't trust him. Do you?"

Leigh got up to refill his drink and sighed as he dropped a single ice cube into the glass. "Not much. He's in it just for the money, and everything, everyone is expendable. If we can make the run and he finds some way of getting rid of us and keeping all the money, he'll do it in a heartbeat."

Kalish had very little in the way of morals, but he did have a fairly decent sense of self-preservation, and something told him things weren't as simple and easy as he'd worked so hard to assure Ritch they would be. Time to admit that they might need a plan B. "So, what happens if we bring in the dope, truck it to his buddy, Tony Reo's warehouse in Michigan, and he decides he doesn't need us anymore? Who are we going to complain to? The cops?"

"That's not going to happen, Steve." Steely resolve filled Ritch's voice as he turned to face his cohort.

Kalish wasn't immediately reassured. "How do we prevent it?"

"When the trucks arrive in Michigan, we arrive with them. I'm not going to risk this much and get beat out of it by a thug like Vogel. I don't like anything about him, but I'm not afraid of him. I'll get our share and I'll make sure he knows we won't be intimidated. Trust me."

Kalish tried to be suave as he downed the remainder of his whiskey on the rocks. If Ritch had cared to, he could have told him he missed the mark by a wide margin. He didn't, instead, electing to go over the plans. "Have you got off-loaders and handlers ready to go again?"

"Yeah, same crew, plus a few new guys from Beaufort and Morehead." Kalish coughed as the liquor burned down his throat a little faster than he was used to. "I've got a new trawler lined up. Ellender is still pissed off about losing his boat. He's actually suing the Federal government to get it back. Talk about balls!"

"Makes sense." Ritch stated absentmindedly as he moved to stand and stare out the window pensively. "If you say you're innocent, like he has, then, naturally, you'd sue to get your 'improperly' seized boat back. You know, he's indignant and wounded. Poor Carl."

Kalish shrugged. "I guess you're right. Anyway, we're not using one of his boats this time. I bought another, bigger boat, and we're refrigerating the hold, again. Don't want the Feds to spot our heat image from a C-130."

"How's our aerial unit?" Ritch was happy to focus on details, knowing that it would keep Kalish from focusing on the risks.

Kalish nodded. "We've got a couple of airline pilots who'll fly point ahead of the boat and keep watch for the Coast Guard. Our radio operator will be using an encrypted signal and will also scan for the authorities." Both men leaned back on the couch and stared at the ceiling, each trying to picture success rather than failure.

Ritch broke the silence. "I'll tell you one thing, if anything screws up this time, we'll never recover. This shit is so damned expensive; it's like running a country. If we don't succeed this time, neither one of us will have to worry about a thing, between our contacts in Colombia, the authorities…"

Kalish snorted. "Don't forget Vogel."
*****

September 10, U.S. Attorney's Office – New Bern, North Carolina

At the blackboard, Doug McCullough began to chalk up every possible suspect as he and Terry Peters conducted an inter-agency briefing on the status of the investigation into the seizure of the *Lady Mauricette*. He wrote the name "Reichey" on the blackboard.

"We have a number of possible suspects. We can't put any of them on the boat at this time. Here's the first: Michael Reichy, a known smuggler, whose driver's license was found in a plastic bag by divers searching the bottom at the Beaufort docks where the smaller boat was pulled over by the Coast Guard.

"Also in the bag was another ID bearing his name and .357 Magnum Colt revolver. This is definitely a smoking, though wet, gun. We currently have Mr. Reichey under surveillance and are trying to tie him to others. Clinton Anderson and Anthony Reo, both less than upstanding members of society, caught a plane out of Kinston shortly after taking a midnight cab ride from Morehead City the night of the bust.

"Reo owns a construction business in Detroit, and Anderson makes his living, so he says, as a car salesman, a between-jobs salesman who stays in a plane almost constantly between the southeastern coast and Detroit. Mr. Reichey, incidentally, is also a citizen of the Motor City.

"Aboard the larger boat were prescriptions from a pharmacy in Louisiana where the boat came from. There were pop bottles from Colombia and numerous other items with a South American origin.

"From the charts aboard and the navigation markings on them, there's no doubt the shrimper came to Beaufort Inlet directly from Colombia.

"With the amount of grass on board, that was no surprise to any of us. Our lab also tells us the weed is definitely Colombian. The problem we have is twofold." He paused and held up two fingers, "If we can't definitively link any of the suspects in the speedboat or the other possible suspects to the trawler, we have no grounds for search warrants or wiretaps.

"Our liberal friends in D.C. have a close watch on how we are conducting investigations and we can't afford to blow this one on some small technicality regarding how we obtain evidence." Doug stepped to the side and nodded to Terry.

"Terry, perhaps you could give us a little insight as to what the agency is doing on this investigation."

Terry stepped up the small table beside Doug.

"It's obvious to us that some of the people mentioned here are involved in this operation. We are watching them closely and will continue to do so till we can come up with enough solid evidence to link them legally to the *Lady Mauricette*.

"As Doug said, we're not there yet and all we can do is stand back and keep an eye on them. However, their records indicate that they aren't new to this business and they won't become Sunday school teachers just because they almost got caught once." Terry paused to let a ripple of laughter roll through the room and waited until everyone had once again settled. "This group is undoubtedly still active, still planning to import drugs, and we will attempt to infiltrate their operation and interdict their shipments.

"My own personal intuition tells me they're a large, active operation and are constantly involved in smuggling drugs. We'll make good progress on this. It may not be as quick as we like, but we are on their trail. Someone will screw up and then we'll get the break we need. If one of them flips, we'll get them all. We figure this load we seized and its supporting cast cost the smugglers at least 200 grand to put together." Someone at the back of the room let out a low whistle, various people nodded as they took in the gravity of the information.

"This isn't two good old boys from Carteret County trying to pick up beer money. These are big-time operatives, and we need to bring in the lot of them, not just the low-level operatives."

*****

Late October, Detroit, Michigan – Michael Vogel's House

Vogel stood drinking beer in the kitchen, admonishing Shine, his underling. Shine, far more intelligent than Vogel, knew when to speak and when to listen. At this moment, he was listening.

"Shine, I'm not a man to be trifled with. Without me, this entire thing would come tumbling down around pretty boy and the kid." Shine nodded, knowing it was what Vogel expected of him.

"You've picked the right wagon, but don't fuck with me. I'm a loyal associate, but you fuck with me, you'll be sharing a drink with Jimmy Hoffa. Now, you understand how important it is to me that our dealings with those kids don't screw up my ongoing business here? You know this is what pays the bills, mine and yours." Shine realized that the reason Vogel was intent on making an impression on him was because he was feeling less than in control. Vogel might not be the smartest tool in the shed, but he was a shark, and an insecure shark was not an animal Shine wanted at his back. He knew he'd need to make damn sure he reassured Vogel that he was dependable and subservient.

"Don't worry, I know where my livelihood comes from. I'm totally on your team. No cocksucker will mess this up for me. I'd plant them for you before I'd let that happen." Shine watched Vogel closely, making sure his words were heard and valued. Vogel, for his part, accepted what he was told and quieted the part of his subconscious that was trying to tell him that his "underling" wasn't bowing to him so much as managing him.

"That's good, Shine. Knowing your place is important. I've put a lot of trust in you and I think you'll agree you're being rewarded suitably. And when some of these next loads come in, you'll be a rich man."

"I know man, trust me, I know."

"You've done your testing thing on everyone involved?"

"Yeah, I got rid of two guys in Carolina right up front. They just about broke the fuckin' needle on the stress evaluator. I think they lied about pretty much everything."

Vogel couldn't care less. He didn't understand Shine's machine, the "science" behind it, or anything about it at all, but more than that, he didn't care. Shine's machine was his "in" with Kalish and Ritch. Beyond that, it didn't matter to him. "How about the military guy? He's got everything ready to go?"

Shine didn't miss Vogel's barely masked disinterest with his report about the lie detector machine. It didn't matter. He knew he just had to keep Vogel happy a little longer to get what he wanted. "He says so. I was there a couple of days back. It's a damned impressive operation. We'll know any move the Feds or the Coast Guard make. He's got the scanners, secret encrypted channels, planes running point ahead of the boat, and a team waiting in Beaufort to unload the moment they hit shore. I feel good about everything."

"What about the surveillance planes they fly over the coast of Colombia? What the hell they call those things?"

"AWACS. We've got a much more reliable tracking system than they do. Ours is foolproof."

"How's that? Those fucking planes gotta cost 100 million each. What do we have better than that?"

"Whores." Shine smiled. "The Colombians have a bunch of whores fucking the pilots of the AWACS. When they're shacked up with them, they tip off the cartel and that's when they send the boats out. No AWACS in the air, they don't get spotted. Pretty foolproof I'd say."

"You can't beat pussy, Shine. That's a fact."

"You ain't telling me a fucking thing man." Shine waited until Vogel turned his back to let his smile fall away. His own subconscious was nagging at him that the authorities might have tagged him during the last bust and he could possibly be under surveillance. He resolved to simply stay as discreet as possible and be careful with all contacts. The biggest payday of his life was just ahead if he had the balls to follow through on it. If there was one thing he could be honest with himself about, it was that he had balls enough to pull just about anything off.

*****

November 1982, Barranquilla, Colombia

A new wrinkle threatened the deal. The trawler *Jason Lee* had been boarded and seized by the Colombian Navy. A frantic series of phone calls took place between the captain, known as "Coon Ass", and Michael Vogel to try to solve the problem.

"Mr. Vogel, from what I can tell, this military guy in charge don't speak English any too good. He's got orders to take us in and not release us till we settle some accounts with what he calls 'prominent local businessmen'."

"Okay, Coon Ass, I know exactly what he's talking about. You stay with the boat and I'll get things worked out."

Vogel paid an urgent visit to Leigh Ritch.

"They've confiscated the damn boat." Vogel paced, trying burn off his anxiety. He knew Ritch was less than pleased to hear from him, but he didn't give a damn. "This is a friggin' nightmare. The first load gets seized by the U.S. Coast Guard, and now the Colombian Navy. What's that, two dugout canoes and a water cannon? You know it's our suppliers that ain't been paid yet for the first load. I can't believe they control their stinkin' navy!"

Ritch sighed heavily before responding. Honestly, sometimes it was such an incredible burden to work with someone of lesser intelligence like Vogel. Having the man show up on his doorstep so stressed he was practically jumping out of his skin was even more inconvenient.

"Why not? They own everything in Colombia. They don't call the stuff 'Colombian' for no reason. The way I see it, we have only one option at this point: We go back to Doc. He's the only one who's going to go any deeper to get his money back. Besides, I've furnished his bands and showbiz friends with great trips to my little island getaway, and also enough drugs to fill the damn trawler. Let's get ahold of him."

"If you think so. You do the talking. I don't think he cares much for me."

Ritch thought that was the understatement of the year, but let it slide without comment. "Doc cares for money, just like we do," Ritch said, dialing, "and we're going to make it for him."

"If we live."

Doc McGhee cut off a discussion with a group of stereotypical rockers to grab the phone.

"Leigh, are we rich yet?" Doc was all smiles and jovial laughter, making sure no one thought he was worried about getting a call.

"One more obstacle has come up, Doc."

"And that obstacle requires more of my money, am I right?" McGhee asked with a laugh, waving the band out of the room. As soon as the door shut, his demeanor changed from friendly to pissed off.

"You guys are fuckin' killin' me! Do you hear me? Dead! I'm dying over here, just waiting to see if I'll ever get back a dime of what I've given you, forget about actually turning a profit. What the hell is it this time? Has the damn boat run into a U.S. Navy ship?"

Doc thought he was being funny. Ritch laughed to himself as he replied, "Not quite, but you're pretty close. The boat has been seized by the Colombian Navy and they won't let it go until we settle up with our previous suppliers."

"And how much do we owe our previous suppliers?"

"I can get them to settle for a hundred grand."

Doc wished he could reach through the phone and strangle the rich little piss-ant like they did in cartoons. "Let me tell you what, Ritch, and you can tell Vogel and Kalish too, I know you might think so, but this isn't a charity operation I'm running. Plus, I'm working with some really hot acts that don't need to see my name on the front page of the paper involved in some drug-dealing fuck-up. I don't have the kind of money you guys are wasting for me. If I do this, I want a three-to-one return, and I want it within two weeks of when this load gets to the States. I'm not fucking with you. Do you understand where we're at here?"

"Yes, Doc. I understand and so do Kalish and Vogel. We're in this too deep to back out now. Our plan is good and we'll get you your money. Thirty days from now, you'll love us." Ritch smiled. Some days, he wondered how he could talk people into things this easily. If it ever backfired on him, he knew he'd be dead, but he didn't consider that a possibility.

"I'm waiting. If this doesn't work, we no longer do business and you guys owe me a hell of a lot of money. You'll be hawking programs at Motley Crue concerts till you die."

"I'll be there in the morning to pick up the money."

*****

The Colombian docks were brightly lit and scores of workers scurried back and forth between the trucks that carried hundreds of bales of marijuana and the trawler, *Jason Lee*. Coon Ass, the trawler captain, stood in the pilothouse with his long-time friend and first mate, Arky.

Coon Ass spoke to Louis, overseer of the loaders, "I'm amazed how bold these people are. This is still against the law in Colombia isn't it?"

Louis smiled benignly, thinking to himself how easy it was to amaze a stupid American. "For most people, yes. They would be arrested and placed in a prison that you Americans would not survive for a very lengthy stay. But the men you are purchasing this load from, control the government. They don't hold elected positions, but everyone here knows who controls our country. It's not all bad. Our people are very poor. This is the only money some of these men will earn this year. They have no jobs, no education, and no future. This money feeds their families and gives them whatever hope they have in their lives." Louis paused to allow the Americans time for that to sink in.

"Before this industry grew into the powerful force it is today, most of these men would be beggars or common thieves, doing anything they could to just stay alive. We are indeed very lucky that these men are engaged in such a profitable and growing concern. We not only don't need to worry about being observed loading your vessel, the guards you see positioned around the dock with automatic weapons are furnished to us by the military.

"So, no need to worry in this country, my friend. You need to focus your concerns on the journey ahead of you. Of course, the dangers that you will be addressing are what make this all so profitable. It is truly a mixed blessing. Is this stormy weather any concern to you? I'm nervous about going to sea any time, but God forbid going out when it's so rough."

Coon Ass stared out the pilothouse window at the dark clouds and the wind-tossed whitecaps finding their way even into the harbor.

"I've been at sea all my life. I think any man who ain't afraid of what can occur out there, is a fool. I respect the ocean and all of its many moods. I listen to the weather reports, and if it seems too dangerous to head out, I don't. Simple as that. No amount of money is worth a watery grave."

"We are in agreement there, my friend. Well, a few more bales and you are free to set sail. It would be beneficial to have the dock area clear for commercial ships that will be here in the morning. If you are not ready to leave by then, just move down to the end of the wharf near the straw market."

"I'm ready to head out soon as you're finished loading."

"In that case, good luck. I wish you success in your venture and will look forward to working with you again."

As the loaders retreated to the collection of ragtag vehicles for their trip home, Captain Coon Ass fired up the trawler's two powerful diesel engines and engaged the sophisticated electronics he would monitor during the course of this two-thousand-mile, open-water journey.

Second Swing

For such a long and risky voyage, its start was beginning to look a bit rough. The sky, previously sprinkled with stars, had clouded over.

In the distance, he could clearly see the periodic bursts of lightning. However, word had come down from the Colombian dealers that the U.S. AWAC pilots were getting laid that evening. It was time to go.

His crewmembers cast off dock-lines, and the small ship slowly eased through the harbor full of anchored fishing vessels and perhaps another treasure ship waiting its turn to be loaded with golden leaf. Coon Ass couldn't help but draw the comparison between himself and the pirates who had amassed their fortunes in these same waters just two centuries earlier. If he could make this run successfully, he could skip five years or more of pulling nets in the middle of winter. He was eking out a narrow living, always risking his life with the vagaries of a fickle and dangerous ocean. Eight to ten days at sea, a successful offloading, and he could lay claim to more than 100 thousand tax-free American dollars; a modern day treasure.

As the trawler cleared the harbor, ocean swells came to greet the bow, sweeping low under the hull of the vessel and causing a gentle lifting action that let all aboard know they were in open water.

Coon Ass turned to Arky, now in the pilothouse with him, and said, "Our Colombian friend on board, what's he up to? Is he any help?"

"He's just a plant, watching over the cargo. He don't know port from starboard, and he's more interested in checking that gun under his belt than whether or not the engines keep running. I thought Kalish trusted us more than this."

"It ain't Skip." Coon Ass told him. Kalish's associates all knew him as Skip. "It's just part of doing business with these Colombians. This is a real serious business with them and one or two lives don't mean shit. They'd kill us all if it meant helping out their bottom line. You keep an eye on the little shit. If he gives you any problems, show him the sea. You get my drift, Arky?"

"Aye, aye Captain. Would be my pleasure." Arky smiled.

As the evening wore on, thunderstorms began to show on the radar monitor. Knowing that a prudent skipper would take precautionary action before it was necessary, Coon Ass gathered his crew in the pilothouse.

"All right boys, we're in for a pretty strong blow here. Let's tie down anything on the deck that needs lashing. Check the hold covers, and secure for rough weather. I believe we can run straight into the seas and still stay on course, but it's probably going to be rough going."

The seas were building even as he spoke. The first rolls of thunder could be heard heading their way, and the unmistakable flashes of lightning lit the dark clouds, creating a surreal background. This was a strong storm. In short order, the crew all gathered back in the pilothouse where they would be dry and have a view of what seas they were in. It was rapidly becoming more of a circus ride than an ocean voyage. Most of them had been here before. Though there was a certain seriousness to the events, they weren't panicked. To work at sea was to live with the ever-present threat of storms. They had seen this many times before.

Strong spray pounded against the windows of the pilothouse. They were not glass, but Lexan, built to withstand the relentless pounding of the heavy seas that rolled over the bow and slammed against the front cabin wall where the captain watched, ever conscious of the size and direction of approaching waves. These were large, already fifteen feet, and growing. Coon Ass looked at the green radar screen above the wheel.

"I see some strong thunderstorms moving in on us. I sure as hell don't want all our electronics getting fried before we even get underway."

Arky offered a thought. "Captain, you want me to shut off the breakers on all the radios and other electrical systems till the storm passes?"

"Won't help a bit. Everything on board is grounded to the hull, even the rigging. If we get a lightning hit, it would all be fried through the grounds. We'll just hope it doesn't like us and stays away from our electronics. Damn, these waves are starting to lose their tops."

The crew had to find handholds in the pilothouse and the movements became something akin to staying atop a bronco at the rodeo. A constant shift of balance was needed to stand up. The Colombian was beginning to get seasick. The others looked at him and smiled at each other.

Arky, feigning sympathy, offered, "Hey Pedro, you don't look too good, man. Can I get you something to eat? How 'bout a bologna sandwich? Might have some sausage left over from breakfast."

The green crewmember opened the door to the pilothouse and disposed of the contents of his stomach for the next ten minutes while the rest of the crew laughed. This wasn't new to them, and they were more concerned about getting the huge paycheck a successful run would bring them all. Strong shots of lightning began to play above the sea's turbulent surface, each burst revealing how large the waves had become.

"We've got some 20-footers out here." Captain Coon Ass said. "Need to play every wave. Don't want a flood of green water finding its way to the hold. Our cargo needs to stay dry. Did you boys get the hold covers on tight?"

Mikey, one of the mates, helped the Columbian gain a good foothold and said, "Yes sir, if we don't go down, she'll be fine. If this trip doesn't result in a large amount of money, I'm ready to go down. Better to just go quickly than to starve to death in Louisiana. I'm tired of poverty. I'm ready to take my money and move to San Diego."

"Still in love with California, 'eh Mikey?"

"I want to live where *Baywatch* is a reality. There's a lot of beauty out there." Everyone laughed.

"Well, first, let's get this old girl through the night."

As the night wore on, the storm subsided. Dawn revealed a sky with only streaks of dark clouds punctuated by bursts of radiant sunlight and the ever-present tropical heat. Coon Ass and Arky, yet to sleep, were relieved the night had come to a quiet end.

"Arky, we're supposed to check in by seven this morning with Miami. Don't forget to engage the encryption unit."

"I won't. Could you use a coffee?"

"Yes, and hit it with a shot of brandy. I need to settle down for a while and catch a few hours of sleep."

Totally drained, Coon Ass enjoyed the feeling of the *Jason Lee* as she rose over the subsiding swells. There was a rhythm to it unequalled by anything else in nature. Arky returned, coffee in hand, with a message from the Miami control center.

"The point planes have picked up a USCG 130 working this area. They advise us to change our heading 35 degrees to starboard for the next two hundred miles or so to avoid being spotted. Damn, Coon Ass, that'll add another day to the trip by the time we get back on course."

"My friend, if this was easy, they wouldn't be paying you 30 grand to do it, now would they?"

"I know. I just want it to be over. I worry about what can go wrong and who would take care of my family if we got caught."

"That's not going to happen. And, if the worst did happen, they'd probably just charge our friends. Prison is for petty thieves, not for members of the organization that pays us. We're protected."

"I hope you're right, I don't want to go to jail, anywhere."

"Not to worry, my friend. Not to worry."

*****

Dawn, A Remote Hunting Camp Near Newport, North Carolina

A number of off-loaders prepared the area for the arrival of the *Jason Lee*. The shore crew numbered around fifty: Handlers, logistics, truck drivers, and miscellaneous crew. Most of the crew knew only one or two other workers at the site. They were mostly from the local area, and a few were from Detroit and Texas. Some had done this before for the same organization. Most of the locals were connected one way or the other to Steve "Big Guy" Fodrie, whose family operated Net House, a successful Beaufort restaurant. He had brought in an interesting mix of local characters, including: Robert Webb, a local karate instructor, Don Nelson, who would handle local small boat logistics, and even a previous mayor of Atlantic Beach, Gary Walters, who ran a local garage and wrecker service.

A few days before, a police vehicle that had been wrecked was parked in his garage. He monitored the police radio in it to determine if there was any activity of concern to the smuggling operation. Walters was also a member of the hunt club that was to be used as the offload site. He had not only furnished keys to the group, but also actually changed the locks on the gate to prevent any other members from wandering in at the wrong time and discovering what was going on if everything went well. That was the key. All the planning, all the connections, none of it would matter if they couldn't pull it off according to plan. Gary Walters was nervous. For that reason, he sought reassurance from his buddies, who had talked him into participating.

"Rob, I gotta tell you, I don't know what I'll do if this doesn't work out and we get dragged into court. You saw what kind of headlines the bust here got in July. There's not much news down here and if an ex-mayor got caught helping to smuggle marijuana into the country, there'd be hell to pay."

"Don't even talk like that, Gary. These guys know what they're doing. This is a sophisticated operation. Even when the Coast Guard stumbled onto the shrimper in July, nobody got caught."

Don Nelson, who'd been listening, spoke up.

"I know for a fact that some of the agencies are still following leads on that case. It's the kind of thing that can make a cop's entire career."

The walkie-talkie Rob carried beeped suddenly.

"Yeah, this is Rob. What's the problem? That so? Okay, we'll be right there."

Walters turned to Wade.

"What's up?"

"The off-loaders say their gate keys don't work."

"Let's go see what the problem is."

The three men got in Walter's pickup and headed to the hunt club gate. As they arrived, they saw a number of trucks with a crew of men they didn't recognize standing beside them. Rob approached them.

"What are you fellas doing here at our hunt club?"

"You're Robert Wade aren't you? We just called you. The friggin' gate keys don't work."

Walters reached out for the key.

"Let me see that key if you don't mind."

Walters compared it to his key.

"Shit, it's the old key. I changed all the locks so that any other club members couldn't get in till they called me."

Robert realized this could be a huge problem.

"How many bad keys did you give out?"

Walters thought hard. "I gave the security guy, what's his name, Shine and some guy named Sharer about twenty of them. They're all going to be bad."

"Shit, this could really mess things up. There's off-loaders coming from all over the place today and tonight. Somebody's got to be here at the gate to let them in."

Gary knew it was his screw-up so he volunteered.

"Okay, I'll stay and let everybody in."

Men streamed into the camp every few hours. Kalish made the rounds, checking small details that could have been overlooked. He realized what was riding on this event, perhaps a lot more than just his financial future. He pulled alongside Gary Walters at the front gate to the hunt club.

"How's it going here?"

Gary didn't realize the size of Kalish's role in this endeavor, but he did understand that his own part was quite far down the ladder.

"I think we're doing fine. People are showing up every couple of hours. We've got generators, conveyors to help offload, several john boats and a lot of people I don't know what the hell they do."

"Nobody you recognize from the area that shouldn't be here?"

"Thank God, no."

"That's good. You blow the whistle if you see anything that might jeopardize this load."

"I'll call right away. But, nobody's getting shot or anything like that, right? I mean, I live around here and I don't want anyone getting hurt."

"Absolutely not. Damn, man, this is just grass. It's not like we're curing cancer or anything."

"Right, right."

Kalish turned to Shine, sitting in his passenger seat. He liked the guy, but realized that he was more an operative of Vogel's than a team player. "What do you think, Shine? Everything going to be okay this time?"

"So far, so good. The weather's beginning to take a turn for the worse though. If this rain gets any heavier, I'm real concerned about getting the trucks and trailers in and out of these old dirt roads."

"Yeah, that's not good. Let's go down to the dock site."

At the edge of the channel, a makeshift dock was in place, and a small group of off-loaders stood around waiting for the *Jason Lee*. It was early yet, but they all were beginning to feel the tension of being somewhere they shouldn't be, and the possibility that this could take a turn for the worse. Kalish had plenty of experience with this and knew what was going through their minds. It was why he was playing the part he played. He turned on the charm, and gave the men the pep talk they needed.

"Hey guys, you're all going to make a shit ton of money tonight. When the boat gets in, just move fast and let's get this load on the trucks, pronto."

One of the men asked, "Any word about the boat yet, Skip?"

"They checked in with our radio operator a short while ago." Kalish advised. "They were getting close to Beaufort Inlet. A couple of you guys give me a hand with this conveyor. Let's move it over by the dock."

As the men hurriedly grabbed the other end of the large machine, it suddenly laid to the side off-balance. Kalish jumped over to help support it and the track slapped his chin with a jagged edge. It sliced deeply into his flesh, causing him to curse.

"Fucking Son-of-a-bitch! I'm split wide open!"

Shine ran over to take a closer look with his flashlight.

"Well, Skip, it ain't life-threatening, but you do need some stitches; probably seven or eight. It's gonna leave you a real pretty scar too. Tell you what, I'll run you down to the emergency room in Morehead and have you back in an hour."

"This fucking hurts like hell. I sure as shit hope this is the last thing that screws up tonight."

Kalish walked back in the rain with Shine to the car. Every minute or so, he wiped the blood from his chin and let the rain wash it from the palm of his hand.

*****

9:00 p.m., Beaufort Inlet – Aboard the *Jason Lee*

Arky was looking through binoculars as Coon Ass alternated between staring at the radar screen and out the pilothouse windows.

"Coon Ass, you think anybody's watching us right now?"

"November isn't a busy time around here. I think the Coasties are probably watching the Sunday night movie and the Feds are already asleep. This is a dead place this time of year. We'll be all right, count on it."

Arky nodded absentmindedly, anxiously rubbing his hands on the front of his pants. "I just want to get it over with and get my money."

Coon Ass knew his friend well, and although he felt the same tension, he knew better than to show it. They were so close to the finish line. Now was not the time to lose momentum. "It'll happen, Arky. What are the rest of the guys up to? How 'bout the Colombian moron?"

"They're all just staring at the coast, looking for lights."

"Well, they won't have to stare long, we're fifteen miles out. See the shoreline on the radar screen?"

"That's great. We going straight in the inlet?"

"Right down the middle of the ship's channel. Just like we belong here."

They maintained a smooth eight knots. The rain was beginning to fall heavier, but rather than being worried, Coon Ass felt that worked in their favor. "Ain't nobody going to be doing routine checks in this mess. We probably won't see another boat." Only a few more tense moments passed before they saw the landmark they were looking for.

"Okay, there's the Number One buoy. We just stay in the channel and we'll be inside in just a few minutes. Help me keep an eye out for the other markers on the radar. I can't see fifty feet ahead in this rain. I sure as shit don't want to run over one of them after coming all this way."

"I got it, about two hundred yards ahead to starboard. We're dead center."

To anyone onshore, the *Jason Lee* appeared to be just another old shrimper, headed back to port to undergo repairs after a long shrimping season. No reason to be suspicious. Coon Ass felt his heartbeat pick up a little with the proximity of a large facility to the port side of the channel.

"Know what that is, don't you, Arky?"

"What's that? You mean all those lights over there? Hard to see much." Arky squinted, trying in vain to see through the darkness and rain.

"That's the Fort Macon Coast Guard station. Those were the guys that got the first load. Looks like all their boats are shut down for the night. We're going to be just fine."

Within minutes, the *Jason Lee* cleared the inlet channel and went under the Beaufort high-rise bridge. Ahead lay the Newport River and Adam's Creek, both small bodies of water that would have no traffic this time of night, especially in this weather.

"Hand me the phone." Coon Ass dialed a number and stood by while it rang. He slowed down the *Jason Lee*, as the water grew narrow and dark. There were very few lighted markers and the area was extremely shallow. Running aground would be about the worst thing that could happen in the short distance that remained.

"Mr. Kalish, it's Coon Ass. We're almost to the house. Everything okay at home?" Coon Ass used the previously agreed upon code, knowing if everything was okay, Kalish would respond in kind.

"Absolutely, Coon Ass. All your friends are here waiting for you to have a late evening drink with us. How much longer do you think you'll be?"

"About fifteen minutes. We're moving kinda slow, don't want to run aground."

"That would be bad, Coon Ass. Take your time. The whole family is here."

Fresh from the emergency room, his now stitched-up chin hurting like a bad toothache, Kalish assembled the men, hoping to make the transfer as quickly as possible. Anticipation was building among the off-loaders, most of whom had never before seen the others. That was an integral part of the plan to reduce the odds of someone being brought in for questioning and giving up names. The running lights of the *Jason Lee* came into view through the driving rain.

"Here she is. Get ready to take her lines."

Several off-loaders stood by on the makeshift dock waiting to throw lines to the shrimp boat. Coon Ass slowly moved her up to the dock. As she touched the edge of the planks, he killed the motor and turned to Arky.

"We're here, my friend. I'm starting to feel rich. What do you say we throw some lines to the boys on shore?"

"Already underway. I think our Colombian friend will never go on a cruise again."

They both laughed at the site of the South American leaping to the dock from the boat. He had been seasick the entire trip.

Kalish greeted Coon Ass at the dock, "Great job, man. I knew you were the one we needed. Anybody get suspicious?"

"Hell, we never seen nobody all the way in. As quiet as it could be. What the hell happened to your face?"

"Ran into a wall. I'm fine. Your guys all okay?"

"It's been a long, wet ride, but we're here and so's your load. It's dry and ready to be offloaded."

"That's great, Coon Ass. We'll take it from here."

Kalish motioned to the off-loaders.

"Okay you guys, let's get this stuff moving. Where the hell's the conveyor?"

"Broke. Won't work."

"That's just great. Not only is that ten grand pissed away, but also the bastard busted up my face. How about the friggin' trucks? Where are they?"

"Stuck in the mud, about five hundred yards from here. We're afraid to bring them in any closer. It just keeps getting softer and softer and once the trucks are loaded, we'd never get them out."

"So what the hell we supposed to do-carry out seven hundred bales on our backs?"

"I think that's the only way we're going to get the stuff on those trucks."

"Shit! What else can fuck up?" Kalish threw his hands up and cursed the sky for his bad luck, before briskly rubbing his face, silently telling himself to move on. "Okay, so be it. Let's get at it."

The rain continued to pour as the night wore on. By two a.m. one thing was becoming increasingly apparent: These were men who had spent most of their lives trying to get away from hard work. Kalish's patience was wearing thin.

"Jesus, we're down to about a third of the crew we started with. What's wrong with these guys, Shine?"

"They're like me, worn out. Two hours of lifting forty-pound bales and carrying them five football fields is about all anybody here is good for."

"What do we have now? Two hernias, five bad backs, two down with the flu? Thank God we're not paying Workman's Comp on these guys or we'd go broke. Are we going to be able to get all this done by sunrise? We need to be out of here before somebody just happens to wander by."

Just down the channel from the loading area, one of the spotters who'd been watching for boat traffic from a small outboard john boat stumbled on the rain-soaked deck and fell out of the boat. He tried to pull himself in and in doing so, got one corner of the small boat too low in the water. It filled and started sinking. He knew he wouldn't be able to tread water for long and the rain was still obliterating his view down the channel. He heard another one of the spotters motoring down the creek past him and took the best course of action his waterlogged mind could come up with. He grabbed his pistol and fired it into the air. The pistol's explosion not only alerted the other boat, but also had a pretty chilling effect on the crew trying to offload remaining bales of dope. Kalish almost jumped out of his skin.

"What the hell was that? It sounded like a gun to me."

Shine recognized the sound also.

"That's exactly what it was. Sounded like it came from down the creek. There's nobody hunting this early in the morning, so it had to be one of our guys. Man, I hope there's not a problem. If they've shot a Fed, we're all fucked. We'll rot in prison."

"Don't jump to conclusions. Here comes a spotter boat."

They rushed to the dock just as the now-drenched and freezing swimmer stepped to the shore.

"Mr. Kalish, I'm sorry. My boat sank."

"Your boat sank? They're all brand new. What do you mean your friggin' boat sank?"

"Actually, I fell overboard and sunk it trying to get back in it. I don't swim so good. I was drowning, swear to God. I didn't know what else to do. You don't think anybody else heard the gun do you?"

"Who the hell knows? What would it matter anyway? The trucks are stuck in the mud, the crew all have bad backs, the conveyor doesn't work, the gate has a lock with the wrong keys, my chin is busted up, and now my drowning spotter is firing his friggin' pistol to get help. If things get any worse, we'll be better off in prison, for our own protection! Let's all just keep moving. Will that be all right with everyone?"

They all knew he was upset. There was only one good answer.

"Yes sir, Skip. Let's just finish unloading and get the hell out of here."

"Thank you, that sounds just great."

By dawn, the four crew members who could still walk, out of the original fifty or so, carried the last bales to the trucks. Shine had a crew laying down plywood in front of the truck tires to keep them from bogging down in foot-deep mud. The rain was still coming down. Even Kalish was freezing.

"Okay, Shine, that's all of it. See if these trucks can roll."

The tractor-trailers, with experienced drivers used to heavy snow in northern Michigan, inched forward. Kalish could feel the pressure fall off his shoulders.

"Don't let them stop moving, no matter what. Keep those wheels turning."

Within an hour, the trucks all made good their departure. Just a couple of guys were left undertaking a thorough search to make sure no traceable evidence was left behind. Kalish walked over to a large smelly stack of cardboard boxes.

"What is this all about?"

"That's the shrimp that was supposed to go in the trucks behind the grass in case they got stopped. It would have a strong smell and throw 'em off. They wouldn't smell the grass over top of them."

"And what's it doing here?"

"We was out of room and time."

"What you're saying is, if someone asks to look in through the back door of one of these trailers heading down the interstate through at least twenty weigh stations, they will just see a couple hundred bales of grass, am I right?"

"That's the way it is."

"And what is going to happen to the thousand pounds of shrimp we bought?"

"It's going to start smelling bad real soon."

Kalish didn't know whether or curse or cry. "Somebody wake me from this nightmare."

- CHAPTER SIX -
THE GREEN, GREEN GRASS

Waterway Construction Company Warehouse, Detroit, Michigan

Kalish, Vogel, and Ritch gathered at the Reo's Construction Company warehouse, known as the Waterway Construction Company. Most of the load had not only made it to the offloading area, but had already been picked up in waiting trucks.

In this cash-only business, a huge amount of money was about to be divided up and distributed. The only thing of more significance to the three men was their mutual distrust, especially between Vogel and the other two. They were each cut from different cloth. Kalish and Ritch felt that Vogel was not only untrustworthy, but also dangerous. All had weapons and the air was thick with apprehension.

"This doesn't feel right," Ritch confided quietly to Kalish. "I'm afraid that this is going to get ugly fast. You think it's just me?"

"I feel it too. Why did everyone have to bring a gun to this? I've done business with lots of people over the past ten or fifteen years and we never brought guns with us to a settlement meeting. This looks like a scene from a James Bond movie. All Vogel needs is a white cat in his lap."

"Sorry, humor escapes me right now. Let's go stand by Vogel. If anything starts, he'll be real close."

"That's a damned good idea."

Vogel had a preoccupied look on his face, as if a lot was going on that he wasn't disclosing to his partners. Kalish asked him what was up.

Vogel pasted on his best "trust me" smile. "I think you'll both be in a very good mood before the day is over."

"Why is that?"

"So far, just by rough count, I'm told that we have taken into our treasury a little over 4 million dollars. I suspect that by the end of today, we will have moved all the product and we should be in the neighborhood of about a million each, after expenses."

Ritch and Kalish liked the sound of that, but wanted proof. "Where are they counting? I'd love to take a look at all the money."

"All right, follow me."

Vogel took them to a small room in the warehouse where two armed men stood guard and Bill Sharer, the communication and accounting expert, stood over a furiously whirling bill-counting machine. He smiled when the bosses appeared in the room.

"Gentlemen, come in. You are looking at the fruits of your labor."

None of the three could help but smile at the sight of a tabletop filled with stacks of money.

Vogel said, "This is the last of it. The trucks that were supposed to be here late tonight came in from Maine early. Some of our customers had concerns about our ability to run this operation as quietly as they like. I think we have eased their minds by now."

Kalish and Ritch were surprised that buyers were hurrying in from that distance.

"How the hell did they hear about this in Maine?"

Vogel was only too happy to use the opportunity to show off his sphere of influence.

"Actually, the medical examiner for the State of Maine is a customer of mine. Been doing business together for some time now."

"I guess if the money's good enough, everybody is a potential customer, heh?"

"That's the way I look at it. And, certainly this time, the money has been good enough. I think it's fair to say that we are all going to be cash millionaires tonight. How does that feel?"

"Good, damn good!"

Vogel motioned to Sharer.

"As soon as you're sure of the count, set aside about two million to finish paying out our expenses and divide the rest up three ways. Ritch, you need to get on a plane and hand-carry Doc's share to him in the morning. He's getting pretty nervous about now and we may well need him again."

"You can count on it. Besides, it'll give me the perfect opportunity to make a call to Miss Locklear."

"Who are you talking about?"

"Heather Locklear, you know that blonde knockout on television."

"You know her?" Vogel asked incredulously.

"A lot more than know her."

Vogel scoffed, "Right, and I'm Richard Nixon."

"Okay, don't believe me. I may still invite you to the wedding."

"You do that."

Kalish drew their attention back to the matter at hand. "I hope you guys have made preparations to get this money out of here. It's a lot to be carrying on your person."

"Just get it divided up. I can handle my part."

By this time, tension had eased. A lot of money seemed to smooth out hard feelings among just about anyone; then Shine entered the office. It was obvious to Kalish and Ritch that Vogel had another agenda involving him.

"Shine, look pal, we're in discussion here right now. How about getting back with me later this evening? I'll be at the house and I plan to have a little of this green stuff for you. You could use a little right about now, couldn't you?"

The Green, Green Grass

Vogel motioned toward the stack of money as he spoke. Shine smiled.

"That sounds just fine to me, Boss. That sounds pretty fucking great."

As Shine left the room, Vogel, sensing that his partners were a little concerned over any side deals, said, "Well, boys. We've had a great outcome to our venture. We need to sit down and decide where we go from here. I have several things in mind, and I'm sure you both do also. How about we get back together in ninety days after we've all had a little time to sit back and enjoy our rewards?"

After the men had secured their portions of the collected money and departed, Shine came back into the room to meet with Vogel. Vogel barely looked up when he entered the room. He was busy practically caressing his pile of bills.

"Cash is an amazing thing, Shine."

"How's that?"

"It's just paper with numbers and pictures on it. It can't do a damn thing other than give off a little heat when it's burned, or maybe you could wipe your ass with it, but that's just about it. And yet, people die for this and the lack of it every minute of every day. It's damn hard to get hold of too. You know how much is in this pile, Shine?"

"A hell of a lot. I know that."

"You're damn right, Shine. A hell of a lot. Enough to retire on for most people. But, we're not most people. That's why you're here."

"What's up, Mike?"

"Ritch, Kalish, and I are planning another load. A mammoth fucking load, many tons bigger than the last one."

"That would be huge. How big are you talking about? The trawler was full to the seams this time."

"That's why we're not going to use a trawler. We're going to bring in a barge, use an ocean-going tug. Maybe 100 million dollars' worth."

"You're shitting me!" The scope of what would be needed to pull off something that large made Shine nervous. Vogel couldn't possibly be serious, could he?

"You know me better than that. This is going to involve a lot of new faces and you're going to have to check 'em all out to make sure we've got the right people. I don't want any crooks in our little family.

"And now, Shine, there's another matter or two. I'm not stopping my own business interests up here just because I'm involved with the Hardy Boys. I've got this network of buyers counting on me and I'm going to have to supply them in the meantime. You'll be working with me on this end. How's that sound? You just cleared over a hundred grand. The money's good, right?"

"No doubt, Mike. I'm happy. I want to just keep my worthless ass busy and keep making some progress financially. I don't want to be doing this, you know, taking all these damned risks, forever. I'd like to set aside a nice piece of change and just quit. Get the fuck out of this."

"I feel exactly the same, Shine. Now, we have to be careful that things don't happen too quickly on this barge thing."

"Why's that?"

"I'm paying a pretty high price for my product in small quantities. I'm still bringing in a plane or two every week straight from Colombia. I've got to get top dollar when it hits the market. So, let's say we bring in a couple hundred tons of grass. It will, no doubt, bring the price down."

"Yeah, but you'll make millions off that load."

"That's right, but I'll also make millions between now and then. What I want you to do is help me control the timing, when that barge comes into port. It's going to be a while yet. I'll keep you posted and let you know when things need to, well, let's say, slow down. You get my drift?"

"Yes, I'll do whatever has to be done."

"And one other thing, Shine."

"Yes?" Shine acted otherwise, but he knew what was coming next. Vogel was nothing if not predictable.

"You do know who you're working for here?" And there it was: The normal threatening, needy reminder of his place in Vogel's world. Shine told him what he needed to hear, like always.

"You, Mike, I work just for you."

"Good. That's all."

*****

December 1982, A Private Jet Bound For Grand Cayman Island

Kalish, his brother, John, and several others were enjoying the fruits of their labor. Kalish was obviously the number one passenger. He relished the position and the success of the recent operation. He walked down the aisle between the individual captain's chairs in the main cabin salon, making sure everyone was enjoying the party, that everyone knew it was all because of him.

"Tell you what. There's going to be a lot of rides in private jets from here on out. You stick with me, do what I tell you, and we'll all be retired in about five years, and not on a pension."

One of the men turned around in his seat.

"Skip, is something else big getting ready to happen?"

"You aren't broke already are you? I mean forty grand for a week's work ain't bad pay."

"That's true, Skip. But that's the only payday like that I've ever had. By the time I got current on my bills, I was just about broke. The damn money don't go nowhere anymore. Just about got to make buckets full of it every week."

"And we will, my friend. And to answer your question, yes. There's a load coming up that makes this past one look small. You'll all make two years' pay for a week of hard work."

His brother, feeling a little more able to press for details than the rest of the men, queried Stephen, "Are you going to be working with Ritch and Vogel full time from here on in?"

"No. My deals with them are a very profitable sideline to my own business. You guys are all on my team. You all work for me, not Ritch and not Mike Vogel. If they ask you to do anything you haven't spoken with me about first, you come and tell me what they want. We're an entity to ourselves. We'll have our own deals, just like before, only this time, they'll be a lot bigger and better financed, and for those reasons, a lot easier. Money does grease the wheels of industry, and we're a part of an industry. Hell, we're probably in the biggest industry in the world."

"So, what are we going to be doing in the islands? How come some of the guys are getting to take their wives?"

"This trip is eighty percent pleasure and twenty percent business. It's our way of saying thank you and letting your family know that you're not working with a bunch of thugs. We want you to have a good time and we've got a few nice surprises planned."

The door to the cockpit opened and the plane's captain walked between the seats toward Kalish. All conversation stopped midsentence as the men stared at the gorgeous young woman responsible for getting their plane to its destination.

Sheila had been piloting Kalish, Ritch, Vogel, and other key members of the organization around for more than a year. She was not only a capable pilot with thousands of hours of flying time, but also offered the added benefit of her own "mile high" club. She was a smart woman who understood exactly what was going on among these specific passengers. Her services were being used more often, and she had instilled enough trust in the organization's hierarchy to serve as not only a pilot, but a courier as well. She had picked up and delivered bags of cash for them. To think that she could perform this job so well and yet be so accommodating with her favors was quite exciting to Kalish.

She walked over to him, stood face-to-face, and said provocatively, "Mr. Kalish, I wonder if you could accompany me to the cockpit for a moment?"

All present concluded that she had stressed the "cock" portion of cockpit a little more than normal. Kalish smiled as he followed her shapely figure toward the front of the plane. She entered, he grabbed the door handle and, as he pulled it closed, he looked back at the men and winked. Sheila came over to him as he stood with his back against the door.

"We're under autopilot, right?"

"That's right, Mr. Kalish, the Lear is quite capable of steering herself, completely on course for the next twenty-five minutes."

She brushed a soft, slender hand against the front of Kalish's pants, an aggressive move by a woman confident in her power over men.

"Anything you'd like to do during that time, Mr. Kalish? I have an idea I think you might like."

"And that would be?"

"You sit right here in the co-pilot's seat and look for oncoming traffic and I'll straddle you while looking toward the cockpit door. It's a highly technical maneuver only the most experienced pilots would ever consider."

Kalish was now stroking her hair and starting to become aroused.

"That sounds like a plan to me, Captain. I mean, you are the pilot. I couldn't begin to fly this bird without your help."

"That's right, Mr. Kalish, you know what I trained on when I first started taking flight lessons?"

"What would that be?"

"An old Piper Cub that didn't have a wheel."

"How did you steer it?"

"It had a very sensitive, stiff stick, right in the cockpit. And you know what?"

"What?" asked Kalish, inhaling her perfume as her hands played with the zipper on his trousers.

"I miss that stick. I miss it a lot. It made me feel in control. For the first time, I learned what it felt like to have a little power in my world. And my, I see you have a stick of your own here, right now. Mind if I show you how well I handle a stick in the cockpit?"

"I want you to show me everything you know."

"You're the boss, Mr. Kalish, I'm here to take you wherever you want to go."

There could be no doubt that the sound of Kalish's head falling rhythmically against the seatback was audible in the passenger seating area. As Kalish felt the rush of intense sexual pleasure wash over him, he could see the moon and stars over the Caribbean streaming at him as they rushed toward the plane's nose at 400 miles per hour.

- CHAPTER SEVEN -
UNLEASHING THE BULL DOG

Grand Cayman Island – Leigh Ritch's Home

A crowd of partygoers arrived at Leigh Ritch's island retreat. The remote estate with its six-sided home was walled in and sealed off with a large gate and security cameras. On this occasion, guards wearing Hawaiian shirts and shorts stood watch at the entrance while a parade of visitors checked in.

Ritch was hosting key players from the recent venture with Vogel and Kalish. Members of all three organizations were present, some eighty people, counting players and escorts. Some were with their wives or girlfriends; but a few arrived solo, looking for someone to share the fun. Ritch was a member of a well-respected and prosperous business family on the island. Locals assumed his own prosperity was derived from the family business, but those within his family privately questioned the recently acquired wealth with no visible source they could detect.

His demeanor and polish were qualities of a man who could never stoop to the level of a common criminal. The last thing he would ever consider himself was a common anything. He moved with a quiet confidence born of privilege and local celebrity. It was a position he enjoyed. He spoke to everyone, greeted each person in a small group at the poolside bar with handshake, a pat on the shoulder, and occasional personal remark. It was no different when he greeted Shine who casually stood next to the bar chatting with a man Ritch didn't know.

"Shine, great to have you here. I trust you have found everything first class?"

"Yes, Sir. This place is fucking first class, man. Hell, the whole island is. I'd kill for a place like this. Your folks are in business here, huh?"

"That's right. We have a wonderful hotel right on the seven-mile beach. I was raised working at the pool and running drinks to the tourists on the beach. Not a bad childhood. Saw some of the most beautiful women God ever put on the planet."

"And I'm sure you got more than your share of them."

"Of course, Shine. I was never one to stand by and watch other people have all the fun. I like to throw the parties myself."

"And this is a great one, Mr. Ritch."

"Thanks. I enjoy sharing my good fortune. And, who is this gentleman with you?"

"This is Larry Garcia. I've brought him onboard to help with all the testing that's lined up. With the size of the organization, I can't keep up with all the new employees. Besides, everyone involved needs to know we can show up anytime and check them for truthfulness. When you're dealing with this kind of money, it's fairly easy for people to rationalize taking a little extra for themselves."

Larry Garcia was huge, greasy, and dangerous looking. Without Shine's invitation, no one like him would ever wind up at a party with Ritch. He looked like he should have a bandana, gun belts strapped over both shoulders, and a sombrero. Ritch knew this was someone he would never have much to do with.

"Very nice to meet you, Larry. I've got to speak to a few other folks, so I'll let Shine show you around. I look forward to spending a little time with both of you later in the week."

Ritch may not have taken a favorable view of Garcia, but Garcia was most impressed with Ritch.

Obvious wealth had always been something he found interesting. He wanted to get to know all of the principles in this operation and share in some of their good fortune. He'd already spent several hours with Vogel and sensed Vogel had taken an immediate liking to him. Ritch moved away toward the rest of the crowd, as they shared drinks and laughter amidst a luxurious backdrop that none of them had ever seen. They all knew they wanted more, lots more. Ritch looked at the rest of the men.

"How about you fellas follow me inside? It's time to talk a little business while everyone else is preoccupied. Won't take but thirty minutes and then we've got a real treat planned. C'mon inside."

As they entered the tropical home, they were greeted by name by Vogel and Kalish, and acknowledged by about ten others, all of whom they recognized as section leaders from the last job.

Ritch then spoke to the group, "If any of you need a drink, let me know. I'll only be a minute here. Just wanted to thank you all for the outstanding work you did for us and inform you of another project coming up shortly."

One of the men spoke up. "Back to North Carolina again? Wouldn't we be pressing our luck?"

"Yes, we would be pressing our luck and no, we won't be going back there. At least, not any time soon. We're going to bring the next load into Louisiana. Now don't forget, whatever you hear is confidential and you're not to repeat anything to anyone, not your wife, not your priest, nobody. This next job will more than likely be the largest single load of marijuana ever brought into the country at one time. I'm talking about several hundred tons."

"Jesus, Mr. Ritch. How can we do that? The trawler was jammed last time and that wasn't anything like what you're talking about here."

"We won't be using a trawler this time. Here, let Stephen Kalish tell you a little about the logistics. That's his arena."

Kalish stood and confidently explained the plan.

"Gentlemen, we call this operation *Bulldog*. We intend to bring an entire barge load of grass into the country from Colombia. We'll use an ocean-going tug, and of course, the most sophisticated equipment and professionals, such as yourselves. We'll have a top crew, planes flying point, a command center on shore, and top drivers and off-loaders waiting for the barge to arrive. We're looking at maybe 20 tractor-trailer loads. You men do your jobs well on this one and you won't need to work again for quite a while. But, of course, we will have other things for you to do, so don't plan on running away the moment you get your money.

"We're planning at least five or six other ventures right now. You're all key players in this operation or you wouldn't be here at this meeting. We'll be utilizing the most expensive electronics available. The Coast Guard doesn't have nearly as good equipment as we do. We'll know where they are and what they're up to almost before they do. We'll slip into Louisiana under cover of darkness and have a shit pot full of men and heavy gear to offload everything in just a few hours.

"You will all be wealthy guys when this one is done. I'm not going to say any more about it at this time. Just be ready to go when we call you. Now, we've got a really nice surprise planned for all of you. After all your hard work on our last operation, you deserve something fabulous and I think we have come up with just the ticket. We asked you to bring along your main woman and some suntan lotion because we have chartered a cruise ship for the next five days. You are all going to be treated like the princes you are and spoiled by the crew of one of the finest ocean liners operating in the Caribbean. So, let's gather up our bags and our ladies and board the chartered bus waiting in the driveway. Let's get at it!"

A look of complete surprise filled every face in the room. As they filed out of the house, a large Silver Eagle tour bus was ready to take them to the waiting ship.

*****
Aboard A Cruise Ship, Eastern Caribbean, Late Evening

The group Ritch invited for the cruise was spread out across the ship. Some entertained themselves on the dance-floor while others carried plastic buckets of quarters from one slot machine to the next in the ship's Caribbean motif casino. The pale-faced truck drivers, trawler crew members, and longshoremen didn't look like the usual tourists on a cruise ship, but more like fans at a stock car race. Others on board had other things on their minds than hitting triple seven on slot machines.

Vogel, Shine and Larry Garcia sat at a table near the bar. A small jazz trio played in the corner and a number of couples danced to the soft, slow rhythm. The three men shared a round of high-priced sipping whiskey as Vogel began talking business.

"Shine, you know how important it is to me that this testing takes a little longer than necessary, don't you? I really need for the *Bulldog* to back off at least a month so I can distribute all the shit I've already taken delivery on. If that much more grass comes my way, the bottom will fall out of the market and I'll lose a ton of money. And you will too. Am I clear here?"

Garcia's eyes grew wide as he heard the large numbers the two men talked about. Shine, slowly taking a sip of whisky, measured his words. He didn't want his almost constant inebriation to become apparent to his principal employer.

"Yes, Michael. I understand. I've told you a hundred times already. I know how much money you're talking about. But, I gotta tell you, Ritch and Kalish seem pretty dammed fired up to get this load to Louisiana. How am I going to get them to slow down? I'm sure they don't give a shit about your schedule."

"They won't move till you tell them you've checked out everybody involved. They're greedy, but not stupid. You do what I'm asking you to do, buy me at least thirty days and you and Garcia here will be glad you did. Right, Larry?"

"Yes sir, Mike. Whatever you say."

Shine noticed the interplay between Garcia and Vogel and it pissed him off to see someone he had brought in as his helper shinnying up to his main source of income. It was a violation of the chain of command and stirred more than a little distrust for his new associate. On the other hand, Vogel was playing the two men against each other to his own advantage and Shine knew it. He was just too drunk to really understand it at the time.

"Shine, you need to take a little direction from Larry and realize that old Mike has only your best interest at heart. Haven't I always looked out for you?"

"Yes, you have been very good to me."

"You're damn right, I have. Now, you and Garcia do what I'm asking and put some brakes on this *Bulldog* thing. Thirty days, no more, no less. Got it?"

Shine took a much larger swallow of the fiery, honey-colored whisky. He swished it around in his mouth, laid his head back, and swallowed. He wiped a small overflow from his chin with the back of his hand and looked at the other two men as he spoke.

"Trust is very important to me. That's what I do for this whole operation. I make sure everyone is trustworthy. I can spot a liar and thief a mile away. I pay my way by helping you find out just who the fuck you can and cannot trust."

He looked at Garcia as he finished that thought. He wanted him to understand what he meant. He had brought him to the group and he could lead him away just as easy. He was determined that a man like Garcia would not stab him in the back.

He continued with slow, deliberate words.

"When it's all said and done, one man, just one fucking guy who's willing to sell out everyone else for money, can put us all out of business and our asses behind bars. So, I think the service I provide is valuable beyond measure. Forgive me if I seem a little too damned proud. Probably had a little too much whiskey."

"I agree with you 110 percent," Vogel said. "Don't you, Larry?"

*****

Next Morning – New Bern, North Carolina

Doug McCullough and Terry Peters sat on opposite sides of an old grey metal desk. Stacks of papers covered almost every inch of the surface except for the spot holding Doug's wingtips. The two men sipped their first round of coffee as they discussed the lack of progress on the ongoing investigation into the *Lady Mauricette*. Doug blew on the rim of his overheated coffee cup and tried a tentative sip.

"Damn, this is hot. Spill this on your lap and it's the Burn Center. What's the word at the Bureau? Your guys making any progress with the tails on these guys? I'm getting the feeling that everything is just getting cold and we're not any closer to finding the main players here than we were four months ago. Tell me if I'm being a little pessimistic."

"Unfortunately, your assessment is about right as far as I can tell. A few months ago, I thought this might be the career-making case I've been looking for. Now, it looks like all we have is a shrimp trawler that we can charge with possession. No captain, no crew, just an old wooden shrimp boat. That'll look great on my resume."

"You know, Terry, this wasn't just a couple of guys who decided to run a bale or two. The cost of setting up this operation had to be in the hundreds of thousands of dollars. There was a ton of sophisticated gear and, even though we got lucky with the Coast Guard guys checking them out, it was just that—a pure luck bust. They were smart enough to not leave any breadcrumbs leading back to the top. I guarantee you that unless we can get someone to flip, we'll never find out who put this together. Remember I said that." Doug pointed his pencil at his friend for emphasis.

Terry wearily rubbed his eyes. "You don't have to convince me. We've had tails on some of these guys for months now and they just go about their blue-collar jobs and routine daily lives. At this point, we don't have anything on anybody. Just a shrimp boat that we can return to the folks in Louisiana who are suing us for it anyway. Do you believe that? The guy has a reputation as a smuggler from way back. *And* he had to be in this thing up to his eyeballs. He's suing to get the damned boat back. Hell, he'll probably say we ruined his shrimp business and collect for lost earnings there too."

Doug spoke between small, hot sips of coffee.

"Yeah, and with the way juries are today, he'll get a million dollar award from the persecuting Feds who are just trying to ruin a poor fisherman. Sometimes I wish J. Edgar was still running things. We could just do what we needed to catch the crooks and everybody else could go to hell."

"Amen, Doug, Amen. So what do we do from here?"

"We just keep watching them all. We might not ever get a direct link to this case, but they'll try again. If any one of them screws up and gets caught, we'll throw the book at them, and then give them the opportunity to flip. Go to jail or do the acrobatics. That's what we're going to have to count on. I can just feel it. There are some real sharp guys at the top of this thing. They're going to keep a low profile, try not to draw any attention to themselves."

*****

Aboard A Lear 35, Somewhere South Of Miami

A young, beautiful woman chatted with Steve Kalish in the main salon as they flew to the Cayman Islands.

"Only real heavy hitters have planes like this, Mr. Kalish," she said. "You do know what they're asking for it?"

"A little over $3 million," he said, "but hey, if your business can justify it, it's not an extravagance. With most of my raw product coming from South America, I have to do a lot of traveling. I like the privacy afforded with this sort of plane."

The young woman, oozing sex appeal, turned on her afterburners for this wealthy young businessman.

"So, Mr. Kalish, what sort of business are you in?"

Kalish, feeling his oats, leaned forward to make sure she caught the sparkle in his eyes. "I'm in international trade. I import items made cheaply in third world countries and then export them for a pretty nice price here in the U.S. It's really a good deal for everyone involved. The U.S. gets a quality product at good prices; the poor countries get the cash they need. I keep a small part for myself. I look at it as almost a sort of charity. But, don't think of me as a saint or something." He winked at her.

Smarter than she looked, the lady passenger had a pretty damned good idea where Kalish's wealth originated, but she played the clueless card well.

"If your 'little part' can put you into one of these Lears, then you're moving a lot of goods. That's for certain."

"I try to sell only hot items. Yeah, I really like this little plane. Tell you what, I'll continue leasing it as I've been doing for the past year and, after my next deal is concluded, we'll talk about getting one of these for myself. You would, of course, continue to be my private stewardess, wouldn't you?"

She moved toward Kalish, pressing her ample breasts against his chest. She threw her arms around his neck and offered her mouth in a deep, passionate kiss.

Kalish responded quickly, slid his hands down her back and gently kneaded her cheeks in a full embrace. She lowered her hands to his belt buckle. With slow, deliberate movements, she unbuckled his belt and unzipped his fly. She dropped his trousers and slipped her hands into his shorts. Kalish's low moans encouraged her and they moved to the private sleeping quarters in the rear of the jet. She would make certain, right now, that if Stephen Kalish ever needed a private stewardess, her name would top his list.

*****

Late Evening, April 1983 – Leigh Ritch's Home, Grand Cayman

Leigh Ritch left a small gathering of friends to take a private phone call from Michael Vogel.

"What's up? Any word from our friends in Colombia? I'm hoping we get a great price on our product this time. A load this big should get the bottom price."

"I've got some news all right. My pilot tells me that he knows a Customs pilot. Said the guy had a few too many the other night and let it slip that the Feds are onto this load. They're watching and plan to interdict as soon as it gets in U.S. territory."

"He's just running off at the mouth. He doesn't know anything about what we've got going. Your man, Shine, could check anybody you think might have talked and clear this up. I say we don't worry about it. I've got too much already tied up in this, millions. Another episode like the Coast Guard fiasco in Beaufort and our contacts will all look elsewhere for distribution. We need for this to be a big success. This will put us in the major leagues. They'll be standing in line to get our business."

"I'm out. The pilot said this guy knew way more than he should. I like money just as much as the next guy, but I don't want to rot in jail over one load."

Ritch knew he needed to talk Vogel down. He might be a slimy git, but his connections were completely necessary to pull of their business endeavor. "This isn't just one load. This is the largest single load ever brought into the country. Don't get scared off."

"Fuck you, Ritch. You know I don't scare. This is credible and I'm just not dumb or desperate enough to risk it. You and Kalish can go on if you want, but I'm out."

Ritch was frantic at this point. "What about Shine?"

"He can do what he wants. I'm only speaking for me. Just remember, I warned you all. Maybe if you backed off for a few months, things would cool off and we could do it then. What harm would there be in doing that?"

"The harm would be that the whole operation gets riskier the longer it takes to put together. The more the crew knows, the longer they wait, the higher the element of risk. We're going to move forward."

"Suit yourself. When you wind up in a Federal prison, don't be calling me for help."

"Trust me, I won't be going to prison."

Ritch set the receiver down, then immediately picked it back up and called Kalish.

"Vogel is out. He says the word on the shipment has gotten to the Feds and they're going to bust it. What do you think?"

"I think we're both a lot richer." Kalish was unimpressed. "I've heard that crap on every load I've ever run. Vogel likes for us to think he's the tough street guy. He thinks we don't want to get our clothes dirty. Let's see who's running scared now. Plus, I have some pretty good sources of my own and I've heard from a number of my people that Vogel has done everything he could think of to slow down bringing the *Bulldog* in. He's still got a lot of product on the warehouse floor and he's afraid this'll cut into what he can get for it. It might, but I don't give a damn. We'll just move ahead without him. Are we together?"

Ritch felt a lot better knowing Kalish felt confident about their chances without Vogel. "I'm definitely on board. But, I suggest we be a little extra vigilant in case our friend Michael decides to slow the *Bulldog* down with a little help from the Feds. I know better than to ignore him."

"What about Shine?" That was the big question. His device was still considered necessary, but keeping him on when his boss was out was a risky move.

"You know he's Vogel's guy. If he's around, he'll definitely be reporting back. I like Shine, but I'm just trying to be realistic."

Kalish knew Ritch was right, but they needed the guy. What else could they do? "I'll keep a close watch on him."

*****

June 1983 – A Tugboat Moving Up the Mississippi In Blinding Rain

"Captain, you got any idea if we're in the channel?" asked a worried first mate named Frank.

Captain Roland Budnikis stared at the radar screen and turned the ship's wheel as he spoke, "I can see a marker on the radar every now and again. I just hope we don't get a thunder storm coming through. It can fill up the screen and then I can't see shit. There's a lot of traffic on the Mississippi and I sure as hell don't want to run into another ship out here; not with what we're carrying. Hell, getting arrested would be the safest thing that could happen. I don't want to have to explain to our bosses that we lost a hundred million dollars for them. Wouldn't be nowheres we could hide that'd be safe."

"You don't think somebody like Kalish would actually hurt us do you? He don't seem like that kind of guy." Frank kind of liked the guy's style.

Budnikis wasn't so worried about Kalish. "Maybe not him or Ritch, but the crew down in Colombia is carrying the debt on this stuff and they'd just as soon kill you as look at you."

Frank realized he hadn't thought about that. Suddenly, he was a lot more worried than he had been before. "Well, you keep a close watch on that screen then."

"Count on it. All this rain might actually help. Patrol boats don't want to be out in this mess either. If it would lighten up just a little and keep raining till we get past all the locks, I'd be right pleased."

"What are we going to do if they want to look in the hold at the locks?"

"I've been knowing that bunch for years. I'll offer them a shot of Jack's finest and they'll tell me about how the fishing is. Then we'll all have a couple more shots and they'll pass me through. Happens that way every time. Why don't you go below and see if any of this water is getting on the cargo? I know she ain't watertight. If you see water coming in anywhere, throw some canvas on the spot and try to contain it as best you can."

"Will do, Captain."

The *Bulldog* made its way throughout the night. After ten days at sea, rough water and continuous rain, the crew was more than ready to get her tied up and get themselves into a bar. It had been a difficult trip with several near misses with the Coast Guard. Their course had been altered at least four times and they had repainted the entire tug and barge at night with compressors and spray guns so their appearance would be constantly different. Every member of the crew was exhausted; mentally and physically. The moment the boat was secure, their job was over. There would be a huge payday and they would never have to take such a risk-plagued voyage again. Captain Roland eased the *Bulldog* tug into the dark boatyard along with the massive barge it had pulled for more than a thousand miles. Shadowy figures could be seen waiting on the dock.

"There's a group waiting on the wharf, Captain."

Budnikis squinted, trying to see clearly out into the night. "That's got to be our crew. The boatyard is closed. Let's just tie her up. I'll get us some well-earned envelopes full of cash and we'll get the hell out of here."

"Amen to that."

Within ten minutes, the waiting shore crew threw lines to the tug and secured her to the dock. Kalish stood ready to greet the captain as promised.

"Budnikis, great job. Welcome to Lafayette, Louisiana. Did you notice anything out of the ordinary? Anyone following a little closer than normal?"

"Nope. Had to give away almost a case of liquor at the locks, but no one so much as peeked into the hold. We're home free. You got something for me and my men?"

"Right here, Roland. If all goes well the rest of the week, there'll be more headed your way in about a month. Sort of a thank you. And remember, no matter how much any of you has to drink, you don't ever say a word about this to anyone. Are we agreed on that?"

"I don't even know what you're talking 'bout!"

"That's what I want to hear. Is the cargo all right?"

"I think you may have some that got a little wet on the edges, but the bulk of its fine. Checked it just a short while back."

"Here's your money. You guys go get some well-deserved rest."

"That's just what I'm going to do, Mr. Kalish, right after I finish off a bottle of Jack. I'll be waiting to hear from you in about a month."

"You will, Captain."

As the captain and his men left, Kalish motioned to the remainder of the crew on the dock.

"Okay, boys, let's start getting this stuff onto the trucks. Time is important."

A dozen tractor-trailer rigs sat, idling in the dark parking area adjacent to the boatyard. The first in line moved forward, turned in a short arc and backed up so off-loaders would have a very short distance to carry the heavy bales of marijuana. The men all stepped quickly to the task. They wanted the windfall they would receive for the evening's work, and they wanted it done as quickly as possible. As the sun began to rise, the last truck was being loaded. A tired off-loader approached Kalish.

"What do you want to do with the wet bales? Probably a hundred or so are drenched. They were under the hatch and a lot of saltwater got through during big seas. I don't think they're worth trying to save."

Kalish shook his head. "Just leave 'em. We've loaded almost twenty rigs. That's small pickin's at this point."

"What if somebody looks below in the barge? They'll know what was going on."

Kalish waved him off. "They'll know anyway. Don't worry about it. They won't have any names or faces to put to any of this. Just finish up and let's get out of here."

"Yes, Sir."

*****

8 a.m. Monday – A Boatyard in Lafayette, Louisiana

A boatyard employee walked into the office where the owner watched a small television while enjoying his first cup of coffee.

"Hey, Mr. Warren, were you expecting a tug to be docked here over the weekend? There's a large rig and barge at the end of the dock. I haven't seen either of them before."

"It's nothing I know about, Art. Nobody called in that I'm aware of. Could have been engine problems. Nobody's onboard?"

"Not a soul."

"What's the barge carrying?"

"Looks empty. She's real high in the water."

"Well, go aboard and check her out. Get the numbers and I'll call the Coast Guard to see what they know."

As the dockworker walked back toward the tug, the barrel-chested and balding boatyard owner leaned back in his chair and continued watching the morning news. About twenty minutes passed before the worker came back to the office, concern now showing on his face.

"Mr. Warren. You really need to come down to the barge I was telling you about. The son-of-a-bitch still has a shitload of pot on board."

"Pots? What kind of pots?"

"Marijuana! That kind of pot!"

"You're shitting me. Show me what you're talking about."

Within the hour, the *Bulldog* was covered with federal agents from the DEA as well as Coast Guard and local authorities. Local police had roped off the end of the dock and police radios chattered everywhere. Two DEA officers met in the pilothouse of the *Bulldog* as rain began falling again.

"What do you make of this? You think they were hauling this stuff and they panicked, just left it here?"

"That's not it at all. There's semi tracks filling with water all over the parking lot. I'm willing to bet that what's left just wasn't worth bothering with. I think this entire barge was full of pot. I'd say we're looking at the residue of what would have to be the mother of all loads."

"Jesus. How much shit could have been on board this thing?"

"Probably hundreds, maybe even over a thousand bales of pot. I think you're looking at a street value of hundreds of millions of dollars. This is a huge operation. I'm going to call this in to D.C. This is enough shit to flood the country with pot."

- CHAPTER EIGHT -
CONNECTING THE DOTS

1 p.m. Doug McCullough's Office, New Bern, North Carolina

Doug was on the phone with Terry Peters. "Yeah, Doug. I just read a report from the home office. A barge was found this morning in Louisiana. They figured more than a thousand bales may have come ashore there. Got away clean. Tractor-trailers were used to haul it away. DEA says it originated in Colombia. Does any of this sound familiar?"

"You think it's the same group, huh?" Doug was immediately interested.

"It sure could be. I say we take a short trip down there and see if we can make any other comparisons."

Doug was up and signaling his secretary that she'd need to take care of things in the office in a flash. "They don't have any concrete leads? Names, prints, anything?"

Terry was already packing. "Nothing yet. We're all over it though. If there's anything there, we'll find it. It would be hard to hide that much pot. It'll be on the streets soon and money will start changing hands. We'll work the streets and try to get a small dealer to flip to stay out of jail. Somebody'll talk. You in?"

"Yeah, let me clear this with the boss and I'm ready to go right now." Doug hung up and jogged to the DA's office, barging in without bothering to knock.

*****

Stephen Kalish's Home – Tampa

A trusted courier arrived at the Kalish house carrying a briefcase. Steve greeted him at the door.

"Good trip, Sharer?"

"The best. I'm getting spoiled being chauffeured around the country in a private jet."

"You ain't seen nothing yet. How much this time?"

"Steve, I swear, while I was there, buyers were literally standing around waiting to hand over the cash. It's only been two days, but I'll guarantee you half of the stuff is already on the road. I've got a little over $4 million here. There'll be another batch ready for you in two days. Took me all night to check the count. That's not easy work, counting old bills one at a time. My eyes are still burning."

"Well, if it makes 'em feel any better, just remember that about a quarter million of what you counted belongs to you."

"Trust me, I was thinking about that the entire time. You know, when you have this much money in your hands, in cash, it almost don't seem real. You know what I mean?"

"It's real, all right. Take it to the ladies in the back room and they'll run it through the money counter. That'll let you know how true your count was."

Sharer carried the briefcase into the adjoining room where money-counting machines made non-stop clatter. The small room looked like the inner vault at Fort Knox. Stacks of bills filled every corner of the room. Two middle-aged women ran the counting machines. They were blurry-eyed from counting.

"Hey, Maria, this machine is on the fritz now. Sounds just like the other one did before it died. I swear we're wearing out a machine every two days. The guy who sold them to Mr. Kalish said they used them in Vegas casinos for years with no problems."

"Well, the casinos must not be handling the same amount of money we are here."

"That's pretty hard to believe."

"The broken machines speak for themselves."

*****

Clinton "Shine" Anderson's Home, Late Evening

With the evening paper in his lap, Shine nodded off watching the news. The phone beside him rang, bringing him back to the realm of consciousness. It was Vogel, and his tone wasn't pleasant.

"Well Shine, you fucked up pretty good this time, didn't you?"

"How's that?"

"All I asked you to do was help slow down this *Bulldog* load and give me two weeks to unload my stuff. You didn't slow it down a day. I wasn't in on it, thanks to my misinformed pilot saying the load was being watched. So, I'm not only out about thirty million bucks there, but thanks to your screwing me over, I'm probably gonna lose a million bucks I've already earned. Pretty bad scenario, eh Shine?"

Shine was getting tired of playing subservient to the belligerent shark. "I don't see how you can blame this on me. I didn't have any control over the *Bulldog* operation. Kalish and Ritch don't ask my permission to do anything. I told them that there were a lot of guys I hadn't screened yet, and they said they had to stay on schedule, no matter what. So, what the hell could I do about it?"

"Shine, you always told me I was paying you big bucks because you were my 'can do' guy. I'd say you owe me a lot of money back. Maybe a hundred grand would help me recover some of what you cost me." Vogel snarled into the phone.

Shine was stunned. "I don't have that kind of money."

"Well, I just wanted to call and give you a chance to come clean and take some responsibility for your failure. I see now that I'm just wasting my time. So, I guess this is where you and I part ways."

"I can't fucking believe this. I've always done everything you asked of me. I always—"

The phone went dead as he spoke. Shine was sweating and his heart was racing at such a bad ending to a long and profitable business arrangement. After sitting down and breathing deeply a few minutes, he was surprised to feel relief replace anxiety. Vogel had been a difficult asshole from the beginning.

He'd set aside enough money to get a new start somewhere else. He knew lots of people in the business now, he could continue on his own. Kalish and Ritch would probably jump right on him if they knew he'd broken off from Vogel. This might be a good turn of events, and maybe he could be known by his actual name instead of the demeaning moniker Vogel has stuck on him all these years.

Shine was exhausted. It had been a very long day and even longer week. The evening news became a background noise droning on as he drifted off to sleep. Throughout the night, he awakened numerous times as every sound alarmed him. A new feeling accompanied his every waking moment. It was fear. He'd always dreaded the consequences of his criminal activities but he'd never really feared for his own safety. Vogel was a dangerous individual and he knew it. He'd have to live with it. Maybe time would dull Vogel's rage.

*****

Tampa - Stephen Kalish's Home

Kalish hit the auto dialer and waited for Ritch to answer his call. Ritch picked up the phone and sprawled out on the designer couch. He peeled a fresh banana, took a bite, and chased it with glass of Merlot as he put the receiver to his ear.

"What's up, Skip? I've heard some rumblings in the last few days over at the bank. What's the problem? They've always been very good to us over here.

Offshore banking is the biggest business on the island, and we're certainly one of, if not the biggest, customer."

Kalish's small-framed, nondescript house had served for years as a safe house. Several armed men moved around the rooms, occasionally peering out the windows. The non-stop sound of counting machines and several women talking could be heard from the adjoining room. Kalish spoke to one of the men in the room.

"Juan, ask the women to shut up a few minutes. I've got Ritch on the line and I can't hear. They can stop counting till we're finished. Give 'em a beer."

He turned back to the phone.

"Ritch, you're not going to believe this, but I called over to the bank yesterday and the guy who runs the place, you know, Roberto, or whatever the hell his name is, told me they can't take any more money. I've got two large bags packed here with $12 million in cash. The girls are still running the counting machines and we've probably got three times that much just sitting in cardboard boxes on the floor. I don't like baby-sitting all this cash, man. There's a ton of damn people that would slit all of our throats here for a grand. If they find out what we've got stashed, well, I just don't feel comfortable sitting on it. What do you suggest? Any other bankers over there you know of?"

"Hey, these are the kind of problems we always wanted, right? How many guys your age are looking to buy their own jet?"

"I ain't looking anymore." Kalish said proudly.

"All right, man! What'd you get?"

"A Lear 35. It's a customized executive model. I mean, it's a beautiful piece of metal. Four hundred knots plus. We won't have to worry about reserving one anymore. You just call and I'll send it over after you.

Midnight, sunrise, whenever, you just call and an hour later, you got your own jet, man. Now, I'd like to load all this fucking cash into it and get it the hell out of my house so I can sleep. You got an idea?"

"Let me sleep on it, Kalish. I'll figure out something. We need to have quick access to a lot of cash because our suppliers don't take checks. We need to keep a lot of green handy. I'll see what I can do. Maybe I can store some of it here in the compound."

Kalish hung up and looked around the room at stacks of money, twenties and hundreds, everywhere. The armed guards kept staring out the windows for any sign of unusual activity. He walked into the counting room and smiled at two women who worked full time on the counting machines. He noticed loose bills on the floor around them and bundles they'd already counted. Each bundle was secured with large rubber bands and a white piece of construction paper with the amount of the stack scribbled on it by a magic marker.

"How's it going, ladies?"

"You know, Mr. Kalish, I read arsenic is used to print money. I go home at night with ink all over me. It isn't going to kill me, or make me crazy, is it?"

"No, Maria. I don't think you have anything to worry about. The lack of money will kill you a hell of a lot faster than too much."

"I hope you're right. Can I ask you a question?"

"Go ahead. Don't know if I can answer it, but I'll try."

"Why don't you just let the banks count the money? Don't you trust them? I don't think they would steal your money."

"That's almost funny, Maria. They don't even want the money, counted or not. I'm going to have to find a new place to take it. Can you believe that? A bank, not wanting money?"

"That's really weird, Mr. Kalish."
"You're telling me."

*****

Private Jetport – Tampa

Kalish was ecstatic as he walked around his new Lear, taking in the magnificence of his new acquisition. It was a spectacular South Florida day, with an intense sun and a comfortable sea breeze coming in off the Gulf of Mexico.

As he made his rounds of the silver jet, Jorge Martinez, a Cuban he'd met at the private aviation facility, approached.

"Ah, Mr. Kalish, this is the new Lear I've heard so much about? She's spectacular. When a man owns a plane like this, it speaks of his entrepreneurial spirit. You obviously have a good head for business. What was it you said you do? Imports?"

"That's correct, Jorge. I import things."

"I would imagine that you must do a lot of importing from South America, am I right?"

It was apparent to Stephen that the implication was that his business must be drugs: He was too young to own such an expensive airplane and southern Florida had a large number of young men who made lots of money importing "things" from South America. He realized he stuck out. He would play along, though, as it would be stupid to acknowledge such a profession.

"South America as well as many other countries. I buy exotic lumber for the boat building business. I broker a lot of teak and Honduras mahogany."

"I was told that you did. Listen, I know of many of the problems associated with the boat building lumber business. I've helped quite a few young lumber brokers, such as yourself."

"What do you help them with? Do you own timber tracts?"

"No. I've found that for South American boat building lumber brokers, banking becomes a huge concern. Not just the money exchange, which can be a problem with all the different currencies, but also just where to find a good bank. A bank that understands the South American boat building lumber business. You get my drift, Mr. Kalish?"

All the double entendres and innuendos were obvious to the point of being comical. This guy knew what Kalish did and knew cash handling was a problem.

"Jorge, if I wanted to talk to someone who ran such a bank, how would I find out this information?"

"Why, for a small finder's fee, I'd be pleased to introduce you to a gentleman who specializes in businesses such as yours."

"Don't tell me he's in the Caymans. I've already done some banking there and it's not what I expected."

"It's not the Caymans. I understand that with such a small island, storage space is at a premium."

"Can you tell me where this bank is located?"

"Panama, my friend. Panama. I have a wonderful contact there who can be of great help to you."

"What can this person do for me?"

"Unmonitored bank accounts, unwatched by U.S. authorities. They have no reciprocal agreement with the United States or the Internal Revenue Service. What you do is just between you and your bank. Not to mention, they offer great assistance in such difficult matters as multiple passports under different names, clearance through their airports with no custom inspections going in or out, and as many legal business licenses as you need to properly address the concerns of your overseas operations. These are just a few things they can do for you. Would you have an interest in meeting such a person? I can arrange this for you."

Kalish looked at the man who appeared to know just about everything about his business. He studied his eyes and countenance. His long-term ability to size up the authorities told him this guy wasn't trying to make a drug bust. He was trying to do just what Kalish wanted to do--make money and lots of it.

"Yes, I'd very much like to meet this individual. How would I go about setting this meeting up?"

"Give me your phone number and I'll handle the arrangements. You're available, when?"

"To meet this person, if he can do as you say he can, anytime would be fine with me."

"Mr. Kalish, you're about to have some very interesting doors opened to you. Be prepared to travel once I call you."

"I need an hour's notice. Call me."

"I will."

- CHAPTER NINE -
BANK OF NORIEGA

Tampa, Florida – Upscale Restaurant

Kalish and two companions sat talking in a dark corner of a plush lounge of an upscale Tampa restaurant where a jazz trio in the far corner attracted an after-dinner crowd. Jorge Martinez was there to introduce Kalish to Cesar Rodriguez, a Panamanian national. He was darkly Latin and covered with gold, from his heavy pendant to the Rolex Presidential on his wrist which he flashed as he talked. Kalish had a drawer full of $10,000 watches at home and handed them out like Halloween candy to associates who won his favor. So he recognized a nice watch when he saw one.

"Ah, Mr. Kalish, what you have been told is true. Panama needs capital. We live off the dollar. American dollars in large quantities can open doors in my country that you would never have access to here in your own country. How much cash are you looking to secure in our banks?"

Without batting an eye, Kalish replied, "Initially, $15, maybe as much as $20 million. If all is as you say it is, and you impress me with your services, a couple hundred million."

The look of utter shock couldn't be removed from the Panamanian's face.

"That's a tremendous amount of money. If I had not taken the time to corroborate some of what my Cuban friend here told me about you, I would probably just get up and leave now, as I must be in the company of a wild dreamer. But, I believe what you are telling me and congratulate you on your business acumen."

Kalish knew he had started the man's mind running at top speed wondering how he could cut himself in on some of this pile of cash.

"It's not all mine, understand. I am a partner with several others, spread across the country and into the Caribbean and South America. I would have to see what you could offer us and then consult with them to reach a consensus as to how much we would be willing to place in your country."

"I understand. Rest assured my country would bend over backwards to assist you and your partners in securing your business interests and safeguarding your profits. We have flexibility, as there is only one person from whom we need to seek approvals in Panama. Totally the opposite of how it is in America where you have to buy off many, many politicians to achieve the same results."

Kalish smiled and replied.

"I believe Benjamin Franklin said, 'The best form of government is a benevolent dictator'. And that is someone with the power to make a decision without seeking approval from anyone and yet having the best interests of his countrymen at heart."

"*Senõr* Kalish, you have just described our President, General Manuel Noriega. A great man. I know he would be delighted to meet you and help you and your associates with your business ventures. If I set up a meeting, will you come meet the General?"

Kalish couldn't believe what he was hearing. This was possibly one of the most exciting things that had ever happened to him. He was determined not to show his excitement, however. Over-eagerness would be bad for this exchange. "I would be very interested in meeting President Noriega. What do I need to do?"

"I will make the arrangements and tell you when to come. Perhaps we can take your jet aircraft? Our friend here tells me that you have a very impressive private Lear. A 35, I believe he said."

"That's correct. I'd be delighted to fly us to Panama."

"That's good, Mr. Kalish, very good. Oh, one other thing I might mention: When you come, you might want to, really you should, bring a token offering to the General, sort of a good will gesture."

Kalish immediately understood, but it always paid to confirm. "Dollars, right?"

"Yes, that's correct."

"How much of a gesture are we talking about?"

"Let's say three hundred thousand. That will let him know how serious you are, and I assure you that will get you the sort of cooperation you are seeking. It's not really all that much, considering the magnitude of what he can offer you. It will just indicate to him that you are worth his time. I, of course, know that you are. Are you all right with that?"

Kalish considered the stacks of bills he was tripping over at his home. "At this point, three hundred grand is not a problem. Just call me when you get things arranged."

"That's very exciting, Mr. Kalish. Waiter, can we have some more drinks over here? That's right, fresh drinks for everyone. Put it on my bill."

Apparently, the Panamanian felt he had made a lot more than a day's wages this evening. If three hundred thousand was all it took to make these people feel like winners, Kalish was thinking maybe this deal would be more beneficial to him that he'd first thought.

*****

Le Club – Grand Cayman

The nightclub was decorated for a very special evening. A private party was in full swing. As usual, Ritch had his contact in Tampa fly in a dozen lovely young escorts. Some were college girls, others, single mothers with bills to pay. Whatever their reason, they all had one thing in common: They were beautiful. Ritch's long-standing arrangement with the escort service ensured that Le Club and all of the businesses he handled were populated with these women. It made doing business with him a pleasure. Many special envoys from the beautiful people were in attendance this evening. Ritch, always the consummate host, made the rounds kissing the women and toasting the men, though several of the men appeared as if a kiss from him might be more to their liking. He was in his natural element; mingling, small-talking, sharing his toothy smile, and schmoozing.

Many famous faces dotted the crowd. Ritch was particularly attentive to an American celebrity couple. The pair enjoyed the tropical paradise, its ambiance, weather, and the royal treatment from Ritch, who seemed to be the de facto prince of the island.

They had long been regular visitors to Ritch's estate and the rumor persisted that he and the actress had been an item. One thing was certain: Ritch enjoyed the celebrity limelight. He walked between the two, linking arms with each, and escorted them through the crowd, stopping to introduce them to anyone he thought might be impressed or helpful at a later time.

Ritch's growing affluence was apparent to the locals but many didn't want to assume the worst. The word was he was making a fortune in the lucrative local real estate market. His family had been well entrenched in island business and it was only natural he would reap the rewards of their contacts, local knowledge and circle of associates. The actress laughed as she turned to look at Ritch. She had his number and she knew it. Of course, she had the number of most men she came into contact with.

They moved off together, still laughing and circulating among star struck patrons and business contacts. After a while, Ritch excused himself and gathered his associates to his office. As they entered, Ritch greeted each man personally, offering a drink or Cuban cigar. After a short round of small talk, Ritch addressed the gathering:

"Gentlemen, welcome to my island. I hope you find everything to your liking. If there's anything you want during your stay, just drop the word and it'll happen. I'm willing to bet that the cash we spread among you this past year has whet your appetite for another venture Steve and I have been working on. We call it the *Master Blaster*."

Sharer, seated in the back of the room, asked, "Another barge into Louisiana?"

"Not quite. An entire shipload. We're talking over a million pounds. This will be the largest shipment ever offloaded in the United States. This could make millionaires out of each of you sitting here this evening. You all know that we're reliable when it comes to sharing the wealth. Our attitude is: Without you, we can't make this work. And this won't be our last project. No, this will be only the first in a major escalation of our endeavors. You will all be an integral part of the growth of our operation, and in just a few short years, you'll be able to retire to any place in the world you want and live like kings. Are you all with us on this?"

Every head in the room nodded agreement. These were not educated men with many opportunities in their lives. There was very little they wouldn't do to have a shot at the kind of money Ritch was talking about.

"I won't go over all the thousands of details that we're working out," Ritch continued. "I will tell you that this'll happen within the next six months and your roles will be carefully spelled out. Your continued confidentiality is crucial to our success and your own good health. If you decide to bow out, your silence in this matter as well as the overall workings of our organization is a must. I won't say any more about that as you have already proven to me that you can keep silent. Either myself or Skip here, will contact you with all the details you will need to know to handle your part. I don't feel it advisable for anyone to know more than his or her own jobs as it creates additional risk for everyone involved. So that's all I'll share with you this evening. The rest of the weekend is yours. Go, have a great time and we'll talk to each of you before you leave. Good evening."

The group dispersed back into the now-quiet bar. Several would remain and drink free high dollar cocktails till they could barely stagger back to their rooms. Their lives offered very little of this luxury and they were determined to miss none of it. Ritch and Kalish remained in the office.

Ritch asked, "So, you fly over in that hot new Lear?"

"You know I did. Don't know how I ever got along without one. Not bad for a poor boy from Florida, eh?"

"You don't even remember what it's like to be poor, Steve. I've never seen anybody get used to being filthy rich quite as fast as you did."

The men laughed and Ritch walked over and put his arm around Kalish. It was apparent both men felt more comfortable speaking just to each other.

"So, what's the big news you have to tell me?" Ritch asked. "I understand they don't want any more of our money in the banks here. Roberto called me, full of apologies, offering to do everything but wash my car, or of course, store our money. What ever happened to banks wanting money and even paying interest on it? They used to give away dishes and crap just to get somebody to put a hundred bucks in a savings account. What ever happened to that?"

"They're concerned that the IRS will cut them off from the U.S. Treasury and they'll be blacklisted if they continue to protect people with concerns such as ours. I've got two words for them, Ritch: Fuck them. We don't need their services anymore. I've located a far more friendly location to do business."

"Where would that be? Colombia? I don't trust them with anything. I wouldn't believe a word they said, Kalish. I know they're talking about helping us with our money problems, but I'm afraid they want to do a lot more with it than store it."

"No, not the Colombians, Ritch. I'm talking Panama."

"I thought Panama was run by some tinhorn dictator who already ran a drug-smuggling concern of his own. Why would he want to help us?"

"He doesn't run anything. He facilitates business that can bring dollars into the country; cut him in for a share and operate freer than anywhere in the world."

Ritch was immediately interested, but cautious. "What do you mean by free?"

"This is from one of his top guys. This is what he tells me. He says they can offer free banking and take any amount of money we want. The government will protect our money in their state run banks. The IRS has no power over them, and they don't offer the U.S. any oversight on American accounts."

"You're shitting me."

"You ain't heard nothing yet, man. Multiple passports in any names we want. Legitimate business fronts. And you're not going to believe this. He says we can use the military runways at the airports without ever going through customs, coming or going. We can rake in millions, give the man a share, and even live there, out of the reach of any law enforcement agency in the world. Not bad, huh?"

"What makes you think they can be trusted to not just take the money and put a bullet in our heads?"

"We always hold back. They want a cut of a heavy cash flow and they know we can give it to them. He tells me that the guy who runs the country, some general or something named Noriega, doesn't have all that much cash to play with. He needs the army to stay in power and the country's too friggin' poor to support it. He used the rent the U.S. paid him for the canal to hold it all together, but it takes all that just to stay afloat. He encourages people like us to set up shop there. I'm going to fly over and visit with him in a couple of weeks and check it out. You want to come with me?"

Ritch took a moment to seriously consider it before deciding he trusted Kalish to handle this alone. "No, I've got too much to do with the *Master Blaster*. You handle it and just let me know what you find. You want some muscle types to go with you?"

"Not just yet. Maybe when I take the first load of cash over, I'll get some help. Don't want it to appear that we don't have our own security force, you know what I mean?"

"Exactly. Nightcap?"

"I'll take a beer."

"That's all great news, Kalish. Now, let's go be the proper hosts. I'm sure several of them will need a strong shoulder just to get to bed."

*****

Aboard Lear 35 Bound for Panama

Kalish and Sheila had just finished conducting a meeting of the "mile high" club. She was enjoying her new position as permanent pilot of the luxurious private jet.

"We're still on course, aren't we?"

"Absolutely. The autopilot is extremely accurate. I don't shirk one duty for another, though I find both quite rewarding."

Kalish caressed her body as she attempted to put her blouse back on. She was a very confident woman; sexy and powerful in her own way.

"I've got to get back to the cockpit. We can pick this up again later. Perhaps, you can show me the town once we arrive in Panama."

"Someone will have to show me first as I haven't got a clue. I'm sure however, that our host will be only too glad to help us find the points of interest. If you need another point of interest." Kalish wiggled his hips in a lewd gesture Sheila pretended to be excited by.

"I'm always interested. Now, excuse me while I prepare for our descent."

After a brief conversation with Panamanian air traffic control, she turned back to Kalish. "They must think we're pretty important. I've been cleared for landing and directed to the military facility on the other side of the tarmac from the commercial passenger terminal. You must have very influential friends here."

"The most influential."

"I see." Sheila purred. "I'm impressed."

After a smooth landing, the Lear taxied over to the military compound as directed. A contingent of military officers stood by as the jet came to a stop. As the steps were lowered and Kalish stepped out, a Panamanian military officer stepped forward and spoke in near perfect English, with only a slight Latin flavor.

"Ah, *Senõr* Kalish. Welcome to Panama. On behalf of myself, and our President, Manuel Noriega, let me extend to you, a most warm welcome. Please, follow me to my car and I'll show you to your quarters. We have a suite reserved for you at our finest hotel. Do you have bags with you? I was told you might have several, well, valuable bags that might need extra protection."

Kalish raised an eyebrow at the none-too-subtle hint. "Yes, my pilot will be coming with us and I'll get my luggage. I only have two bags and I believe my pilot has a small overnight bag."

The officer was more than impressed when he saw the pilot step out of the plane behind them.

"Your pilot, I am greatly surprised to see such a lovely creature who has set aside the concerns of women to pursue a man's occupation."

"Do not worry, my friend. She combines the two quite nicely." Kalish enjoyed being envied, completely missing the look that passed between his pilot and the Panamanian military officer.

The officer drove Kalish to his hotel. For a third-world country, it was surprisingly well appointed, and his suite on the top floor had to be the premiere location in the entire country. It was quite apparent that Noriega was expecting great things from him. As the military host left, he reminded Kalish that he would return later that evening.

"Around 6 p.m., I will either come by personally or send a member of my staff to pick you up, as the president has arranged a small social in your honor. There will be bankers, politicians, prominent people from Panama, as well as myself and others from our military. I'll look forward then, to this evening."

"Very good. I never did get your name."

"Corso. I am Colonel Raphael Corso. Nice to have made your acquaintance."

"Nice to meet you, also. I'll look forward to this evening."

*****

After passing the afternoon with athletic bouts of sex with Sheila pressed up against the windows of the hotel suite, Stephen Kalish grew optimistic over his reception as he showered and dressed for the evening. By the time Colonel Corso returned to drive him to the capitol, his mind was churning with all the possibilities this meeting could present. The town itself was a mixture of old government buildings punctuated by small shops. The streets were pockmarked and in need of major repair. Like many third-world countries, Panama was a mixture of the few wealthy elite that ran the country and the masses of very poor who suffered under the authoritarian rule that helped the rich stay in power.

They arrived in less than twenty minutes to the capitol building, itself an older structure, not large but surrounded with enough guards to signal its position. The colonel's driver pulled up to the main steps. As they exited the car, guards at the street and at the main entrance to the building snapped to attention. The place had more of the feeling of a military base than a seat of government. Kalish figured that since the president of Panama still referred to himself as a general, the military had to be on the top rung of the local ladder.

As they entered, more guards came to attention. The colonel returned their salutes and escorted Kalish to a small gathering of distinguished-looking attendees seated near a quartet the provided an elegant musical backdrop for the evening. He motioned for Kalish to follow him and they sat down at the table. Small talk ensued, along with the expected questions that Kalish fielded.

"Yes, Mr. Kalish, I understand you are from Florida. What part? I'm told you have a private jet, what make? You're so young. Did you inherit your fortune? How did you become so successful this young in life? Are you married? Would you like to meet a beautiful young Panamanian woman? Yes, our daughter."

After an hour of such light fare, the band stopped playing and the assembled cast all leapt to their feet, applauding as a small, rotund uniformed man entered the room with bearing so regal that he could only be the General, and President Manuel Noriega.

Polite applause erupted from the crowd. The General shook hands, smiled, and gestured with a trained political eye to the appropriate guests in the room whose sponsorship he enjoyed. He came to the group where Kalish was seated.

"You must be Stephen Kalish."

He extended his hand.

"Yes, Sir, General Noriega."

"It's a pleasure to have you here with us in our beautiful country. Let me extend to you the warmest of welcomes. I will see to it that your visit here is memorable, and profitable. Panama is a great place to conduct business. But, we'll talk more about that later. Let's be seated, shall we? And tell one another all that is good today."

The group waited till Noriega seated himself and then followed suit. Kalish did likewise. Drinks flowed. Gossip of all sorts, political as well as social, filled the next two hours. Several young women were brought over to Kalish to dance with, but each time he begged off, claiming two left feet. He was gracious, however, and charmed the crowd with the skill he had accumulated while mingling with the wealthy in southern Florida, many of whom were also of Latin descent. They were very similar in speech and thought in this gathering. The general appeared comfortable among the group, but seemed to grow restless and after a while, he offered his apologies.

"Beautiful ladies, gentlemen, I would love nothing more than to while away this entire evening in your company, but I'm afraid the duties of State call and I must leave to take care of Panama's business. Mr. Kalish, I will be heading to my office. Would you be free to accompany me so that we may go over our common interests?"

"Certainly. Ladies, gentlemen, it's been a pleasure and I'll look forward to getting to know you all far better in the days ahead. Good evening."

Noriega grabbed Stephen's arm as they walked, making it clear to the gathering that he was a very special guest. He had to admit he enjoyed the attention. He had been in the presence of numerous wealthy and powerful men before. Hell, he was one. *But this is different*, he thought. Here he was being wined and dined by the president of an entire country. To his mind, he had achieved a new level of accomplishment.

They continued to General Noriega's private office guarded by young elite troops armed with automatic rifles. They saluted as Noriega and Kalish approached, then opened the door for them, and shut it quietly upon their entrance.

"Come in please, Stephen. This is my office. Make yourself comfortable. Can I offer you a brandy? I have some of the finest you will ever taste. I fancy myself an expert of sorts on brandy and cigars, two of my passions."

"Yes, I would love one. This is a very impressive facility you have here, General, and your troops, very sharp."

General Noriega shrugged, "After all, Stephen, my background is the military. It got me to where I am today. The training, the discipline and understanding of power and respect, all lessons I learned in the army. In

Panama, to be in our army is a privilege. These young men are from some of our best families."

The two men sat down in plush leather chairs and sipped their brandy. It was a little stronger than Kalish enjoyed, though he knew better than to let on to the general that he wasn't enamored with his choice. He set the brown leather attaché case he had brought with him beside the chair, which didn't go unnoticed by Noriega.

"I see you have brought your case with you. Might I assume that you have brought something for me in the way of an introduction?"

"You would be correct. I'm told that your favorite color is green so I have brought you an entire briefcase full of green."

He bent down and opened the briefcase, revealing it was completely full of U.S. dollars. He pushed it toward the general.

"There's a little over three hundred thousand dollars. It's a gift for you for offering us, my associates and myself, the opportunity to conduct business in your country."

"Very impressive, Stephen. You realize, I'm not a poor man. I control all the monies in Panama. However, as a caretaker of the people here, many of whom are uneducated and poor, so much of what I have I use for the benefit of my people. For that reason, I encourage entrepreneurs such as yourself to locate their operations within Panama and I will guarantee their protection; not just from the ordinary criminals who seek to take what you have, but from the prying eyes of other governments who are not as understanding as I am when it comes to free enterprise. For example, your government considers itself the owner of your business and you, merely the hired operator who gets to keep a small part if you should find a way to become successful in spite of their constant interference. They make the old Mafia insurance racket look like a legitimate business. You'll find Panama a far freer place to do business.

"Of course, we expect this to be profitable for us also, but not nearly so oppressive as other governments. You allow us to keep just the icing, say only fifteen percent off the top of your profits, and we will see that you are able to keep all the rest of your money and not have to worry about who is coming after it or you."

"General, it is very true what you say about the climate of business in the States. It sometimes seems as if the banks, the government and all the major corporations are one and the same. They work together to keep the financial hierarchy status quo."

"Very, very wise, Stephen. Let me offer this to you also. I really don't care what a man does for a living. I don't want to see children get hurt, poor people abused, you know, that sort of thing. However, all that said, a man is judged by where he gets in life, not how he got there.

"Even though I am now a respected leader of my country, I've done some things in my life that I'm not proud of. But, today I am in a position to help my country so it all works out. I've spent many years, many sleepless nights trying to put Panama into a safe position in a rather hostile and unsafe world. It has taken a lot out of me. I'm not a young man anymore.

"I'm trying to now think just a little of myself. I have a small ranch located in the interior of the country. It's quite beautiful and I love it there. I hope to be able to retire there in the not-too-distant future. It's very quiet. I have some horses and even raise a few crops, mostly for the staff to take to their homes. Even in my own backyard, I am thinking of my people. I'd like to spend a lot more time there. Would you come visit me there on your next trip? I'd love to show you around my ranch. A place that needs a little money spent on it to make it as it should be. You see where I am going with this thought?"

"I think so. You're saying that where my money comes from isn't your concern, it's where it winds up, being mainly your banks. Am I right?"

"Exactly. Let's say for example that your business was primarily the importation of illegal drugs into the United States. I already have friends who I suspect am involved in such activities. They have legal accounts in our banks; they are good citizens and friends of Panama and if they break the laws of the United States, that's not my concern.

"Even though I may allow associates of this sort to operate freely in Panama, the U.S. sees me as a leader and a front-line partner in their war on drugs. I have received awards from their DEA, you know, the Drug Enforcement Agency. They love me. Why? Because I have helped them catch many drug dealers trying to use my country as a platform from which to conduct their business without coming to me and having their operation legitimized by my personal endorsement, such as you have."

"What you're saying, I believe, is that if you aren't a partner with them, then you have no problem turning them over to the United States authorities. If you're sharing in the profits, you protect them. Am I correct?"

"I don't like to express it quite so bluntly, but you understand how things work. You will never receive a public endorsement from me regarding your business, but you will have my complete cooperation while you and your money are here. You will be protected and assisted by every means possible. For myself, and my total support, I will require from your organization a fee of $4 million dollars: One million up front, the rest when we have delivered to you the state of affairs we promise. Sound fair, my young friend?"

Kalish didn't hesitate.

"More than fair, General. If all is as you say it will be, my partners and I would love to set up shop in Panama. We have a deal as far as I'm concerned."

The general smiled, took a deep puff from his Cuban cigar and followed it with a strong sip of his cherished brandy. He'd made this proposal to many others before Kalish.

"Do you have any questions I might answer for you?"

"It all sounds good to me, General. I will be in contact with my associates tomorrow morning and I feel certain they will endorse this deal. When can we begin to work with local banks? I've got, well, sort of a storage problem back in Florida."

"I specialize in solving that sort of problem. We will introduce you tomorrow to our local banking community and tell them of my personal endorsement of your operations. You should be ready to conduct business immediately thereafter. Is that soon enough?"

Kalish held his brandy up in a toast.

"To a long and profitable venture."

Noriega smiled again, and raised his glass.

"To Panama."

- CHAPTER TEN -
GENERAL ECSTATIC

Four Months Later – Private Estate, Panama

Steve Kalish and Leigh Ritch sat in the plush drawing room, sipping *El Presidente's* favorite brandy in a palatial estate in the cool hills above Panama City.

Ritch took a deep sip of brandy. "Not bad," he said, "Not bad, at all. So, you've decided to call Panama home, eh, Kalish? Not that I'm getting a third-world feeling here in your new humble abode."

"Why not?" Kalish said. "We're golden here. The good general handed me the country on a silver platter. For the first time, when I go to sleep at night, I'm not lying awake wondering if narcs are going to come busting into my home after midnight and haul me off. Hell, they love me here. They don't give a shit where my money, our money, comes from as long as we store it here, and give them a little off the top. For the sort of cooperation we're getting here, that's a small price to pay. Very small. How do you like my place?"

"Lovely. I've got to admit I never saw you as the domestic type who'd want to settle down to something of this sort, but hey, you're not getting any younger. Why not?"

"Actually, I always wanted a place. I just didn't want *any* place. If I couldn't get something like I wanted, like this, then I just didn't care. How are things with you and the lovely Miss Locklear? You want to become Mr. Locklear and join the Hollywood crowd? I never saw you doing that. So, we're even."

"Not hardly," Ritch said with a frown. "She's head over heels for Tommy Lee, the tattooed drummer. No way can I compete with a rock star. However, you ought to see the woman I'm entertaining now. She's one of the most beautiful women I've ever seen. She's

Miss Colombia. You know, like in the Miss Universe contest. She's smart, loves the Caymans, and me, I might add. You'll meet her soon. Listen, about the *Master Blaster*. We need to firm up a date and get things ready."

"Vogel's back in?"

"Yeah, he's pissed about all the cash he didn't get out of the *Bulldog*. You know, it's funny. He's the one everyone thinks is so friggin' tough. Yet, he's the one that got cold feet and chickened out. Doesn't bother me any. I not only don't like him, but I trust him about as far as I can throw this house; and he's dangerous. I don't mind running drugs, but I don't want to be involved with getting people killed."

"Yeah, my sentiments exactly. Especially getting me killed. But we can't afford to piss him off. He still has the distribution set up and the warehouse contacts."

"Speaking of warehouse contacts, what's up with the Reo Brothers? I heard they got busted. Man, they could lead right to us if they start running their mouths."

"I'm concerned, but Vogel says there's no way they'll talk. They've been busted before for small bananas and that's what they're looking at now. The Feds don't have a clue how close they are to us."

"Hey, the way things are going right now, I can set up the entire deal and never leave Panama. You can stay in the islands and we'll never show up as suspects anywhere."

"Listen, Kalish. While we're on the subject, there's something I want to mention to you. I think it's important and I hope you'll heed my advice."

"Go ahead, big brother."

"I'm serious, now. I know that you are still doing some small loads of grass. I hope it's only grass. In the past, I've done it; we all have. Vogel has always had a ton of jobs going on, but I think you should really consider just doing our stuff. We're making enough money on these big loads that we don't need the cash. So, why take the additional risk for a small payout that you don't even need? I think it's risky and if everyone keeps their own deals on the side, somebody's going to get busted and then we'll all be tied together. It just makes sense to stop the small loads while we have these big operations underway. The *Blaster* will pump several hundred million more into our pockets. How much money can we spend?"

"Here's my problem," countered Kalish. "If I pay my regular guys enough that they don't have to work the rest of the year, then they would love to just do the big jobs. But we'd be taking home a hell of a lot less money ourselves. I keep a few small loads coming along, and they make regular money. I don't even care if I make anything on them. It's just to keep them fat. We've got these small loads down to a science. Regular distributors, safe houses, nobody's doing stupid things. Hell, I've been working with some of these guys since high school. They count on me to feed their families. I'm like their Don, you know, the Godfather. Don't worry, nothing's going to happen."

That wasn't the answer Ritch was looking for. The lines on his brow grew heavier.

"Remember, I asked you not to do it."

"No problem, man. I fuck up, you'll never be blamed."

"Blame isn't what I'm concerned about."

Ritch looked out the window and noticed two black Mercedes pulling into the drive. The lone guard, furnished by Noriega, waved them in.

"You have company."

"Who's out there?"

"Looks like Colonel Klink."

"Klink?"

"You know, from Hogan's Heroes. It's a joke."

"Gotcha. Oh yeah, it's the general's assistant. Colonel Eduardo, or something like that. Pretty nice guy. A little on the primate side, but okay. Wonder what he wants? I'll get the door. You need to meet him anyway. He's the guy for getting stuff done around here."

The doorbell rang and Kalish asked Colonel Eduardo in. Always proper, he removed his hat, placed it under his arm, and followed Kalish back into the parlor where Kalish introduced him to Ritch.

"Ah, *Senõr* Ritch. I have heard *Senõr* Kalish speak kindly of you. You are from the islands, am I right?"

"Exactly, Colonel. The Caymans. You should come and visit me sometime. I'm told that you have been an immeasurable help to Stephen and our business ventures here."

"*Si*. I was instructed by *El Presidente* to make your stay here as smooth as possible. You are to be treated as the great asset you are to Panama. We want American businesses to prosper here in Panama. To that end, we will spare nothing. I think you have already seen that, have you not, *Senõr* Kalish?"

"You and the general have bent over backwards to make this work and, I might add, it's working very well. We could not be more pleased. Now, sit down. Can I pour you a brandy?"

"I'm still on duty. I really should not."

Kalish poured him one anyway.

"I'll never tell. Enjoy. It's the good stuff the general sent over. I'm developing a real taste for it. Now, what can I help you with this afternoon?"

"*Senõr* Kalish, *Senõr* Ritch, I have two things to ask of you. First, the general is going to Washington D.C.

to receive an award from the drug agency, I believe you call it the DEA."

"Yes, the Drug Enforcement Administration."

"That's correct. They are going to be giving a medal or award of some kind to *El Presidente* and he was wondering if you might like to accompany him."

"Why, I'd be honored. Would we be taking a military plane?"

"No, that is actually the second problem. The general does not have a plane worthy of such matters of State. He was wondering if you would consider flying him there in your private aircraft?"

"No problem, Colonel. Tell the general it's a done deal. Anything else I can do to help, just let me know."

"Well, there is just one other thing he wanted me to mention."

"And that would be?"

"It's a little sensitive and I was instructed to feel you out on this. I don't know how to do that other than just ask."

"I'm sure I won't be offended. What is it?"

"Well, as I mentioned a minute ago, we really don't have a plane that would be suitable for our president to use as he visits other countries. He has a helicopter and any number of military transport planes. But, as our president, it would be a real boost to the country's prestige and that of the general if he had a plane like...well..."

"Like Air Force One? The plane that our president uses?"

"*Senõr*, that is exactly what I mean."

"And how could I be of help in this matter?"

"The general wanted to make it perfectly clear that he does not expect you to buy him a 727."

"Well, that's good."

"But if you might consider loaning Panama the money, or how you say in America, 'co-signing' a note so that the general could acquire such a plane from the Boeing Aircraft Company in the United States. Is this something you would be able to do?"

Kalish considered the request for a moment.

"Tell you what, Colonel. You go back and tell the general that I was hesitant about undertaking such a huge obligation, but you convinced me that it was in the best interest of everyone involved to underwrite this for Panama. It was your persuasive manner and sincerity that turned the tide and made me see the necessity of doing this."

The colonel knew very well what Kalish was doing for him. Such a big task accomplished would raise his stature with *El Presidente* to a new level.

"Thank you, *Senõr* Kalish. Your assistance to Panama, *El Presidente* and myself will not be forgotten. I think I will try that brandy after all."

The men finished their brandy; and as the colonel was escorted back to the waiting car, Ritch and Kalish contemplated the afternoon's developments.

"I'd say you made a powerful ally there, Steve. At what cost will this little gesture be underwritten?"

"A good 727 will probably run six to seven million."

Ritch whistled "That's a lot of money."

Kalish soothed him. "The way I see it, it's not much risk, though."

"How's that?"

"The plane is its own collateral. If the good general stops making the payments, they'll just come get the plane, in theory."

Ritch laughed. "I hope 'they' bring some military equipment with them. That would be a repossession I wouldn't want to make."

"Even if we had to make the payments for them, it would probably be small potatoes for the benefit we get out of operating here carte blanche. I like the general realizing he owes us for keeping him flying in Panama One."

Ritch thought about it a moment. "You have a point there. But, there's one thing that I think might offer up some possibilities and you're just the guy to make it work."

"What's that?"

"Colombia and Panama have had some significant disagreements recently that keep them from being able to benefit from each other's unique market positions."

"Unique?"

"Yes, the world's largest manufacturer of cocaine and the former U.S. territory that's willing to offer 'duty-free' importing for a piece of the action."

"And they haven't been getting along?"

"The way I've been told, the Colombians don't want a partnership with Noriega. They don't want to be a junior partner with anyone, and with *El Presidente*, they would never have the upper hand. This is second-hand information, mind you, but I'm told that they're about to pay off a Colonel Melo to do away with General Noriega and then support him as the new leader."

"Do away, as in assassinate?"

"That's exactly what I mean. They'd hold all the cards then, and have their own people on Melo's staff. With your relationship with Noriega, you could alert him to this. I think the gratitude of *El Presidente* would be of great value to our operations."

Kalish immediately saw the value in it. "I agree. We aren't talking the Colombian government here, are we?"

"Of course not, we're talking the Cartel. They couldn't give a shit about who the leader of Colombia is. They need the cooperation of the guys who own the country, and I know them by name. Can you work this to our advantage without the Colombians getting wise as to who tipped off the general?"

"I think so." Kalish took a moment to consider the possibilities. "I've invited him over here to see my new home. I'll spring it on him during a quiet moment."

"That's great. Let me know when you have some feedback. Another shot of the general's brandy?"

"I'm beginning to grow fond of it, myself."

*****

Exclusive Club in Tampa

Steve Kalish was back in his old stomping grounds. To frequent the best clubs and the most exclusive restaurants and have the wait staff fight over who would be receiving his gratuity had always been high on his want list. With his money, he could play in any game anywhere. This particular scene was especially sweet for him because he still considered Tampa home. He was known by just about everyone there, and his wealth made him the object of "Who is that?" questions young and beautiful women often asked. This evening, he made the rounds; pressing flesh with the city's well-heeled. The club manager came over to him.

"Mr. Kalish, good to have you back in town. How long are you here for?"

"Just a day or two."

As he spoke, he was distracted by a blonde woman with imposing looks who was talking to a small group of people gathered at the far end of the polished mahogany and brass bar.

"Robert, who is that incredible-looking woman, just at the end of the bar?"

"Talking with Hans and Rueben?"

"I guess so. She's got long, blonde hair, very beautiful."

"I think her name is Denise. She's not here very often. Kind of quiet, doesn't say much, and not a top catch from a financial point of view."

"Robert, a woman that beautiful has a commodity far more in demand than money. Can you arrange an introduction?"

"I'm certain she would be interested in meeting you, Mr. Kalish. What woman wouldn't?"

Robert moved through the elbow-room crowd to where the two men were speaking with the woman. Kalish watched as Robert politely interrupted the group and pulled the young woman aside. She appeared casual, not interested in meeting another man. She'd had many such 'he wants to meet you' opportunities in the past. Robert kissed her hand in a thank you gesture and moved back toward Kalish.

"She says you could come and join her and her friends for a drink if you like. I explained to her that you were a very special customer."

"She didn't seem overly impressed."

"No, Sir. I don't think that means a great deal to her. Maybe she doesn't have the maturity to understand the value of wealth."

"Perhaps, but she just may have the wisdom to realize that all the money in the world can't help a relationship that isn't meant to be. I think I'll take her up on her offer. Thank you, Robert."

"My pleasure, Mr. Kalish, anytime I can help. I, of course do have the maturity level we spoke of."

"Let's wait till I see how well this works out before I decide the value of your contribution for the evening, shall we?"

"Of course, Mr. Kalish, of course."

Kalish was normally confident with women. His experiences, however, had been clouded by the fact that most not only knew he was wealthy, at least in recent years, but also because most knew the source of his income. Generally, a woman willing to spend her time with a drug lord, no matter how wealthy, was of questionable morality. Kalish had enjoyed the company of many beautiful women in the past, none of whom cared where his money came from. He didn't understand why, as he approached this woman, his hands felt cold and sweaty. She didn't acknowledge his approach until he was beside her and opened with a casual, practiced greeting.

"Good evening, I'm Stephen Kalish."

He was taken back when she didn't turn around immediately to acknowledge his presence. Instead, she held up a finger toward him as though to say "Just a moment", without stopping her conversation with the two men. Then, she slowly turned, smiled pleasantly, and waited for Kalish to continue. Her show of control and confidence caused him to sweat a little more and stumble for the next line.

"I, I'm Stephen Kalish."

"I know, I know. You just told me that, as did Robert previously. Is your name supposed to ring some sort of bell with me? I'm sorry, but I just don't remember you."

"No, that's not it at all. I just wanted to meet you."

"And why is that?"

"Well, because....I, er, uh."

"Perhaps because I'm the only woman here you haven't already been out with?"

Kalish drew a deep breath and collected himself. She was going to be a challenge.

"I'm sorry. I thought you were someone else. You have a remarkable resemblance to a young woman I've flown with, a pilot, and I was just going to say hello. I'm sorry. I didn't mean to interrupt you. Just a case of mistaken identity. Could I buy you and your friends here a bottle of champagne to make up for my mistake?"

He was quite proud of the transition, as he had maneuvered from defense to offense. *Very subtle,* he thought, *yet effective.*

The woman couldn't easily read Kalish and wondered how much she was hearing was true, and how much was a great opening line. She decided to test him with a few questions.

"You often rent planes that require you to hire your own pilot?"

"Actually, I don't rent planes, I have my own. Several, but I prefer the Lear 35. It's quite fast and with the amount of traveling my business requires, the faster the better."

Not knowing at this point whether Kalish was a bullshit artist or telling half-truths, Denise took the bait, as he hoped. He knew a number of women might not be attracted to dollars alone, but money intermingled with mystery and adventure made a combination few could resist. He sensed at this moment, he had her right where he wanted, until he made a slip of tongue that put her on the offense again.

"If you would like to go for a test flight at some point, Denise, I'd be delighted to have you as my guest."

"I assume the pilot you mistook me for was named Denise? Since I haven't told you my name, our host Robert must have. You knew I wasn't Amelia Earhart when you came over."

"You got me. I just wanted to meet you," he admitted. "I'm guilty as charged. If it makes any difference to you, I was drawn to you from the first glance and didn't want to leave without an introduction. Robert, my old friend, was nice enough to indulge me. I apologize and won't bore you any longer. Good evening, Denise."

Knowing his best course of action was to be contrite and slip away, tail between his legs, Kalish smiled at her. She was far more beautiful than he first thought. He turned, and slowly walked away. His second gambit worked and Denise called after him.

"Mr. Kalish, if you promise to keep your lies to a minimum, I'll let you buy me a drink. Only the finest champagne."

Kalish turned, gave another warm smile, walked back to her, approaching a little closer than one might ordinarily.

"I never buy anything that's not the best. Robert, your finest champagne."

Denise continued pressing him.

"I'm not going to wind up having to buy this bottle myself when you realize you forgot your wallet, am I? I know it's not as expensive as a private jet, but I'm sure Robert has something in the cellar that can push a couple grand."

"Let's just say, my credit's good here."

After a few glasses of champagne and a great rendition of songs from the band setting a romantic 'Sinatra-ish' mood, a truce was declared and their conversation slipped away from cute opening lines. Kalish studied her as she talked. Her hair was long and thick; natural blonde tresses contrasting perfectly with aqua blue eyes. Her fitted dress revealed a well-endowed, but athletic shape. There was nothing about her looks he didn't find perfect. He was charmed. She was bright, confident, and offering him the chance to get to know her better. They sat at a small table, just far enough away from the band to talk.

"Well, Stephen Kalish. I'm surprised. You are quite personable. What's your line of work? What do you do for living?"

"I'm an international investor. Mainly banking. I broker investments for people who want to invest out of the country for tax purposes. My office is in Panama City, Panama."

"And, you fly commercial, am I right?"

"No, I'm not a pilot, but I do have a Lear 35 and I'd be delighted to take you up in her. I could have my pilot meet us in about an hour."

She searched the face of this brash young man. He wasn't joking and she knew it. He was a mystery and this could be the sort of adventure she sought.

"You're on. But, if this turns out to be a Piper Cub, I'm not going to step aboard."

"I would never exaggerate. Trust me."

"For no good reason, I do."

She had no idea that the flight she was about to take would forever alter her view of adventure and mystery.

*****

Later That evening – Aboard Lear 35

The sleek luxury jet cruised at 350 knots. Even Denise, who never saw wealth as an enhancement to a person's character, was impressed. His opening line may have been contrived, but the rest of his story appeared to be the truth.

"Where are we going?"

"What time do you have to be back?"

"I'm a big girl now. I don't answer to anyone but myself."

"In that case, how about a nightcap with friends on Grand Cayman?"

"Grand Cayman Island?"

"The very same. You on?"

"I'm on."

"How about another champagne? I have several vintage bottles in the cooler."

"I'm impressed. Surprise me."

As Kalish poured her champagne, the pilot announced to him quietly over the intercom.

"Mr. Kalish, you have a call. Would you like me to transfer it to the lounge?"

"Do you know who it's from?"

"Yes, Sir, Mr. Ritch."

"Put him on the speaker phone in the lounge."

"Steve, where the hell are you, Son?"

"Headed your way for a nightcap. I have a guest on board. Say hi to Denise."

"Have you ever visited Grand Cayman before, Denise?"

"No, I'm really looking forward to a short visit."

"Several days?"

"No. Probably just this evening."

"Well, Denise. One thing you can be sure of."

"Yes?"

"You're not a cheap date."

"I'm flattered. I honestly thought Steve was jerking my chain, but so far he seems to be on the level, other than the bit about the beautiful pilot."

"You mean Sheila?"

"There is a beautiful female pilot?"

"She's fine all right."

"This is getting harder to believe all the time. At least she's not a Denise."

"Well, either way, glad to have you visit us. I'll be there to pick you up. By the way, Steve, I have a few business items I need to speak with you about while you're here. Don't forget to set aside a moment before you head back out."

"That's fine, Leigh. See you in about an hour."

"Right on."

*****
Grand Cayman Island – Le Club – Later That Night

Steve Kalish convinced Denise to stay in a luxury suite kindly provided by Leigh Ritch. She turned in for the evening and Kalish, not wanting to pressure her so early in the relationship, was alone with Ritch in his private office.

"The *Master Blaster* is getting very close. Are the folks on your end ready to go?"

"Absolutely!" Kalish declared. "Most of them have been bugging me lately about when the next big payday was coming. They're ready now."

"I know that I've expressed my concerns to you before about other smaller jobs potentially leading to trouble on what we do together. I understand that you've been doing this a long time, but I just want to stress that any foul-up at all, and I mean anything, even one of your off-loaders getting busted for possession of a single joint, could jeopardize this entire operation. Not to mention the possibility of a federal retirement home for all of us instead of somewhere like where we are right now."

"Leigh, how many times do I have to assure you that I'm just as concerned about these things as you are? I don't want to see an end to this life we've carved out of basically nothing. I'll do what it takes to protect our interest. Nothing, and I mean nothing is going to screw it up."

"One more thing."

"What's that?"

"The Reo brothers. I'm still thinking that they might be talking. They'll sing to stay out of jail. I just know they'll spill their guts."

"What do they know? All they can do is say Vogel stored shit in their warehouse. There's nothing in them now and Vogel will deny everything. It'll stop right there. Besides, as slow and pathetic as the Feds are, the *Blaster* will be finished and you and I will be safely out of the country with cash out the wazoo. I'm not worried about it."

"I guess I'm a worrier. I am worried. Do you ever have your house and phone lines checked to make sure you're not wired?"

"I haven't in my new place yet, but tell Shine I want him to take a long weekend in Panama and check things out, ASAP. That make you feel better?"

"It helps. You know, even Shine is not the same as he used to be. He seems distant, a little too quiet."

"Hell, our old pal Vogel has disowned him. I know Shine has been straight with us. Vogel's been bad-mouthing him constantly for the past year. I don't know what he did to piss Vogel off so much, but I'm sure it would make us all love him if we knew. I wouldn't blame him if he didn't have anything to do with any of us. He's got to be wondering who the hell he can trust. We have the good fortune to have never trusted Vogel. There's no way to lower my opinion of him."

"You're right. I'm just jumpy. Seems like everything has just been going too good. But we've got enough to quit now if we wanted, right?"

"Whatever you have put away plus another fifty or so in our accounts in Panama, thanks to *El Presidente*."

That reminded Ritch, "Speaking of the good general, have you mentioned to him the possibility of a traitor on his staff?"

"He'll be coming over very soon to take a look at my little palace, and I intend to spring it on him while he's there. I have to pick my time and words very carefully. He's a pretty volatile guy."

"Good luck, Steve. So, who is this new lady?"

"Beautiful, huh? I actually just met her this evening. She was interested in a plane ride and I was interested in her. The rest is history. This one could be special. She's got class and a lot of attitude. I like a little fire in a woman; someone who doesn't just roll over for me."

"Beautiful, she certainly is. But be careful, man. She shouldn't know a damn thing about what we do."

"You're looking at Stephen Kalish, international banker."

Ritch laughed, "The jet is a great fucking aphrodisiac, am I right?"

"All it got me tonight is a long way from Tampa and this late night with you. Not that I'm complaining. I've been looking for a spectacular woman for a long time, and I think I might just have found a candidate." Kalish relaxed into the plush cushions of Ritch's luxe couch and let out a contended sigh.

Ritch stared as his snifter contemplatively. "If that's what you want, man, I'm happy for you."

"And you're currently between movie stars and beauty queens?"

Ritch smiled like a man who knew he was the envy of all other men. "I always have several of both around." Ritch waggled his eyebrows, making Kalish laugh. After a few moments, he settled. "I'm not in the mood right now to settle down. I enjoy my freedom and the delights offered by a life filled with options." Both fell silent, thinking about the job ahead.

"We're on our way to becoming very, very rich, my friend." Ritch said to Kalish, holding his glass out for a toast.

"I don't know about you, but I already have more than I could spend. If it weren't for airplanes, I don't know what I'd do with the money." Kalish clinked glasses with Ritch before settling back into the cushions.

"Don't sell yourself short, Steve," Ritch said with a laugh. "I have great confidence in your ability to squander a fortune." Kalish laughed and nodded at that. Ritch enjoyed this comfortable conversation between the two of them. "But, I agree. We're getting way beyond small fortunes. I moved some of my stash the other day. It took a pallet and a forklift, and the smallest bills were hundreds. I've got enough on the island to open my own bank. You're setting some aside for the time when you retire, are you not?"

"I don't know if I can retire. The folks I'm working with aren't ready to quit, and they probably wouldn't like it too much if I just announced my retirement. Besides, I kinda like the political intrigue. Who would have ever thought little Stevie Kalish, pot-smoking high-school flunky, would wind up spending a lot of time with the presidents of countries, flying all over the place on his own jet? This is the kind of life everyone wants but only a very few ever get. I'm a very lucky man."

Ritch was incredulous. "You actually like the general?"

"He's not bad. I don't trust him for shit. He'd have you killed as quick as look at you if you crossed him. Even if he just *thought* you crossed him. Two weeks ago, I flew him to D.C. to accept that award from President Reagan."

"I knew you were doing something like that. What was it all about?"

Kalish leaned forward, "You're not going to believe this shit. He accepted an award from the DEA for his efforts supporting America's war on drugs. Swear to God!"

"You're shitting me!"

"It's the truth. He has turned in a goodly number of smugglers. None that worked with him, of course. But if they didn't pay him off, they were fair game. Only one guy in D.C. has his number. Good old Jessie Helms from North Carolina. He called him a 'thug' and a 'drug lord' and the democrats and hand wringers all called Helms a moron for pointing it out." Kalish shook his head sadly. "I swear the U.S. just gets a little dumber every day."

"Was the general pleased with all your support and flying him there?"

"I think the award touched him. But in all truth, the side trip to Vegas on the way home and the love and admiration of several high-priced hookers seemed to make him far happier."

"No way!"

"That's exactly what happened. I think of him not so much as a president, but a lonely sailor on shore leave." They both laughed at that.

The two men sipped brandy and continued catching up till very late. The morning would find Kalish back in Tampa and then quickly on about his business of "international investing."

*****

February 16, 1984, En Route to Noriega's Ranch – Panama

A young Panamanian soldier drove Steve Kalish and Denise through the jungle in a vintage Jeep. Kalish sat in the passenger seat up front, and Denise sat in the back with the luggage. The road was very rough and they had been traveling for more an hour since being picked up at the airport.

"*Senõr* Kalish. I'm very sorry about the rough ride. Recent rains have washed out a lot of the road. *El Presidente* was upset when he saw how bad it was. I'm certain he will want improvements made immediately."

"Don't worry about it. How much further?"

"Just ahead. Not too much longer."

The interior of Panama consisted of sections of rich farm pastures separated by very dense and equally green jungle. The beauty of the country was undeniable. Kalish could see himself spending a great deal of time in Panama. After a few more minutes, the driver slowed down and approached a crossing gate. Beside it stood a small wooden guard shack and four uniformed soldiers with automatic weapons at the ready. One of the guards approached the Jeep. After a brief exchange in Spanish, the crossing bar was raised and they proceeded down a now very smooth road, recently paved with asphalt.

"Much better, eh, *Senõr* Kalish?"

"Very nice. So this is the general's ranch?"

"Yes, we are here. Notice how manicured it is? He is very particular about the grounds and the house. The house is almost a palace! You wait and see. I think you will be impressed." Their escort smiled widely, his pride in working for the general evident in his attitude.

As the road curved and the house came into view, Kalish felt over-whelmed. The Mediterranean-style stucco building with its red tile roof would have been a match for one of the grand houses in South Beach. The Jeep stopped at the front door where a young man in a floral shirt and white shorts greeted them.

"Ah, good afternoon, Mr. Kalish, and you must be Miss Denise?"

"Yes, I am." She flashed a smile at young man. "What a fine home the general has."

"Thank you." He gave a slight bow, his eyes glued to her chest.

"It is quite beautiful, is it not?" Denise rolled her eyes.

Kalish had the good sense to say nothing. Finally realizing that no one was talking and he'd perhaps stared a bit too long, the young man cleared his throat and gestured toward the door. "The General is expecting you. A wonderful dinner is being prepared in your honor."

"How lovely." Denise swept forward, taking Kalish's offered arm. "I'm very excited to meet General Noriega."

"Miss Denise, he is a very great man," their escort chattered.

"I'm sure." They all entered the immaculately-kept home. The general had more than enough staff to keep every blade of grass outside and every corner inside flawless. Kalish put his arm around Denise's waist as they walked down the hall to the great room where their host was waiting. Kalish was a little surprised to see that he wasn't in his usual military garb, but rather an untucked, white silk shirt and khaki pants. He now looked more the part of the South American drug lord than the military dictator he portrayed so well in Panama City.

"Stephen, my good friend. I'm so pleased to have you visit me here at my ranch. And this beautiful woman must be Denise, whom I've heard so many good things about?"

"Yes, Tony. This is Denise."

The general reached for her hand and kissed it. It was immediately obviously that the general was smitten by her beauty.

"I can see why Stephen is so enamored of you. Rarely do I meet such a beautiful woman. I'm honored to meet you."

"Thank you, General." Her eyes lowered, lush eyelashes brushing cheeks lightly flushed from the humid heat of the environment. The general was completely taken in. "Please, call me Tony."

"Yes, Tony." She smiled, genuinely charmed by the man, "And you must call me Denise."

"It is settled, Denise. We shall be close friends from here on. If there is anything you need, anything at all, you call Tony. I will handle it. Come, let me show you around my home."

El Presidente spent the next hour showing his home and grounds to his visitors. There were times when it was apparent to Kalish that Tony was more interested in looking at Denise than showing them anything. He did, however, pause a while to show them his collection of exotic firearms, both rifles and handguns.

"What do you think of my collection, Stephen? Is it not one of the finest you have ever seen?"

Kalish didn't miss the chance to ingratiate himself. "I'd have to go to a museum to see anything comparable, Tony. You have a remarkable assortment of weapons here. How long have you been collecting them?"

"Years, many years. When I was a young soldier, I became fascinated by them. After all, a gun has saved my life more than one time. They are very special pieces of equipment. Not only are they functional, but they are, to me, works of art."

All three admired the collection in silence for a moment. Kalish knew the moment was intended for them to take in the collection and make certain assumptions about the owner.

"Now, shall we move to the dining room where my cook has prepared a wonderful meal for us?"

"Absolutely, Tony. I'm starved," Kalish said.

"Very good, follow me, will you?"

The trio walked to the immense dining room. There was a very large, polished mahogany table, long enough to accommodate eight chairs on either side. A meal befitting heads of state was set before them. They ate and chatted for an hour. Afterward, Tony called for his valet.

"Manuel, please take Denise to her quarters and help her to get comfortable. I need to speak with Stephen on business for a while and I'm certain she would find it boring. Denise, there is a large whirlpool tub in the guestroom for you to enjoy, as well as fresh flowers cut here on the ranch. We won't be long."

"Thank you, Tony. I would enjoy a hot bath. Stephen, I'll wait for you in the room, smelling the flowers."

"It was a delight meeting you, Denise. I'm looking forward to showing you the countryside tomorrow."

"Me too. Goodnight, Tony."

Both men watched her leave the room.

"My God, Stephen. I had no idea your woman would be such a beauty. You are a very lucky man, very lucky."

"I know, Tony. I have been incredibly lucky in finding her."

"Let's go into the study, shall we? I'm ready for a shot of my favorite brandy. How about you?"

"I'm growing to appreciate it. Let's have a go at it."

The two men sipped brandy and talked about many subjects. The general needed to talk with someone he considered an equal since everyone else around him felt compelled to agree with him on everything. His temper was well documented. They would say anything they thought would make him happy, when what he needed was a little blunt honesty.

"You know Stephen. It is men like us, who have built the world. Where most men see only problems, we see opportunities. We are, in one respect, artists. We create business and wealth from nothing but ideas. To us the world is a great orchard. We collect the fruit. Do you see what I'm saying?"

"Yes, Tony." Kalish was careful to smile just enough. "For a man such as yourself to wrestle the control of an entire nation from established rulers and recreate it, is truly a remarkable achievement. I'm in awe of what you have accomplished."

"Ah, Stephen. You are a flatterer." The general accepted the flattery as his due, going on to return the favor. "It is no wonder you have done so well for yourself." He leaned forward, gesturing with his glass to show emphasis. "Words create power. Say the right words to people and they will support you and push you to a position of leadership. Just words. The words will cause the actions needed to gain control." The general leaned back comfortably. "Panama is in a very unique position."

"How is that?"

"Thanks to your country, we possess the only passage across the continent by ships, both commercial vessels and warships. That is a commodity of untold value. Yes, we have natural resources and we are a beautiful country, but the value of a dollar cannot be underestimated. It is what makes the world turn.

"I get so many, many offers from other governments that you would find hard to believe. These are governments that do not appreciate your country as I do." This got Kalish's attention. It wasn't the first time the general had mentioned other governments and their requests, but it was the first time he'd given any kind of detail and Kalish was curious to see what he would say. "They would rather see the United States crumble than share in its wealth. Myself, I realize that the world needs a superpower to keep the little nations from destroying each other and making life on the planet more stressful than it already is." The general got up and poured himself another glass of his precious brandy. "The U.S. fits the bill perfectly as far as I'm concerned. I have the world's greatest superpower extremely concerned over the well-being of my country and therefore, myself. And we are also right next door to the greatest consumer market. You have a lot of product to sell there, am I right?"

Kalish nodded. "I have been very fortunate in that regard."

"Don't sell yourself short, my friend," the general said with a laugh. "A lot of others have tried to do what you have accomplished. Most either failed or wound up in prison. You have flourished and prospered. I have a great deal of interest in your abilities, Stephen."

"Why's that?" Kalish accepted a refill when the general offered it.

The general waited until he was comfortably situated back in his chair to continue. "Panama is still a poor nation, dependent on the United States for most of its economy. I want to change that. I want the Panama Canal given back to my country, to let the free market determine its value, not your government. Many other countries are interested in having a say in use of the canal." The general waved off that idea. "I'm just a businessman, like yourself. I want what's best for Panama and for Tony. Panama was poor. I was poor. I don't like poor, and I don't intend for either myself or my country to stay that way. I need men like you as partners to help me with my vision of a free marketplace where vendors from all over the world find a friendly place to do business. They will find a government and *Presidente* who want to help them. As for you, Stephen, I want you to be my man in the States."

"How's that?" Kalish was both stunned and excited. This sounded very much like real power the general was offering him. The scope of what he was talking about was nearly overwhelming, and yet, Kalish knew he wanted to be a part of it.

"I need someone whose name is not Manuel Noriega to front my business interests in the U.S. I have many ideas and yet, because of my position in Panama, I cannot act on them. Many would think I'm using my position to enrich myself." The general waved off Kalish's protests. "Let me ask you, Stephen, why else would anyone subject themselves to the constant hounding, the personal risk to their very life if not to gain somehow? To do otherwise would be idiotic. There are no Mother Theresas running governments. You can trust me on that." The general wisely gave Kalish a moment for the whole idea to sink in before he continued. "Are you with me, Stephen? You could become one of the most powerful businessmen in America."

"We have the same vision, Tony. I look forward to a long, prosperous association with you and Panama."

The two toasted and settled back in their chairs, both wearing smug, satisfied expressions for the same reasons.

*****

Later That Evening

Kalish and Denise were a tangled web of arms, legs, and hair under silk sheets in the guest room at Noriega's ranch. They had just finished a rousing hour of lovemaking that was over the top for both of them.

"You're one hell of a woman. What in God's name are you doing here with me?"

"Well Stephen, you're a pretty cute guy."

"Cute? Is that what I am?" Kalish pretended affront. "Was Clark Gable cute? How about Jack Nicholson? What does it take to be a 'hunk' with you?"

"Okay, if your fragile pride is injured, you're a hunk. There, feel better?"

"Much, thank you. You're pretty much a hunk yourself."

"I'm a hunk? I'd rather be cute."

"How about beautiful beyond words? I think that describes how I see you."

"You're good with words, Mr. Kalish."

"You're good all the time. I've been thinking a lot about you these past couple of months and I've come to some conclusions."

Denise froze, all thoughts of playful banter erased from her mind in an instant. "About me?"

Kalish took her hand and rested it on his chest. "More about us."

"And these conclusions were?"

He pulled her face to his and whispered. "I'm twice the man with you, make that ten times the man with you, than I am without you. I want to keep you with me, forever."

Denise's heart was nearly pounding out of her chest. "You know I don't believe in playing house? We've been over that."

"I know, you want it official or not at all. I've thought a lot about that, and I keep coming up with one question."

"Which is?"

Kalish reached down under the bed and brought up something in his clenched hand. He slowly opened his hand, one finger at a time and revealed the largest diamond ring Denise had ever seen.

"Will you wear this ring forever and ever? Will you be my wife?"

She gasped as she took the ring and slid it on her finger.

"You know I'd never consider marriage unless I was sure it was forever. You know the words, 'in sickness and health...'"

Stephen finished for her. "'...for better or for worse till death do us part'."

"If you really mean it with all your heart, then, yes, I will marry you Stephen Kalish. I will be your wife, forever. Can I ask you one question?"

Feeling like king of the world, Kalish would've given her anything in that moment. "Ask away."

"Is this thing real? It looks like the Hope Diamond."

Kalish laughed wryly. "Yes, it's a real diamond. All six carats."

Denise swore, unable to take her eyes off the rock. "I'll need a sling to carry my arm with this on."

"Yes, but every man in the room will know you're taken."

Denise felt the tiniest hint of apprehension bloom in her heart. She had always seen the value in using her body to get what she wanted, but this man...this man was different. She had shared her deepest desire, to be a man's one and only for the rest of their lives. She had opened up and told him how important marriage vows were to her. Here he was offering her the dream she had not really dared to dream and yet... "Diamonds are beautiful, but they won't hold a marriage together."

"I know. I'm not counting on it to keep you with me. I intend to spoil you with attention, love, and affection every day of your life. No one could offer you more."

Denise's heart overflowed with happiness. "Now, you're talking. And when will we get married? And where? Any ideas?"

"I'll let you pick the time and place. Any time. Any place. But the sooner the better. I don't like sleeping alone. Especially since I met you."

"You will never have to sleep alone again."

"Is that a promise?"

"Yes."

- CHAPTER ELEVEN -
IN LOVE IN PANAMA

April 1984 – Kalish Estate – Panama City

Steve Kalish and his new bride, Denise, entered the great room as chimes rang to announce the arrival of guests. "I got it, Beautiful."

A Panamanian officer stood at the door under an olive drab umbrella sheltering him from a downpour.

"Senõr Kalish, *El Presidente* is here. Are you ready to receive him and his escorts, Sir?"

"Of course, we're delighted he's arrived. Please come in."

"I'll inform the guards to escort him this way."

Denise and Stephen watched the general approach. This was all new to her and she was quite impressed by all the security precautions. "You know, I'm used to security with my father's job, but this is extreme."

"Why did your father's job involve security?"

"I told you, he's with the Secret Service."

Kalish was stunned into momentary silence. "No, you didn't."

Her revelation took his breath away, but he would have to panic over that later. The dictator of the country they lived in who helped them pull off the largest scale drug smuggling chain the world had ever seen, was arriving. Grilling Denise about her father would have to wait. Noriega entered, flanked by high-ranking officers. Kalish could only hope he didn't look as stressed as he suddenly felt.

"Ah, Stephen, my friend. How nice to see you again. Your hacienda is truly beautiful, as lovely as any in Panama City."

"Thank you, Mr. President. We are delighted to have you visit us. You remember Denise, now my bride."

Noriega took her extended hand and stepped back to admire her.

"And a magnificent wife you are, Mrs. Kalish. Stephen is a lucky man to have such beautiful surroundings for a home, and now a spectacular woman to accompany him here. Lucky indeed! I shall require a dance with you before this evening is over."

"Of course, Mr. President," Denise replied. "I'd be delighted." She was entirely flustered, feeling like a princess with his praise and her new position in life.

"Denise, call me Tony." The general gently chided. "I have told Stephen to do this many times. He just insists on the formality of my title. I think he enjoys the company of *El Presidente* more than a Tony. Am I right, Stephen?"

"You are always right, Mr. President. Please, make yourself at home. Our butler, Artiste, will be delighted to get you a drink, food, anything you need. Please, help yourself to a comfortable seat and relax."

Noriega stood, surrounded by his staff. Before the moment could get awkward, Kalish rushed into the only topic that came to mind at the moment.

"So, General, I was speaking with my aviation broker yesterday and I think we can arrange the purchase of a Boeing 727 for your use. I've seen her, and I think you'll be most pleased. Any head of state would be proud to have such an aircraft."

To his relief, the general seemed to take the change in conversation in stride. "Well, Stephen. I have to say that our relationship has become one of the most gratifying that I have encountered through my business ventures beyond my duties as president. And, I might add, this appears to be a very profitable arrangement, am I right?"

"You are, General. I hope that it continues to be so as I intend to make this my home. I have grown very fond of Panama and its hospitable ways." Kalish was at this point wondering why the conversation was staying so formal. He was used to getting the formal stuff out of the way but on this day, the general seemed to be drawing it out, and it made Kalish just a bit nervous.

"I am pleased that you have come to that decision. If I can assist you in any way, feel free to call on me."

Knowing something was up and he needed to get the general in private to talk about it, Kalish linked an arm with Noriega and turned to Denise.

"Darling, I'm going to walk out to the water with the general. Would you please entertain our other guests? We'll be back in a short while."

He kissed her on the cheek, but didn't wait for a reply. He was beginning to understand that he would either have to tell her the truth about the real nature of his occupation, or live a life of constant deception. It wasn't a choice he wanted to make at the moment. As he walked through the landscaped tropical garden with Noriega, he broached the treachery Leigh Ritch mentioned.

"I have some information that you need to know. I don't really know any correct way to say this other than it's something I've heard that could or could not be true. I'd bet it is, but since it involves people in your government and their attempt to betray you, I feel a need to choose my words very carefully."

"Stephen, I hear these things all the time. My life is always in danger and I know that it could come from anywhere, even a most trusted ally. What have you heard? I will weigh it in my own mind and decide if I think your information is correct. You will bear no responsibility for its accuracy."

"In that case, I'll just tell you outright. I'm informed by reliable sources that the Colombians have arranged a $5 million bribe to your Colonel Melo to protect their cocaine operations in Panama. It is strongly implied that he plans a coup and that you will be assassinated. He intends to take over the country and go into a limited partnership with the Colombians who would be the de facto rulers."

A noticeably different expression came over Noriega's face. Having dealt with him regarding only business matters, and under favorable circumstances for them both, Kalish hadn't had the opportunity to see the ruthless side of his dictator friend. Noriega's eyes were steely as he took a deep breath, paused for a moment, and responded.

"Thank you, very much, Stephen. This really does not surprise me. Melo is a very ambitious man. A good soldier, but as you confirmed my suspicions, not to be trusted. I will deal with him immediately. You have endeared yourself to me and my country with this act. It was courageous to come to me, but somehow, I would expect this from you. You are not a man easily frightened and you are loyal to your friends." Feeling a bit better now that he'd gotten that off his chest and it seemed to go well, Kalish took a slow, deep breath, and tried to release some of the tension in his shoulders before responding.

"I try to be honest in all my dealings, General. I just hope this information is helpful."

"You may have saved my life. I will not forget it. I'll handle those who are involved. Now, shall we go back inside? I don't want to miss my dance with the lovely Mrs. Kalish. And please, Stephen, call me Tony as all my close friends do."

Later that evening, Kalish presented the general with an expensive, rare, gold-plated rifle and revolver to add to his already extensive collection. Noriega was impressed. After the general and his entourage departed, mostly inebriated, Kalish and Denise lounged on the large Louis XIV bed. When Denise picked it out at the auction, Kalish remarked that it looked like a throne lying on its back. It fostered a sense of grandiose overindulgence.

Beautiful Denise was now his wife; the wife he always dreamed would one day share his life. He was in love, but knew this marriage could pose a danger. He turned to her and asked the question that had been on his mind for weeks.

"What if I told you I'm not in the banking business?"

"What kind of question is that? I don't even want to think about you not being all that you said you were. You didn't lie to me, did you?"

"No. I am principally involved in international banking. It's just that some of my clients are under the microscope of U.S. authorities. They may be involved in some dealings that would be illegal under U.S. law—not in Panama, where we do business."

"What sort of illegal businesses are you talking about? Please tell me they're not running guns or drugs. That's not it, is it?"

Kalish took a moment before responding. This was of the utmost importance to him, and he truly feared losing her in the process of trying to be open and honest with her. "I want to be honest with you in every way, Denise. I'm not sure what all of their business dealings are. They bring hundreds of millions of dollars into Panama where the government doesn't seem that interested in where it comes from. I do their banking for them, handle and invest their money, as well as mine, ours. Some of what they do could possibly be drugs, I don't know. I haven't asked them. Hell, back in my younger days I got busted for selling a little bit of grass."

"You got busted?" Denise was immediately alarmed. "As in going to jail?"

"Just for a short time," he assured her. "I've turned around. I wouldn't expose you to anything that would embarrass you, or get you into any sort of trouble." He meant it with every fiber of his being, even as he accepted that he couldn't tell her absolutely everything. Her reaction to this small revelation told him all he needed to know.

"God, I hope not. My father would die. You're certain that we will never be brought into whatever things these business people you work with are doing? Especially anything that would be illegal?"

"I'm dead certain. I'm even thinking about getting out altogether, you and me retiring together here in Panama. What would you think of that?"

"That would be nice. I don't like the way you said 'getting out', though. It sounds like you're in the mob or something."

He pulled her close. "That couldn't be further from the truth. No self-respecting Mafioso would have anything to do with a southern, pasty-faced WASP like me. I'm not their type."

He kissed her and started stroking her face.

"Hey, how about a little lovin'? I have a hard time lying here beside you and talking business. My mind has turned to sexy, soft, gentle things like you. You know, Mrs. Kalish, you are much beloved. Beautiful, smart, loving; you are all the things a man could possibly want in a woman. I will stay with you till my last breath. Till death do us part."

"And you are my beloved husband. Till death do us part."

They embraced and devoured each other as if they knew their time together would be too short. When they were spent, Stephen Kalish dropped into a deep sleep.

Denise Kalish lay awake, staring at the ceiling, unable to put the night's revelations out of her mind.

*****

May 1984 – Tampa – Kalish's Florida Home
Kalish and Ritch talked alone in the house.

"It's the Colombians, Steve. They know about your close relationship with Noriega, and they want a favor."

"The Colombians want help from me? That's a switch. They're bound to suspect I tipped off the general. But, I'd like to get them on the 'owe me' side for once. What do they want?"

"Two Colombians were arrested during the Colonel Melo fiasco. They're related to some heavyweights in the Cartel and they want you to try to intervene with Noriega on their behalf. One of them is Guia Ochoa. I don't have to tell you how powerful the Ochoas are. They'd owe us plenty if you could persuade Noriega to let him out."

Kalish wasn't eager to get involved. "I don't know. He was livid when he found out what was going on. There are a lot of horror stories in Panama about what happens to anyone who fucks with the general. They say a quick bullet in the head is the best that can happen. To say he was pissed off about their attempt to have him killed would be an understatement. He refers to them constantly as worthless bastards and the two in prison are more than likely reminded every day of just how much he dislikes their country. Poor Colonel Melo. I've heard from officers that his death was long and very painful. I cringe every time I hear his name, knowing that I was involved in it. But with the money I'm putting in *El Presidente's* wallet, I'm sure he'd be willing to consider anything I put before him." Even as he said the words, Kalish knew he didn't really believe them. No matter how much he was doing for the general, he had a feeling what Ritch wanted him to ask for as a favor would put him on the general's shit list. At the same time, what choice did he have?

"Don't get paranoid. You really didn't have much choice. We've practically our entire life's savings in Panama, dependent on *El Presidente's* favor. I could only imagine what having Colonel Melo in power might have done to our operation. If he had taken out Noriega and you hadn't warned him, you would have felt just as guilty, so just worry about today."

"You're right. I'm sure he'll be expecting them to offer him some sort of remuneration. He'll work with just about anybody willing to cut him in on the action. Even people he can't stand. Bypass him, though, and he'll bury you. I think this is something we can get done. Tell them I'm working on it. Think about what we want in return." Kalish knew he had to make this happen. He just hoped Ritch didn't detect how reluctant he truly was about it.

*****

The Following Week – General Noriega's Office – Panama

Whenever Stephen requested a meeting with Noriega, it was always granted immediately. When they were together, Stephen was treated more like a close friend than a business associate. Noriega met him at the office door, all smiles. Instead of a handshake, he threw his arm around Stephen's shoulder and walked him to an overstuffed leather chair. Stephen sat down and chatted a moment before raising the Ochoa matter.

"General, I have a situation that I think could benefit us both a great deal. It requires some action on your part, a conciliatory gesture that might pay off handsomely."

"I'm always interested in matters such as this. What do you want me to do?"

"It's the Colombians. You know I have done business with a number of them over the years as suppliers. I don't like them or trust them, as you know. Well, there has been, to their way of thinking, a misunderstanding between themselves and Panama."

"Oh, their attempt to have Colonel Melo assassinate me, eh? They thought they would use Panama as a platform to smuggle cocaine into the United States without informing me. If it weren't for you, I might not be alive right now. They wanted me out of the way. I know almost everything that goes on in my country. I have eyes and ears everywhere, and they couldn't hide such a secret for long. But this, I did not know. Now mind you, just as I expressed myself to you early on, I encourage everyone to do business in my country. I don't really care what a man does to make a living." This was exactly the line Kalish was counting on, but the general didn't give him an opening to turn the conversation yet.

"The world is a hard place and money is not easy to come by. I have pulled myself up literally from the gutter to run my country, so I will never put someone down for trying however they can to achieve success. It's just that now I run Panama and if you want to do business such as this here, you must inform me and be willing to share with us what you make. Have you not found me fair in these matters? A benefit to have on your side?"

"General, I agree completely, and certainly, your support is the key factor in the success of my operation here. I would never dare to think I could make this work without your help."

Ego suitably soothed, the general finally gave Kalish the opening he needed. "So, they want to make amends at this late date? Am I right?"

"You are, General. You have two of their men in prison. They're related to very powerful men in Colombia and they would ask you to forgive them and send them home to their families. They wish you to forgive their improper start in Panama and request the privilege to work with you on future dealings. They have asked me to intervene on their behalf and try to persuade you to overlook their impropriety and help them to rebuild a working relationship here."

The general paused for a long time. He took a drag from his ever-present cigar and followed it with a sip of brandy. He looked directly into Kalish's eyes as he spoke, "Stephen, you are a very smart man. And so young. If I had the same wisdom that you have at this early age, I could have run the world, much less, Panama. You have tact, diplomacy, and a keen business mind. I will do this for you, for us. We will do business with these people. You may call them as soon as you leave and tell them their associates will be on a plane for Colombia tomorrow. They will be back with their families by dinner.

"However, I will never completely trust the Colombians, either. A man would be a fool to trust men who have helped so many government leaders in their own country to an early grave. But, they do know how to make money, lots of money. I will not turn my back towards them, but I will let them do business with me. I want you, Stephen, to monitor their actions and tell me immediately if you see them up to anything that you think might harm our mutual interests or the stability in my country. Are you satisfied with this arrangement?"

"Yes, General, I think you're making a wise decision." Kalish enjoyed the rest of his visit and counted his lucky stars that it had gone so well.

- CHAPTER TWELVE -
NOTHING GOOD EVER LASTS FOREVER

July 26, 1984, Tampa Jetport – General Aviation
Leigh Ritch and Richard Landis waited for Kalish at the private jet terminal in Tampa. They saw him approach in his red Ferrari, ignoring the speed limit and taking turns too fast. His recklessness always bothered Ritch. The Ferrari roared into the parking lot and stopped on a dime. Kalish, all smiles, walked briskly toward them.

As he approached, he reached over, placed his arm around Ritch and asked, "How 'bout a coffee before I hit the road? I've got some news you'll be delighted with."

"I'm always in the mood for good news, Stephen. And it seems Denise is keeping you in great spirits."

They walked into the small office, helped themselves to free coffee, and took a table in the otherwise empty private waiting area.

"She's the best. I'm ready to settle down and enjoy the fruits of my, or should I say our, labor? Money is no longer an issue. She still believes me to be the highly successful investment banker and I want this marriage to work. Hell, I'm ready for kids."

Ritch shook his head in disbelief. "Are you hearing this, Landis? Kalish wants kids."

"I didn't think we'd live this long. I guess everyone gets old."

Kalish laughed. "Assholes, you're just jealous. That drummer, what's his name, Tommy Lee, is going out with Leigh's great love, Heather Locklear, and he hasn't found a suitable replacement as of yet."

"You don't think Miss Colombia is a catch?"

"Hey, she's beautiful. The question is, does she want to have babies with you?"

The three men were jovial, and having known one another a long time, they enjoyed each other's company. Ritch changed the subject to business.

"So, what's this great news you mentioned?"

"My friends, thanks to General Noriega's gratitude for us saving his neck, and the Colombians' for getting their guys out of a Panamanian jail, we're the main banking pipeline for a principal branch of their U.S. operations. We've solved our banking problems and they want us to solve theirs. They have been depositing an average of about a $150 million a week into our accounts."

"No shit!"

Kalish decided now was the time to make the pitch he'd been considering for months. "We have enough money going through the accounts to take a small piece and make as much money—safely—as we're making running drugs. This is big, really big. It's like we have become international financial brokers. We don't need to risk our necks anymore. I'm happy with Denise. I don't want to risk our marriage or our lives by taking chances running drugs. We don't need the money, and I want to settle down with her. She doesn't know all that I do, and it would probably kill our marriage if she found out. I don't want to take that chance." Both men stared at him dumbly.

Kalish thought maybe he'd lost them in his speech, so he tried again. "I'm on my way to being a gentleman banker in Panama. Why don't you join me?"

Ritch was the first to break the silence. "I'm happy in the Caymans. My family is there and I have friends to watch my back. I'll be fine there. That doesn't mean I won't come visit with you. What are you going to do about all your stuff here in Tampa?"

"I'm going to sell the real estate. I want my boat moved to Panama and I'm going to have my Ferrari and the other cars shipped there. I am concerned about my computers and files at the house."

"Is there anything on them someone would find incriminating?"

"Well, there's an address list of contacts and some of the accounting I don't want to fall into the wrong hands. I was wondering if you could have them packaged up and sent to me? I don't trust a moving company with that sort of stuff. Hell, half of our off-loaders and drivers do that kind of work between jobs. I hear them bragging about all the electronics they've scored during moves. I just want to be careful."

"Okay, done. I'll get to it before I go home in a couple of days."

"Well, gentlemen, my plane and the lovely Sheila await on the tarmac."

"That's another thing, Steve. Just how long is Denise going to put up with Sheila flying you around? She's going to figure it out at some point."

"I'll be talking to pilots soon. You can have Sheila full time. I'm going to leave the jet based here in Tampa so we can justify the cost by leasing it out. I'm only a short hop away if I need it. Besides, the Colombians gave me a helicopter as sort of a thank you for helping them."

Ritch laughed. "How many does that make?"

"Just four helicopters. Then, of course, the Lear, the 727 I got for the general, and a couple smaller prop planes for short hops." Kalish laughed. "A guy can't have too many planes, my friend. Well, I better get on the road."

"That's pretty impressive stuff, Skip. You're still in on the *Blaster* aren't you? We're just a few days away from the biggest score ever."

"Of course, man. I won't bail out now. But, it is the last run for me. I don't need the adrenaline rush anymore. I'm done after this. If you want to talk to me, it will be about football or sailing, not business. I will give you guys my interest in the operation. I'll just be the rich, retired American banker living in Panama City." Kalish smiled the smile only a man completely satisfied with his place in life could muster.

"I'm happy for you. I really am."

The men started out of the lounge and walked toward the waiting jet. Kalish looked over to where he expected to see Sheila performing her last walk-around visual, but she was nowhere to be found. Beside the plane he saw a plain grey Ford sedan, a very bad sign. Two men sat in the front seat. Sheila sat in the back by herself. Ritch knew this visit had nothing to do with airplanes or the FAA. He quietly suggested to the others, "Let's turn around slowly and leave before we're noticed."

They turned in unison only to be stopped in their tracks by two dark-suited men standing behind them, guns drawn. One man held up identification.

"Federal Bureau of Investigation. Place your hands behind your heads and do not move. Stephen Kalish, you are under arrest. All of you stand where you are."

The officers approached, pulled Kalish's hands down behind his back, and handcuffed them. One of the two federal agents began to read the Miranda Rights to him. The other approached Leigh Ritch and Landis.

"Do you gentlemen have identification on you? If so, I'd like to see it, please, one at a time. You first, Sir."

Ritch strained to hear the charges being read to Kalish while still paying attention to his own predicament. As best he could overhear, the charges were "importation and distribution of narcotics" and something about "criminal conspiracy".

As Kalish was led to a waiting car, Ritch and Landis produced identification. The agents undoubtedly suspected their involvement somehow with Kalish, but since neither had any warrants outstanding against them and no crime had been committed at the airport, they were released. They watched as the first car carried Kalish away and the remaining officers began searching Kalish's jet. Soon after, the pilot emerged from the other car and it sped away. Shaken, she approached Ritch.

"Mr. Ritch, they're FBI. They have been questioning me for at least two hours. I had to tell them Mr. Kalish was coming. They already knew a lot of things. Somebody has been talking to the authorities. Am I in trouble?"

"Not if you don't know anything. You don't, do you?"

"I didn't tell them a thing. I just said I fly the plane, that's it. I didn't say anything else. They grilled me. I mean they came close to threatening me, telling me I'd go to jail, never fly again, my life was ruined. But I still didn't say anything."

"If you don't know anything bad about anybody, if you just flew the airplane, and stayed in the cockpit, then you're in no more trouble than if you were a pilot with any airline. You don't know anything, right?"

"That's right."

"Then you have nothing to worry about. Go home, get some rest, and I'll call you when I need you. Otherwise, fly for whoever wants to hire you. Just remember that these people often pretend to be someone they're not, so be very careful not to talk with anyone about our business dealings."

"Yes, Sir. Mr. Ritch."

"Fine. I've got to run."

Sheila walked to her car and left quickly. Leigh Ritch and Landis got into Ritch's car, their concern more than evident. Ritch was now left to figure out how to hold things together and avoid prison himself.

"Look, remember what Kalish just told us about the computer at his home here?"

"Right, about the addresses and accounting stuff?"

"Yes, no telling what Kalish has on those computers. We need to get over there now and remove them. Can you go with me to help?"

"It's my ass too. Let's go do it."

Kalish's home was dark and empty. The guards were no longer needed since all the cash now rested in a Panama bank vault. Ritch had a key to the back door and entered.

"I'll get the lights. You go around to the car. I'll open the garage door, you pull in and no one will be able to tell we're even here."

"Let's hustle. I'm pretty nervous about all of this."

Ritch opened the door and Landis pulled the vehicle in. They found the computers in the living room, which now resembled an abandoned office.

"God, it stinks in here," Landis said. "Smells like rotten marijuana leaves."

"That's the smell of money. Grab just the computer decks and don't worry about monitors or printers. Hard drives are all I'm worried about. I think these two are all we need. I'll give the rest of the place a quick look while you load these in the trunk."

"Right."

Ritch found nothing else he thought might be of concern. He killed the lights and joined Landis in the garage. He pressed the garage opener and waited for the door to open. Since he didn't have the remote, he told Landis to back out and he would hit the close button, then go around the house and join him. Landis did as instructed. Ritch locked the back door to the garage and ran around the house where he found Landis and the car blocked by another grey Ford, one of the two they'd seen at the airport. He recognized two FBI agents, one of whom approached him as the other went to the car door where Landis sat in stunned silence.

"Mr. Ritch. You are under arrest for interfering with a criminal investigation and suspicion of attempting to alter or destroy evidence. I will read you your rights."

Both men were taken to the Tampa jail and booked. Within an hour, Ritch's attorney had both men released on bail. Suddenly, all Leigh Ritch's concerns about being cautious and keeping a low profile slammed him in the face. He was smart enough to know that given the people arrested that day, even if they all managed to get out of jail, the authorities could now connect the dots. The FBI had possession of Kalish's computer files. Undoubtedly, the name and phone number of everyone connected with him would be there. Ritch's first priority was to get home, out of the states and back to the Caymans where the authorities were not only tired of the dictates of U.S. authorities, but were friends of his as well. His attorney was experienced, and within two days, the charges were dropped against Landis and Ritch. After all, he explained, Ritch was just doing a favor for a friend, shipping his computer to him. He had no idea what Kalish was arrested for or what was on the computer. Unless there was some evidence to the contrary, there was no case. The Tampa district attorney agreed and Ritch used the window of opportunity to get out of the States.

*****

Next Morning – Michael Vogel's House – Detroit
Vogel was on the phone with Ritch.

"Stupid son of a bitch. I knew you guys would eventually bring this all down around us. Ferraris, yachts, mansions, jets, and women all over the place. Did you think the Feds were totally stupid? Why couldn't you just wait till you had your money before wearing the 'I'm rich' billboards everywhere you went? I can't believe this shit. So, what do you want from me? I don't want no more contact from either of you guys. You're dead men."

"Look Mike, I just called to tell you the *Blaster* is off. It's too hot. With Kalish in jail and the authorities watching him, we can't use his off-loaders or any of his people. It can't happen."

"Brilliant, that's just truly brilliant, Leigh. I guess to agree that running drugs with the DEA and FBI sitting on the fifty-yard line would probably not be a very good idea. Any more revelations you want to share with me?"

Ritch decided to take this opportunity to lay it all out on the line. He didn't plan to do business with the man ever again. Why not tell him off? "Just one, Mike. You're probably the biggest single asshole I've ever known in my life. Nobody in the world trusts you or wants to spend more than a second around you."

"Please don't hurt my feelings, shithead. You know how sensitive I am. Tell you what, at this point; trusting me wouldn't be a very good idea. So why don't you just get the fuck out of my life. We're at the end of the road, amigo. Comprende?"

Vogel hung up the phone. He never liked his partners and never trusted anyone to start with. This would change nothing in his life. Thank God he had kept his organization separate from Kalish and Ritch. He could wait a while for the air to clear, assume that Kalish and Ritch knew better than to talk, and eventually resume operations without them. He was, however, about to make a few changes in his own organization.

*****
Larry Garcia's House – Detroit

Shine beat on the door to Garcia's small clapboard house. He was stoned and in the mood to tell Garcia that he'd had it with him trying to come between him and Vogel. He was positive Garcia had soured his relationship with Vogel and it was going to cost him a fortune. He knew the big Mexican was large, mean, and dangerous, but Shine had reinforced his confidence with the better part of a fifth of Jack and was ready to tell Vogel what he thought.

"I'm coming, I'm coming. Quit beating on the fucking door. What the hell do you want, Shine? It's late! I don't feel like fucking with you tonight. You're drunk, ain't you?"

"How about letting me in? I've got some news for you. Kalish, he's in the slammer. Let me in."

"All right, give me a minute to get this latch undone."

Garcia threw the deadbolt and opened the door for Shine. He stood in the shadows of the porch in a slow, freezing drizzle.

"What in the devil are you doing over here so late? You're asking for pneumonia out on a night like this. Get your sorry ass in here."

As Shine entered the dimly-lit room, it was apparent Garcia had a shotgun tucked under his arm. He knew Shine always packed a gun. Maybe he knew what was on his mind.

"What the hell is that for, Larry?"

Without hesitation, Garcia raised the weapon at point blank range and pumped a round straight into Clinton.

"That's from Mike Vogel, Shine. You're out, I'm in. Sorry, that's the price you pay for fucking over your boss."

There was no expression on Shine's face other than surprise and intense pain as he fell to his knees and then forward. Garcia knew the wound was mortal at that range, but the amount of blood emptying onto the beige carpet surprised him. Looking just once more at Shine on the floor and hearing him gasp for breath, he quickly backed out the door and ran out to his car. In seconds, he'd made his escape, leaving Shine in a bloody sprawl on the floor. He would come back later and find Shine dead. He would say that Shine was staying with him and that someone came over, got into an argument, and shot him. Or, maybe he wanted to rob him. Shine always bragged about how much money he was making. Better yet, he would just dump the body in the Detroit River. That might be the best idea of all. He just didn't realize Shine wasn't dead yet.

With each movement bringing monumental pain, Shine crawled to the phone and dialed for help.

"911, how can I help you?"

"I've been shot. I'm dying."

"Sir, where are you? What is your address?"

"Fourteen zero six Decatur. You better get somebody here quick, I don't have much blood left."

"Yes, Sir, please try and stay on the phone, help is already dispatched. Someone will be there in just a minute. Please talk to me, Sir. What is your name?"

"My name, my name....I'm fading, my name...Shine, Clinton is my name...can't stay awake, I'm fading..."

"Sir, Clinton, do you hear me, Clinton, can you hear me?"

*****

7 a.m., Henry Ford Hospital Intensive Care Unit

An emergency room surgeon came to check on Clinton Anderson while a nurse changed the intravenous glucose container connected to his arm.

"Clinton, can you hear me? Are you awake?"

Through Shine's dense fog, the dim voice came from a distant ship alerting him to rocky shore ahead.

"Clinton, are you awake?"

Clinton tried to open his eyes. They were stuck tightly.

"Miss Owens, get a warm sponge and get his lids clear, they're stuck together."

"Yes, Sir."

The nurse unwrapped a sterile sponge, soaked it in warm water, and proceeded to wipe hardened sleep from Clinton's eyes. Slowly, he began to see light and the young doctor at the end of his bed.

"Clinton, you're in Henry Ford Hospital. Can you hear me? Do you understand what I'm saying?"

Clinton nodded slightly.

"You're going to make it, but another minute later getting here, and I'm afraid you wouldn't have survived. You're going to recover, hopefully without more surgery. No major organs were destroyed. You lost about half the blood in your body and were close to checking out. A vascular surgeon happened to be here to meet his wife. You were lucky. If he hadn't just been here, no way you would have survived. There's a detective wanting to speak with you, soon as you're able. You want to talk with him now? I'll be glad to tell him to come tomorrow if you want to wait."

"Tomorrow," Clinton murmured.

"Okay, I'll handle it. You try to stay awake a while and eat something if you can. As soon as you're able, I'd like for you to try to sit up, and then tomorrow, try putting some weight on your feet. The sooner we can get you moving, the better off you're going to be. I know you've to be hurting a lot right now. Your nurse, Sarah Owens, has a pump set up for you that'll give you a nice hit of the finest painkiller, just by touching the button. You'll have this for a couple of days and then you'll have to do without it. Hopefully, you'll be a lot better by then. I'm going to tell the officer you'll talk with him in the morning. I'll check in on you throughout the day."

"Thanks, Doc," Clinton replied. "I'll be right here."

Throughout the day, Shine drifted in and out of sleep. Every time he awoke, pain shot through his heavily-bandaged legs and abdomen until he hit the morphine pump. A good shot of painkiller and he would drift back into deep sleep. Late in the evening, just as he was beginning to have a major dose of pain, two large, bearded bikers appeared at his side.

"Shine, what the hell have you done, Son? You look like a damn octopus with all these tubes running into you."

Clinton was pleased to see Whiskers and Mackie, his drinking buddies and members of one of Detroit's major motorcycle gangs. He never chose to hang out with their borderline civilized friends, but at this moment, they were a welcome sight.

"You guys, I'm glad to see you. I'm pretty messed up, heh?"

"What the hell happened to you, Shine? The doctor who operated on you said somebody shot the shit out of you."

"Don't say nothing to anybody here. I'm just saying I shot myself screwing around with my gun."

"They're not that stupid, Clinton. Who did this to you? I thought you said the guys you dealt with were above all this sort of thing."

"Look, this goes nowhere, but it was that greasy son-of-a-bitch, Garcia, the guy I helped get a job who tried to kill me."

"Why would he want to kill you?"

"He's greedy and stupid. Never made more than ten grand a year in his whole fucking life, and now I get him in a position to make ten times that every year, and he wants more. He obviously wants to move into my place."

"There's more to it than that, Shine. I've talked with Larry and he's just not that smart. He's really what I'd call a dumb motherfucker. He's just following orders. You pissed off one of the guys at the top, trust me. If anybody knows how a gang works, it's us. You were set up."

"Vogel. It had to be him."

"Mike Vogel, your boss?"

"Yeah, he says I blew a deal for him. He called me the other night, practically in a rage. It had to be him. I didn't think he'd do this to me."

"You got to be kidding, brother. Everybody in Detroit knows he's a muthafucker of the highest order. You ain't safe here, either. He'll definitely be wanting to finish you off to save his ass. And Garcia better cover his, too. He ain't gonna want to leave no trail back to himself. We'll stay here with you till you get released."

"I can't ask you to do that. What about your job?"

"Job? Who's got a job? We're full-time associates of our biker organization. We can come and go, as we need to. We'll be right here. You've really pissed off one of the baddest guys around, Shine."

"You're probably right. Let me think about this."

Mackie approached Clinton and put his hand on his shoulder.

"Listen, buddy. You get some sleep and you can relax. You ain't gonna be left alone one minute. Just get well."

Clinton, overcome by pain and the show of support, teared up.

"I'm really pleased you guys are here."

He was surprised by their offer of protection and concern for his welfare. They were the last ones he imagined showing up at the hospital and volunteering to look out for him.

Another night of unparalleled pain followed, but Clinton slept soundly knowing Mackie and Whiskers were close by, covering his back. It also dawned on him he had serious problems that weren't going to go away. He needed to figure out what to tell authorities who wanted to talk to him and how to stay away from Vogel's long arm. There was no proof Vogel ordered Garcia to hit him, but his playing the two underlings against each other could have led up to it. His dreams rambled from one chase scene to another, with scattered visions of his past mingled with growing fear of what his future held.

Clinton awoke to the movement of a nurse in the room changing his IV. She was a large, friendly black woman with a smile.

"Why, good morning, Clinton. How you feeling today?"

Clinton was stiff, but improved in pain level.

"I'm feeling a little better this morning. I don't want to go jogging, but I'm coming around."

"Well that's real good, 'cause there sure are a lot of folks wanting to talk to you."

"The police?"

"Yeah, and your two tattooed friends are in the next room waiting for me to give them the all clear also."

"Please, send them in."

"Clinton, now you take these pills I'm leaving here with a cup of water."

"Will do."

As the nurse left the room, the two bikers came in, followed by a tall, well-dressed young man with 'government' written all over him.

"Hey, pal, I'm not up to an interview yet. Besides, my friends are here to see me. Make an appointment."

"Sorry, Clinton. I have to ask you a few questions."

"It was an accident. The gun fell and went off. That's all that happened. Nobody shot me."

The soft-spoken young man interrupted.

"You know, Clinton, you don't have a very good track record. You've already have one killing on your record."

"I was acquitted. I was only charged with manslaughter. The jury agreed with me that it was an accident. It was a bar fight. I hit the guy and he fell down and hit his head."

"And then there's Garcia. His string of arrests and convictions makes you look like a Sunday school teacher."

Shine wasn't going to take the bait that easily. "It was an accident. I was playing with his shotgun and it just went off. I didn't realize it still had a shell in it."

"That so, Clinton? What happened to the gun after you shot yourself? The police report says it was on a couple of nails above the door. The kind of place that someone would store a shotgun so that it would be available to welcome folks to the front door on quick notice."

Shine said nothing, so the agent decided to try a different track.

"Let me get this straight: After you shot yourself and crawled to the phone, you put the gun up and crawled back to your spot on the living room floor to wait for the ambulance? That's it?"

"I don't remember. Maybe someone else put it back up." Shine didn't know what else to say at that point. The agent was zeroing in on him.

"Clinton, you may be in a hospital right now and you'll probably recover, but you're a dead man."

"How you figure?"

"Whoever shot you knows you're not in the morgue right now and you are a link to them and whatever they're up to. Since you're still alive and now realize they want you dead, you're even more of a threat to them. They'll be back and without some sort of protection, they'll probably succeed in putting you away next time."

Shine stared at the wall at the end of the bed and remained silent a long while. The detective could see wheels churning in his head, and sat back waiting for a response.

Finally, Shine said, "It was an accident. The gun fell and shot me. That's my statement."

"You know, Clinton you're more of an idiot than a bad ass. I'm sure I'll be back investigating another shooting involving you before long. You probably won't be answering any questions next time. Very few statements are taken in the morgue. You think about that."

"Like I said, it was an accident."

"Have a good day, Clinton."

"You too." Shine watched the agent walk out the door, wondering if he'd just avoided a problem, or turned his back on his only chance to stay alive.

- CHAPTER THIRTEEN -
INFILTRATION

Low End Neighborhood – Detroit

With his athletic frame, shoulder-length blond hair, and gritty demeanor, Ned Timmons fit right in with the Detroit crime scene. He knew the city from his youth, its citizens, its crime, and the language of the street. Danger was constant, but he was young, restless, and, in his own mind, bullet-proof.

After ten years undercover, his uncanny ability to gain acceptance with smugglers, thieves, and organized crime, brought him to the FBI's attention.

When they recruited Timmons to infiltrate the local chapter of the Hell's Angels motorcycle gang, he signed on, but only if the FBI let him pick out a big Harley to ride. He knew the exact model and style a biker would kill for, and that's what he was riding today. His leather chaps and jacket, coupled with a moustache and three-day stubble, completed the package. He was well on his way to investigating the bikers for a string of crimes, from drug peddling to murder.

The deep, unmistakable rumble of his Harley filled the street lined with overgrown shrubs and unkempt small houses that had been going downhill for twenty years. It was a crime-riddled neighborhood, known for petty drug dealers who worked out of flophouses and took advantage of their proximity to the public high school around the corner.

Ned pulled his bike up to the porch of the dealer he was after, Tumer Brown. Tumer was a biker, a long-time gang member, and their main meth dealer. Ned had made at least eight purchases from him over the past several weeks. Each time, he'd been wired and Tumer was about to hear the bad news.

Infiltration

"All right, Ed, my man. What you doing out this early? You don't usually need to score until after lunch. You down low today? Need to fly a little bit? I got your medicine right here, Captain."

"No Tumer. I actually came to talk with you a minute."

"Talk? What you want to talk about? I ain't much of a talker. I'm here to make a buck, man. This is my fucking job, you know?"

"I know, Tumer. I know exactly why you're here. And guess what? Guess why I'm here?"

"I know why you're here. You're on the stuff man. You can't do without it and I'm the guy who helps you get your hit."

"Wrong. Take a look over there across the street. See that grey sedan? The one that looks like a cop car?"

"What about it? The cops around here don't bother us. We have an understanding with them. They don't fuck with us."

"Those aren't cops, Tumer. They're Federal agents, just like me. I'm wired and you're busted." This was the part of the job he loved. Something about turning the tables on the people he arrested made the job just that much sweeter. Tumer had the predictable reaction.

"You sorry bastard! What do you mean wired? You better be fucking joking or you're a dead man."

"Don't be a fool, Tumer. Watch the car. Guys, how about showing Tumer here you're listening in."

Both men in the front seat of the car turned their heads and raised their hands in a half-hearted wave. They hated when he called them out like that, but they were just his backup and had to let him run the op how he saw fit.

"You can be downtown and in the joint within fifteen minutes. I've made at least eight or nine buys from you that were recorded. You've been dealing within a thousand yards of a school. You're looking at close to fifty years in the joint. Let's see, you'll be around ninety-five, maybe a hundred when you're back out on the street. Sorry, Tumer. It's my job."

"You're an FBI agent?"

"That's right."

"So, what do I have to do? What do you want? I'll die before I go back to the joint. I've done time already and I ain't going back alive. You can count on that." Tumer thumped his chest for emphasis.

"It doesn't have to be that dramatic, Tumer. There are options. I can get you out of this, at least most of it. Maybe get you a short stint in the county jail for possession. Two years, maybe even less, depending on what you get me."

"You want me to rat out my friends, right?"

"You're going to have to give me something big, really big, not to die in prison. What can you tell me? What do you know that'll buy your way out of this? Hell, Tumer, if you're willing to sell drugs to kids, you certainly shouldn't blink at just selling me some information."

The fat, bearded biker, overcome with the severity of his situation, sat down on the worn-out couch behind him. He ran his mind through the memories of the time he had already spent behind bars. His present life wasn't much, but prison was far worse. To rat out the Angels meant quick death if he got found out. He'd be better off in prison, but there were a few other players he knew who wasn't in his gang. He would offer them the one loud-mouthed asshole he couldn't care less about: The guy who liked to play the big shot and who constantly bragged about the scope of his operations. Shine.

"Yeah, I know about a guy who's big, real big. He's making millions and running dope all over the country.

He makes what I'm doing look like shit. I could take you to him right now if I wanted to."

"I'm interested. You need to come with me this morning. We're going to take you downtown to our office and record every word you say. If you put me on to something big, we'll deal with you. Otherwise, you'll rot in jail."

*****

Four Days Later, Clinton Anderson's Home – Detroit

With a case of Jack Daniels and the flipped biker, Tumer Brown, in tow, Ned Timmons set off to pay a house call to Shine.

"From what I hear, Shine's just getting over getting shot. He says it was an accident, but I heard from some bikers I know that Larry Garcia pumped one into his gut with a twelve gauge shot gun. Word is, Garcia was promoting himself to Shine's job in his organization. He might be too spooked to talk."

"Never can tell, Tumer. He might just be ready to flip on the whole group, seeing as how one of them tried to waste him."

"Maybe so. Be careful how you handle him now. Shine can be crazy. He stays whacked out on alcohol and coke about half the time."

"You just get him talking. Convince him I'm with your biker group and that we want to do some business with him. I'll take it from there."

"I'll do what I can. Remember our deal. I bring you something big, I walk."

"You have my word on it."

Shine's wife answered the doorbell. Worn looking and used to unsavory characters at the door, she pointed them to the dining room where Shine sat with a bottle of beer, reading the paper.

"Tumer, what the fuck are you doing here?"

"Just came to check on you, man. Somebody told me you got whacked, almost killed."

"Yeah, that shithead Garcia tried to plant me. He'll get his. Damn, stomach still hurts when I move too fast. Who's this with you?"

"This is Ed. He's with the Angels too. We was just out this way. I remember you lived here. Just thought I'd drop by for old time's sake. Brought you a little something to help recuperate."

"No shit? What you got?"

"Left it on the porch. How 'bout grabbing it, Ed?"

Ned left the room and grabbed the case of liquor. He retrieved it and set it on the table in front of Shine.

"You gotta be kidding me. A case of Jack?"

"Yeah," Brown said, "Turns out a truck of the stuff had some, er uh, suspension problems and had to unload it in a hurry. Me and Ed here helped out with the unloading. We got about ten cases each. Thought one might make you feel a little better."

"Just doing me a little favor, 'eh Tumer? Somehow, that don't seem like you. What am I missing here?"

"You're right Shine. I swear you're the best. That's why you do that lie detector thing so good. Hell, you don't hardly need it."

"Okay, Tumer, cut the crap. What do you need?"

"We're looking to do some out-of-state work, maybe offloading or driving for some importing companies. Word is, you're connected. You told me to get up with you if I ever needed to get hooked up. So, me and Ed here are looking. Need to make some cash."

"What happened to your little lab downtown?"

"Getting too hot. I'm afraid the place is about to get jammed by the cops. Some kids OD'd a week or so ago and the narcs are coming out of the fucking woodwork. I need to move along. So does Ed. Can you help us?"

"Well, let's try one of these bottles and then we'll talk about it some. I can probably do you some good. But you'd owe me big time."

"I wouldn't ever forget. You know me."

Over the next two hours, the three men went through not one, but four bottles of liquor. Ned held back, occasionally excusing himself to the bathroom or kitchen and dumping his glass. He was, nonetheless, feeling a strong buzz. Shine and Tumer, on the other hand, were three sheets to the wind. Shine was getting loud and obnoxious.

"You fuckers come to me 'cause you know I'm the man. I run the pipeline. Hell, I am the pipeline. Without me, the biggest damned drug-running operation in the world would just fall apart. Yes sir, I am the man. I fly all over the fucking world making deals, showing Vogel, Ritch, and whatever the fuck...Kalish, yeah, that's him. I run the whole show for them. Last load came in on a friggin' barge in Louisiana. The organization made over a hundred million bucks. I got my share too. Yeah, without me, they'd be dead in the fucking water."

For the next hour, with some gentle prodding from Ned and Tumer, Shine spilled his guts. He ranted and raved about how Michael Vogel had fucked him and that he was going to take over the whole operation if they didn't do right by him. After two hours of wired conversation, Ned had enough. It was confrontation time.

"Shine, guess what?"

"What's that, Ed? You need another drink? We got plenty here."

"Nope, I'm just fine, but you're not."

"How's that, Ed?"

"I'm with the FBI and you're fucked."

"You're kidding, right?"

"No, I'm not kidding. Here's my badge."

Ned produced his identification and Shine got sober fast.

"I can't believe this. Tumer, why the fuck did you bring this guy over here? You've set me up. You've fucking screwed me good."

"I'm sorry, Shine. They got me too. They own us both."

"Well, I'm not saying another word. Fuck the FBI and fuck you, asshole!"

"Sorry you feel that way, Shine," Timmons said. "Your wife over there, and your kids in the other room are going to miss their old man. You've said enough to hang yourself tonight. Got it all recorded. You ready to go now? I'll have you booked within the hour. Shouldn't bother you none, though, Shine. You know lots of the folks serving time there already, right? You'll fit in real good. Let's go. Need a coat?"

Shine sat motionless for several minutes without a sound. It was a reaction Ned had seen before. Even the most violent and emotionally disturbed knew when they had reached the end of the road. It was decision time. He generally let them sit and think it out, watching for any sign of them going over the edge and trying to find a gun. He sat back and just stared at Shine. He could tell the moment that resignation appeared in his eyes. Shine was trash, but he wasn't completely stupid. He had made the only smart decision.

"You made some sort of deal with Tumer or he wouldn't be ratting me out, am I right?"

"What's your point, Shine?"

"You want me to do the same. You want to know what I know, who I know. I'll talk for the right deal. I know stuff you won't fucking believe. I work for guys that are bringing in at least $100 million worth of pot twice a year or more. Hell, maybe $1 billion a year. I know all about them. I got names, faces, and details. I know it all. But, I ain't going to jail. Not one day. Not one single day. I got a wife, kids, and a home. They need me here. I can't do no time. You cut me an ironclad deal and I'll give you what you're looking for. I'll give you more than you ever thought about. Do we have a deal?"

"If you can produce this information, facts, names, faces, times, all the details, and there are no bodies in your past, then we have a deal. But, you lie, you try to wiggle out of this, and you'll be doing forty years at Sing Sing. That's a promise, not a threat. And, when the word gets out, if it should, that you've flipped, you're dead. I'm your safety net." Ned needed that last bit to be the part that stuck with Shine the most. He only hoped he was sober enough to grasp it.

"What do you want from me? What's in it for you to keep me alive?"

"That should be obvious. You're undoubtedly in something up to your ears and I can't offer you protection unless you're willing to cooperate with me. You tell me what you're involved in, who the players are, and you furnish details to back up your story. As long as you're truthful, whether we get a bust or not, I'll see to it you have protection. You need to think about this carefully, Clinton. There's not a lot of places to go when you need protection. We're one of the few organizations in the world that can keep our promises."

Shine sneered at Ned. "Like, for example, Bobby Seale?"

Ned shook his head. "We're not perfect. But, there are a lot of successes, and they can't make movies about the successful cases because you don't hear about them. There are a lot of them. All I can guarantee you is that we give all we can to live up to our promises. We are your best avenue if you want to keep on living."

Shine made his decision. "I'll do what you say. Now, pass me the Jack. I need another drink. Hell, I need a lot of drinks."

Ned stayed more than twelve hours, talking and drinking with Shine and Tumer. Shine relayed, through his stupor, a tale of an organization so large it was almost inconceivable. If it was real, it was huge.

*****

Office Federal Bureau of Investigation, Detroit

A piece of work, Shine acted as though he was a guest on The Tonight Show. He talked into a tape recorder with three witnesses, Ned Timmons, an assistant U.S. Attorney, and a court stenographer who took verbatim notes. When sober, Shine was crafty and deceiving, but with no course of action left except to cooperate, he relished the limelight.

If the drug ring he described was only a tenth as large as what he said, it would be one of the largest ever discovered operating in the States.

A number of the drug operations Shine described were real, unsolved cases under Bureau investigation.

"That's the truth of it," he said. "The last load, which Vogel didn't even take a cut of, was for over $100 million bucks by itself. And all his partners have individual operations as well. Together, they've done more than $1 billion.

"I can give you a complete breakdown on probably the largest marijuana smuggling operation in the country, maybe the whole world. The guys I've been working with are smart. They've done a great job of keeping out of trouble and not making enemies. They're good to their help and make everyone feel like they're actually interested in them. And the money, hell, some truck drivers were making up to $40 grand for two days' work. That instills a lot of loyalty in working people."

Infiltration

The Assistant U.S. Attorney quizzed Shine.

"Mr. Anderson, first just give us an overview of the scope of what you were involved with. What was your role? Where did the stuff come from? How many people are involved? How long has this operation been going on? How was it brought in and then distributed? Let's start there and then we'll know what other questions to ask."

Shine took a deep breath before starting. He paused as if to gather thoughts. He began slowly, choosing every word with care.

"I've been working with these folks about five years. I've helped them with security issues. When you've got over a hundred people involved on a daily basis, you have to know everybody's on the up and up. I'm sort of an expert in lie detection. I use a stress analyzer and periodically test anybody who'll be working with the organization. A hint of a lie and they're out. And, it's been working. Nobody has turned on the group yet. At least, not till now. If that son of a bitch Vogel hadn't had me shot...stupid, how friggin' stupid can he be? Anyway, there's almost two hundred guys involved here, and even some women."

"Women?"

"Yeah, including a knockout of a pilot. She flies one of the partner's private jets."

"Private jets?"

"Oh yeah, they use them all the time. And off-duty airline pilots who fly ahead of the ships to scout for the Navy and Coast Guard."

"They're using ships?"

"Several times. And tractor-trailers, warehouses, conveyors, longshoremen, encrypting radio transmitters, you name it. If it makes it easier, they do it."

"What size would a single load be?"

"This past one they brought into the bayou in Louisiana was about 500 thousand pounds."

"A half million pounds?"

"That's right. Took almost twenty tractor trailers to haul it up here."

"I'll tell you what, Clinton. If all this is as you say it is, this could very well be the largest organization of this kind in the country."

"It's exactly what I say it is. Probably even bigger than I know 'cause I really have only seen the operations that Michael Vogel works with. The other two guys, Leigh Ritch out of the Caymans, and Stephen Kalish out of Florida, have their own things going on separately from the group. So did Vogel. That's why I ended up here."

"How's that?"

"He was pissed 'cause I couldn't slow down this last load coming into Louisiana till he sold everything he already had stored up here. Said it lowered the price and he lost money when they brought in such a large supply. They'd been running stuff into North Carolina, Florida, Texas, and Louisiana, and shipping it all over the country. Buyers would line up twenty deep when a load came in. Most times, it was gone within twenty-four hours after it arrived up here. Garcia seen Vogel was upset with me and tried to move in on my spot. Bastard shot me."

As the morning turned to afternoon, the agents listened wide-eyed to what was either the biggest and best-told lie they had ever heard, or the start of the largest drug-bust in history. When a guard reappeared with lunch for Shine, Ned Timmons and the Assistant U.S. Attorney excused themselves for an hour to go to a nearby diner and digest what they had been told during the morning. Neither could get to a phone quickly enough to call their superiors and relate what they had been hearing for the past four hours. After making their reports, the two men went to the diner and discussed what approaches they should follow.

"How much of this do you think is true, Tony?"

"I'm willing to bet that a lot of it is. Vogel has been in our sights for a long time and we could never get anything solid on him."

"But a billion dollar pipeline?"

"Hey, almost any school kid will tell you that they can buy it anywhere in the country, anytime they want. To have that much stuff available, you'd have to have a trucking line as big as UPS along with an airline and a shipping line to keep it coming. You're talking the McDonald's of pot. This could be that main organization we always felt was there but couldn't get a hold of. This might just be it. If it is, this will be one hell of a case. It's what's called a career case. Every federal, state, city, county, and even park police will want a piece of this. There'll be a fight for jurisdiction that will make the Super Bowl pale by comparison."

"You think so?"

"I know so."

*****

Doug McCullough's Office – New Bern, North Carolina

Deep in concentration, Doug pored over a stack of cases on his desk. The constant flow of paper and relentlessly dull depositions that flooded his office were almost mind-numbing. The phone interrupted him continually. This morning was no different. Two pages into the stack and the phone rang again.

"U.S. Attorney's office, McCullough speaking. Yes, I'm the assistant attorney for the district. What can I help you with?"

A stunned look came over his face as he listened.

"Yes, I investigated that case and have the file on my desk at this moment. Your agent, Terry Peters, and I have been trying to connect the dots to Louisiana and a couple of guys we tracked to the airport in Detroit. So far, we're dead in the water. We'd both be very interested in meeting with you. You name the time. I'll be there."

Next, Doug had Terry Peters on the line.

"I just got a very interesting phone call."

"Is that right? I'm supposed to guess from who?"

"You couldn't if you wanted, so I'll spare you the suspense. One of your people in Detroit called our guys in D.C. and they forwarded it to me. We've got a solid lead on the *Lady Mauricette* and perhaps a lot of other cases we're working. Tampa and Carolina are both being advised that this leads to open investigations in their districts."

Terry didn't understand the magnitude.

"They find another half-sunk shrimp boat with some pot?"

"No. They found an insider who's in it as deep as it gets. He's got names, faces, and places and he's talking to save his skin."

"We nail him?"

"His own people nailed him. Left him for dead. He needs us to protect him and he's willing to flip for that and immunity. He knew all about the abandoned trawler, and get this: His name is the same as the guy your agents talked to in Charlotte the night the shrimper was found. This guy's for real."

"How is Tampa involved?"

"They're probably tied in somehow on other cases. I'm going. You coming? I thought that might get your attention. What's the chance of grabbing one of the Bureau's jets? Check on it and get back with me ASAP."

- CHAPTER FOURTEEN -
LIKE DUCKS ON A POND

Federal Building – Tampa

From Detroit to Texas, the federal prosecutors, each from their own district, came by invitation to Tampa's Federal Building for a bird's-eye view of the widening investigation. On a green chalkboard full of names and arrows Ned Timmons outlined intelligence gained in the interrogation of Clinton "Shine" Anderson.

"Before we begin," Timmons said, "everything you are about to be told here is confidential. If any of this gets out, bodies will be found floating face down. The entire operation will be compromised.

"That would make me very upset, as I'm about to go undercover and collect enough hard evidence to indict every major player in this smuggling enterprise.

"You agents have been invited from Detroit, Tampa, Texas, and North Carolina because this organization has successfully smuggled large quantities of marijuana in each of your regions.

"Top of the chart, you see the names of Ritch, Kalish and Vogel. Remember those names. The Detroit office is familiar with Vogel. Stephen Kalish is in custody at the moment. Leigh Ritch is from a prominent family in the Caymans and as far as the Bureau is concerned, as pure as the new fallen snow."

Terry Peters looked quizzically at Doug McCullough.

"You have any idea what he's talking about?"

Doug shook his head.

"You're undoubtedly wondering if that was an accurate statement and that 'you missed one'. The answer is, in a nutshell—yes. A lot has been missed that we all had no idea about, until now.

"Our informant, a gentleman named Clinton Anderson, aka 'Shine', was, until very recently, a key player in this three-pronged group.

"He was responsible for staff security. He conducted routine lie detector tests on every member of their organization, and even potential investors.

"Don't be surprised. We always figured they had to be pretty sophisticated to run such huge quantities under our noses. This informant has confirmed that in spades. Ocean-going vessels with refrigerated holds so our infrared detectors couldn't pick up a signal from the fermenting weed.

"Aircraft accompanying them to spot Navy and Coast Guard reconnaissance ships, encrypted communications, even toll-free 800 numbers for their haulers to check in with.

"There're construction warehouses in the Detroit area and a far-flung distributor network, supplying buyers nationwide.

"We're looking at a $1 billion dollar plus syndicate. Gentlemen, if we succeed in bringing down this group, it'll be the largest drug cartel prosecution in the history of the country."

Doug McCullough raised a question. "Is there a plan to gather evidence without blowing the whistle and jeopardizing a bigger prosecution at this point?"

"That's why you're all here today," Timmons said. "We will formulate a surveillance plan and hopefully determine the workings of this entire operation before they discover we're on to them."

Doug's next question silenced the room. It was forthright and on the minds of many in the room.

"Who will be the lead in the investigation and where are you thinking that prosecution will rest?"

"I know that'll be a hotly-contested point," Timmons said. "I'll leave prosecution up to the U.S.

Attorney's office to argue over. Since we broke the case in Detroit, we'll continue as the investigative lead and see what develops. We will liaison equally with all of you and share information as we acquire it."

Doug turned to Terry and whispered, "The fight over jurisdiction on this one will rival Vietnam."

"You're telling me?"

Almost as if on cue, an assistant U.S. Attorney from Tampa stepped up to suggest they would be the prosecuting office.

"Tampa holds places of residence for two of the three principals, and the conspiracy charge is viable here, given the large number of meetings between conspirators in the district. I believe everyone here in this room would have no problem with that, am I correct?"

Doug had a problem with that. "That's not the way we see it at all. So far, the only hard case of importation that has any corroborating evidence that would stand up in court is North Carolina. That's where the crime was committed and we will be prosecuting the principals there, and for importation, not conspiracy. We are not going to move off of this position either. I can assure you of that. We will, of course, assist all investigating agencies in any way possible."

Timmons intervened, "As I said, these are matters that will be decided down the road by the attorneys from the involved districts; not here, not today. Let's drop that line of discussion for now."

The jurisdiction fight was on.

It was obvious to Doug and Terry Peters that the much larger Tampa office felt the smaller Eastern North Carolina district didn't have the resources and expertise required to prosecute a case of this magnitude.

There were tight jaws as the meeting closed.

*****

August 1984 – Prison Interrogation Room, Tampa

Stephen Kalish, clad in an orange prison jump suit, sat quietly, and said nothing as two FBI agents pressed him for details.

"Why don't you tell us something worthwhile? Give us some names. Make things lighter on yourself."

Coaxing information out of Kalish was futile. It was time for a new tactic.

"Your wife is beside herself, Steve. She can hardly talk for crying. This is killing her. A few years in prison and there's a chance you could save your marriage and turn your life around. You love your wife don't you?"

"You know I do," Kalish said. "I'd prefer to leave her out of all this, though."

"We all know that's not possible. She wants to be with you, to grow old with her husband who, right now, is looking at growing old in the joint."

Kalish stared at the wall.

"I've got to tell you, your name has come up in some other investigations. Other folks are talking to save their skins. They don't mind giving you up. Why don't you look out for yourself, for Denise? Give us some details, some names. We know that what you were booked here for is small shit compared to what you're really involved in. Your man, Shine, he's talking. You know Michael Vogel had him whacked don't you?"

"Vogel tried to kill Shine? I don't believe it. Clinton was his guy. Besides, I know their names, but I never had any dealings with them. Everybody dealing on almost any level has heard of them. I might have wound up with a little grass that started out in Detroit, but I was never large enough to deal with them directly."

"You're hurting yourself, Steve. Small timers don't have jets hauling their ass around, or Ferraris, or estates in Panama. That's right, we've checked you out thoroughly. Your computers, the ones you wanted Leigh Ritch to grab for you, they've already provided us with a lot of names."

The agent tried to pad the case with a little exaggeration, doubting Kalish knew any better.

"Leigh Ritch and Landis have been very helpful too. They're willing to give you up to save their own necks. They say you're the top guy. You made the big bucks while they just picked up the scraps and helped you with a little distribution. I think you're the one who's going to take the brunt of all this if you don't try to help yourself. What do you say, Steve? Think about it. We can't wait indefinitely for an answer."

Kalish stared at the fluorescent light fixture on the dirty ceiling, reflecting against the government grey walls. It reminded him of an old black and white Cagney movie. Where was the proper bulb? Surely, they knew the room needed an unshaded hundred-watt bulb hanging by a single lamp cord if they were going to interrogate him and force him to talk. Had they never been to a movie?

He inhaled a deep drag from a cigarette and blew the smoke into the soft light overhead. He wasn't as simple a man as they thought. If they knew everything they said they did, why would they want him to flip? He didn't need to cut any deals too quickly. He would bide his time, play them along.

"Guys, I want to tell you that somebody's feeding you a load of shit. It's pretty small of you to use my wife, that you know I love dearly, as bait to get me to talk about things I'm not involved with. I don't want to hang some innocent just to save my own skin, not even to be with Denise. I would only be too glad to cut a deal with you if I actually had some sort of valuable information like you think I do. Want me to lie?"

Stalemated, the two agents backed off to decide on another approach. Time was on their side. Stephen Kalish wasn't going anywhere.

*****

Shine's Home in Detroit – Late Afternoon

After three weeks, Ned Timmons won approval for an undercover operation in the Cayman Islands and now, it was in jeopardy because of Shine.

The plan called for Shine to introduce Timmons to Ritch as his cousin, and pose as an international arms merchant whose last deal involved selling gunboats to Saudis.

The two were booked on an early morning flight to Atlanta to make the Caribbean connection, but the night before, Shine grew anxious and started hitting a fresh bottle of Jack Daniels. Within an hour, he was a screaming drunk.

He mounted his son's ATV and started stunt riding down the road to his house, and wrapped the machine around an oak tree in his front yard. The collision slammed Shine into the tree trunk. He sounded drunk, hurt, and still in shock when he called Timmons.

"Yeah, Ned. It's me, your man, Shine. Look, I can't be going with you in the morning. I'm hurt, bad."

"You sound drunk, Shine. I think that's your biggest problem. You've got to leave the bottle alone. When you drink, you talk and act like a wild man. With our trip coming up, saying the wrong thing to the wrong person could jeopardize what we're trying to do, maybe even get us killed. Sober up, man."

"I'm really hurt, Ned. I think I broke some bones."

"Okay, I'm on the way over. Leave the bottle alone."

"All right, I'll be waiting right here."

By the time Ned arrived, Shine had killed the bottle to kill the pain and was barely conscious.

"Shine, you son-of-a-bitch. You said you'd leave the bottle alone till I got here."

"I was hurting bad, Ned. I need to go to the hospital. My shoulder is all fucked up."

"Let me see it."

Shine unbuttoned his dirty torn shirt. He'd been correct in his diagnosis. It was apparent from the bone almost pushing through the skin that his shoulder was cleanly broken. This opened up a new set of problems for Timmons.

"This is just great. It's taken three weeks to get permission to go undercover in the Caymans. We have to go early tomorrow. Leave the bottle alone. I'll get you some painkillers and you can get it looked at when we get there."

"Man, you're shitting me. I'm over here suffering and you don't want me to go to the doctor? I can't fucking believe it. This is killing me."

"I'm real sorry, Shine. You were drunk; you ran into a tree like a stupid kid. You did this to yourself. I'm going to stay right here with you tonight and put you on the plane with me in the morning. Nothing, not even you, is going to screw this up. Here, take five aspirins and try to fall asleep. The time will go by faster and we'll fix the shoulder tomorrow afternoon."

"I can't believe you're letting me die like this."

"You're not dying. You just think you are. You'll be all right."

By morning, Shine was sober and in severe pain.

"Shine, get dressed. Here's some more aspirin. I'll bring the bottle with me. Hurry, the plane leaves in two hours. We need to hustle."

Ned went to the kitchen, put on a pot of coffee, and got out two cups while he waited on Shine. He took a hot cup in to Shine.

"Here you are, man. Sorry you're hurting. Wish I could help more. What the hell is that under your shirt? Tell me you're not wearing a gun. What the hell are you thinking, man? You can't wear that on a plane."

"I do it all the time."

"Take it off. Don't ever pack a weapon while we're working together. That's something I don't want to worry about. No drugs and no alcohol either. Not even a beer unless I give you the okay."

"You're shitting me. This is never going to work. I can't ask permission to drink a beer."

"Shine, you need to remember, there is 'no' beer in prison. Understand?"

"Heartless bastard."

Shine dutifully removed the shoulder holster and grimaced with pain as he put his shirt back on. He took a sip of the coffee, followed by four more aspirins.

"I can't believe all this. My life is ruined."

"Well, Shine, just remember, it can always get worse; a lot worse."

The two men left for the airport.

*****

Grand Cayman Island – Le Club

Shine and Agent Ned Timmons arrived at Le Club, the resort where Leigh Ritch maintained food and beverage concessions as a front. Ned immediately took Shine to the clinic and had his shoulder treated. Shine was most pleased with the strong, prescription narcotic pain killer. He didn't like the doctor's instruction to avoid alcohol while taking it.

Most members of the Ritch organization hung out at Le Club routinely. Shine introduced Ned as his cousin, Ed Thomas to everyone present. He cornered a couple of Ritch's key employees.

"This is my cousin, Ed, from my mother's side of the family."

The response to a new face from anyone involved in major drug smuggling was always suspicious.

"I'm Jason. This here is Mark. How come we haven't heard of you before? I've never known Shine to be able to keep his mouth shut about anything or anybody."

Shine was prepared for any question with a long line of bullshit, at which, he was unequalled.

"He's been in Saudi Arabia for the past couple years selling gunboats to the royals. Some folks back home would like to ask him a few questions he don't want to answer, so I thought I'd bring him down and introduce him to Leigh. He's almost as well versed in security as I am. Hell, he's probably better; just don't promote him as well. How 'bout a drink, Ed?"

"I'll take bourbon, with a beer chaser, draft will be fine."

Shine motioned for the waiter and ordered the first round for the group. He was relishing the fact that the only way to be social with the crew was to drink with them. Ned watched him closely so he would know immediately when his sobriety had vanished enough to loosen his tongue.

Within an hour, more men that Shine knew as associates joined them. Before long, there was an impromptu party in full swing. Ed, based on Shine's recommendation, was slowly accepted by the others. He knew that he would be suspect for a while, but for the moment, he was blending well and his knowledge of police matters, drug operations, and security issues learned during his long tenure with the bureau, helped convince them that he was as billed.

The drinking and socializing continued till way after all the regular customers had departed for their rooms at the upscale resort. Shine and Ned retreated to their respective rooms, confident of their charade. By

10 a.m., Leigh Ritch was trying to reach Shine. Finally, the persistent phone ringing awoke him from his tequila-induced sleep.

*****

May 26, 1985 – Seven Mile Beach – Grand Cayman – Leigh Ritch's Estate

Shine and Ned drove beside the main beach as they made their way to Leigh Ritch's estate.

"This is quite some place. You say Ritch's family is in business here?"

"Yeah, they're well connected and well thought of. For that matter, Leigh is kinda the local golden boy. You know, he lives in the big house, has movie stars and celebrities over for dinner, that kind of stuff. He's generous with the locals and they love him. Money can certainly buy respect."

"They don't have a clue where his money comes from, eh Shine?"

"Most of these folks aren't well off. If you spread a little money around the island, nobody's about to ask where the hell it came from. For that matter, I guarantee you they wouldn't ask back in Detroit either. I know I don't care where you get your bucks if you're giving some of it to me. Now listen, Leigh is going to buy into you one hundred percent if I tell him you're okay. So don't fuck up. He's sharp as hell and if any of this group finds out what you're up to, and that I helped you, we're both dead. Got it?"

"I've spent a lot of years doing this, Shine. If I can squeeze my way into a biker's gang and not ever be found out, this won't be any more difficult than that, trust me. Ritch knows you were shot, doesn't he? How'd you explain that?"

"I told him that Garcia hit me, trying to move into my deal with Vogel. I don't like either one of them, so I came down here. They've never arrested Garcia or

Vogel for it so as far as anybody knows, I'm clean; unlucky, but clean."

As the men drove along West Bay road, which paralleled Seven Mile Beach, they passed a string of luxury hotels and tourists. Four miles beyond, they passed the Cayman Turtle Farm, widely known for saving endangered species. In another mile, an immense gray wall appeared on the west side, surrounding Leigh Ritch's opulent estate.

The main house, a six-sided contemporary with decks and a large, elaborate pool included an equally-impressive guest house and dock where Ritch's yacht, *Post Time*, was moored.

Shine pulled up to the main house and the men approached the front door where Bertley, Ritch's butler, awaited, with the door open and a large smile on his dark-skinned face.

"Gentlemen, welcome. Mr. Ritch has been asking for you all morning."

"Sorry 'bout that. We were up late."

"You were on island time, as we say."

Leigh Ritch entered the room, walked briskly up to Shine and Ned, hand extended, first to Shine.

"Shine, my friend. I've tried to reach you all morning. I knew you were down. Got a job for you."

He looked at Ned Timmons.

"You must be the gunboat dealer I've already heard so much about."

"Ed, Ed Thomas, Mr. Ritch."

"Call me Leigh. Well, what do you think so far of our little Island? Quite beautiful, eh?"

"From what I've seen so far, this is a most beautiful spot."

"I am quite proud of my little piece of the island. I'm very happy here. What brings you to the Caymans?"

"My cousin thought I might be of some help. I've got a pretty long resume of 'special' jobs over the years. I've got a rather unique set of skills, if I do say so myself."

With a charming smile, Ritch probed further into his guest's credentials.

"Exactly what can you do better than most people?"

"If I'm allowed to do a little bragging: Security. I'd say that I qualify for the description of expert when it comes to security."

"How's that? What do you know that Shine doesn't?"

"Not to put down my cousin, because I really don't do anything with lie detectors and voice stress analysis, but I'm extremely up to speed on wiretaps, bugs, electronic surveillance, radio detection, infrared technology, anything in the way of telecommunication. I'm also pretty damned good with weapons and my first love, boats."

Ritch studied the undercover agent for a full minute. He stared him square in the eye and then, once again, smiled.

"I can use a man with that sort of background in my organization, Ed. Matter of fact, the reason I wanted to talk with Shine this morning is to debug my place."

"How do you know you're bugged?"

"I don't. I was watching a cop show on television, and that's what brought down this guy's operation. He, of course, was a bad guy, whereas I'm just an international trader with enemies whose business I've taken in several countries. They'd love to put me out of business. Now, I'm not doing anything here that's illegal, but I realize that some of my associates might walk a fine line in that area. You understand, bend the law to increase their profits.

"As a matter of fact, a very close business associate, Steve Kalish in Tampa, and the Reo brothers from Michigan, associates of mine in the past, have recently run afoul of the law. The Reos are in the warehouse business and, from time to time, I've stored some goods with them for very short periods of time. I've heard that they're under investigation for storing illegal commodities in their warehouses. Since I've done business with them in the past, and I'm from the Caymans where the Feds already think we operate the entire country just to evade the law, I'm afraid my name might come under scrutiny from these same people. Not that I have anything to hide. I just got to worrying about the possibility of my being overheard during some delicate conversations."

"I understand, Mr. Ritch."

"Call me Leigh."

"So, you want me to check your entire compound to make certain your conversations are private? That you're not being watched in any way?"

"Good, you understand completely. How about starting with my private phone line here? I get a lot of business calls every day and I don't want to have to use smoke signals to do business. How long will it take to check this out?"

"Let me get a piece of equipment out of my luggage and I can tell you pretty quickly if your phone is safe. It's in the car."

"That's great, Ed. I think you're going to fit into my operation in a big way. Shine has to come and go quite a bit. He works for several of my key associates as well, but I'd like for you to stay here, watch over my day-to-day security. How would you feel about that? What do you say, Shine, is he up to it?"

Shine knew the ramifications of what was occurring. He was knowingly endorsing a plant; a mole within the organization that had been the financial highpoint of his life. This would be the downfall for everyone involved. Maybe a hundred or more people would be looking at jail time and wanting to know who set them up. It weighed heavily on him, but not as much as the fact that Vogel had already tried to bury him. What could be any worse than that?

Besides, when it all came apart, he'd be on the side of the fence that housed the Feds and the courts. He wouldn't be going to prison, and they'd assured him he could hang onto his winnings until then. He had set aside enough to retire comfortably. This would be a nerve-racking, gut-wrenching time, but there was no other way out. It was every man for himself now. He smiled at Leigh Ritch.

"He's top drawer, Leigh," Shine said. "Other than lie detection, he's light years ahead of me when it comes to security. He can keep your place clean. You'd be lucky to get him. You got to pay him pretty decent though. He's used to working for Saudi princes, you know."

"I think I can match what they were paying. I'd say you should be good for three grand a week to start and a number of sizable bonuses when I have a good turn during the year. You'll go over two hundred a year, no doubt. Would that work for you? And don't forget, you'll be staying in my guest house here in the compound and enjoying the most beautiful place in the world every day."

Ned knew he was in. It was so much easier than he thought it would be, and it almost unnerved him. Not to mention, Leigh Ritch seemed to be a great guy who just happened to run drugs for a living. In another situation, he would've enjoyed just hanging with him.

"You have a new face in security, Leigh. I'll get my gear and start checking out the place."

"That's great, Ed. Don't forget to start with my phones."

"I'll be on it in a minute."

Over the course of the next three hours, Ned checked out Ritch's compound. He not only would get a first-hand opportunity to look over the whole place, but he would also be able to determine if anyone inside or outside of the Ritch group had actually been eavesdropping on him. He quickly ran an electronic sensor through the phone lines and was certain they were clean. He immediately informed Leigh Ritch of that result. Ritch was visibly relieved. For the next hour, Ned pretended to be checking everything in the room from the wet bar to the electrical outlets. The phone rang non-stop and he listened to Ritch's side of the conversations. What he heard was adding a great deal of credibility to the tale that Clinton had told him. This was a drug operation of mammoth proportions. After a lengthy conversation about the most remote ports in the Gulf of Mexico, Leigh Ritch hung up the phone and walked over to Ned who he knew had heard every word of his conversation.

"Finding anything, Ed?"

"Nope, your fears weren't justified, though your need for precautions is."

"By the way, Ed, you do realize that you'll see and overhear a lot of my private affairs since you're going to be dealing with my security. Everything, and I do mean everything, is private. It goes no further than these walls. You understand?"

"Completely. I've listened while prime ministers and sheiks made billion-dollar oil deals and funneled money all over the globe to less than desirable functionaries. You know what I'm talking about, right?"

"I'd say you're talking about terrorists."

"You'd be right. I know how to keep my mouth shut. You buy my services, you buy my confidentiality. You can rest assured that whatever I overhear will only be repeated where it should be."

Ned laughed to himself at the remark he had just made to Ritch. Things had progressed so much faster and easier than he could ever have imagined. Leigh trusted Shine and had bought into Ned's story completely. From here on out, he would be privy to the inner workings of Ritch's organization. If he handled things properly, he could establish a drug cartel sting operation greater than any ever undertaken.

- CHAPTER FIFTEEN -
GRABBING THE MARBLES

Doug McCullough's Office – New Bern, North Carolina

Doug McCullough, Terry Peters, and several other attorneys from the United States Attorney's Office knew they sat in the catbird seat. They had come to Doug's office to monitor a phone call to Tampa.

"This'll be an interesting call, I assure you," Doug said, dialing. "Tampa thinks that their prosecution of this whole thing is a foregone conclusion. I hate to upset their apple cart, but we need to make our viewpoint clear on this right now."

Doug winked at his colleagues as his call was answered.

"Yes, this is Assistant U.S. Attorney Doug McCullough in the North Carolina Eastern District. Right, good to speak with you, too.

"Listen, following the recent events and direction the Clinton Anderson case is going, we want to let you know that we intend to prosecute in our district. We're firm all the way up to the top on this."

He paused as a long dissertation from the Tampa attorney attempted to explain why that was not workable from their viewpoint. Doug finally interjected.

"That's all well and good, but the fact is, you cannot establish an actual importation in Florida. The best you could hope for is conspiracy. We've got at least two confirmed imports here and a shit pot full of co-conspirators still living here.

"Common sense dictates that this is where it should be tried. Well, I'm sorry you feel that way, but our position is not negotiable. We intend to prosecute the moment all of the pieces are put together. We're hearing a repeat of the same names that Clinton Anderson offered up from several other investigations in Texas, Louisiana, Michigan, and now from Ned Timmons.

"I'm just giving you a head's up. This is all going to come together quickly and we're ready to move forward here. Sorry you feel that way. Yeah, you too."

Doug smiled broadly as he hung up the phone.

"Whew! You're talking about a really pissed-off prosecutor there. He was already tasting the headlines he just knew were heading his way."

Terry walked over to Doug and sat opposite him on the corner of his desk.

"Did he recognize that we've got the best jurisdiction? It only makes sense that we try the case here."

"He knows. He just doesn't want to give up without a fight. There'll be a turf war over our heads on this one. But, I'm confident we're going to get this case. He's just a little disappointed right now."

Others in the office began to laugh out loud at the plight of the prosecutor in Florida. One of the younger attorneys patted Doug on the back and remarked, "Doug, you'll end up on the Supreme Court before it's all over with. You just have a way about you that's hard to argue with."

"My friend, it's called the law."

After a few more rounds of self-congratulations, everyone left but Terry Peters and Doug. Terry grew more serious.

"What do you think, Doug? Is this as big as it seems right now?"

"The first reports we have back from Ned Timmons indicate it's ongoing, far larger, and more sophisticated than Clinton Anderson knew. Ned is apparently getting in tight with Leigh Ritch. He said he's been put in charge of his entire security operation. You talk about a major screw-up by Ritch. Can you believe he meets some guy and three weeks later, puts him in charge of his security?"

Terry shook his head. "That's why we win, Doug. No matter how smart they seem to be, they always fuck up."

"I guess you're right."

*****

Grand Cayman

Ned, aka Ed, carried out his assignment on two fronts. First, he made sure Ritch's security was being impeccably managed. Then, with a well-trained eye and loyalty to his real employer, he set a trap for Ritch. He hoped his efforts would ensnare a large collection of smugglers, money handlers, and assorted criminals. Not many agents ever received the opportunity his charade was creating. That morning, Ritch asked him to ride with him to town and then to Le Club where he was setting up for a party later that evening.

While he drove, he nonchalantly dropped a bomb on Ned.

"Ed, there's an FBI agent on the island."

Ned almost choked as he heard the words. They were on to him! Or, at least to the fact there was a mole on the island.

"Be careful."

"Right, Leigh. I will."

Nothing else was said as Leigh and Ned made their rounds. Jason, who had introduced himself to Ned the first night, came up to him a while later as he did a routine security check at Le Club.

"Ed, you know there's an FBI agent on the island?"

"I heard already. What do you know about it?"

"That's all. Word is out to all the guys. Keep an eye open."

"I'll certainly do that, Jason. Thanks for the word."

"No problem, Ed."

Later that afternoon, a dense fog moved in. Leigh came over to Ned and asked.

"Ed, I want you to help Bertley get some conch for a special dish I'm craving. It needs fresh conch and Bertley knows just the spot. He's up at the house. How about running up there and giving him a hand?"

"Sure, Leigh. But is that more important than checking out the club?"

"Right now it is. Shouldn't take long."

"Okay, if that's what you want."

"Good. See you later."

Ned's mind raced overtime.

This is it, he thought. *He knows. He's going to have Bertley take me out. Got to keep on guard. Got to be careful.*

Ned found Bertley in the old truck used to haul supplies. He looked over at Ned as he approached.

"Good, you're here. Leigh said you would be. He's always right. A good man. I'd do anything for him. Anything."

"I'm sure you would."

They drove down to a small lagoon where an old wooden rowboat sat upside-down with oars laid over the top. Bertley reached for one end of the boat.

"Here, Ed, you grab the other end and let's turn it over."

"Right, Bertley. Listen, isn't it getting too foggy to go out?"

"I know this lagoon like the back of my hand. This won't take but a few minutes."

As the boat fell over on its bottom, Bertley pulled out a large machete from behind him. Ned thought, *This is it. Stay mobile. Be ready.*

Bertley threw the machete in the boat and said.

"Okay, let's row to the middle. You take the oars."
"Sure, no problem."
Ned now considered the oars his weapon. He'd be a hard man to handle if Bertley decided to make a move on him. He slowly rowed and maneuvered the small boat to the center of the lagoon. Bertley reached over and grabbed the machete. Ned braced himself and tightened his grip on an oar like a baseball bat. He was ready. Bertley took the machete, tucked it under his arm, and rolled backward into the water. In moments, he surfaced, depositing two live conch shells in the boat. As promised, in a few moments, the boat had conch enough to satisfy Bertley.

"Okay, let's go. We've got enough."

Ned rowed back to shore with such alacrity, he almost beached the boat. Bertley would never know Ned's anxiety.

Nothing else was said about the FBI agent that afternoon. Ned started his security sweep of the club again and saw neither Bertley nor Leigh Ritch until guests started to arrive at the party. Ned circulated, made small talk with employees, and observed partygoers as they arrived.

A natural showman, Leigh made a grand entrance with a gorgeous woman on his arm, fifteen minutes after everyone arrived. That was his style. He came over to Ned.

"Ed, let me introduce you to my lovely and wonderful friend."

Ned couldn't deny that this was one good-looking gal.

"A pleasure to meet you. I've enjoyed your show. I wouldn't blame Leigh if he tried to hold that arm all night. I know I would."

"Well, Ed, he certainly seems to be doing a good job of it so far," she smiled. "Of course, I've always enjoyed Leigh trying to hold onto me."

Ned scanned the crowd not only to make it look like he was doing his job, but also to make note of anything that might give him insight into the Ritch organization.

As the evening stretched on, diners and the late party guests merged to make one merry crowd; among them, Leigh's close associates.

Ned knew his cover could always be blown. What happened next underscored that belief. Entering the bar from the restaurant was another FBI agent Ned knew well from a prior operation.

With his wife in tow, the agent walked straight toward him, smiling, about to greet him like a colleague. Ned looked him straight in the eye, took his right hand, ran it flat across his throat as if to imply, "stop right there." To his great relief, the agent got the message and walked away.

Beads of perspiration on Ned's forehead reminded him how fast his masquerade could end with dangerous consequences.

Odds another agent would be on holiday in the middle of Ned's surveillance had to be one in a million, but it was a relief to clear up the mystery of "agent on the island". It wasn't Ned.

On the surface, Leigh Ritch seemed to be a happy-go-lucky fellow with great personality and style. However, Ned didn't have to remember back very far to recall Shine in a hospital bed with his guts sewn up. He'd never underestimate the danger of his situation.

The sweat had barely dried from Ned's forehead when Ritch came over and asked him and Shine to join him in the club's office. He now stood ready to discuss business with intimates of his organization. *How bizarre,* Ned thought, *that I, so new to the group, would not only be included in conspiratorial discussions, but also be in charge of overall security, too.*

Within moments, several associates brought in for the weekend, joined Leigh Ritch, Ned, and Shine.

"This isn't a good time for our organization," Ritch began. "If you've not heard, Stephen Kalish, and a number of our associates have been arrested. At this time, I don't think the authorities have an insight into the total workings of our operation. I can't help but feel they would already be on the island if they had any information. But this does make it necessary for us to stop moving any product and curtail our association with one another till we see where all this goes. The *Blaster* is off for now. It's just too risky. We need to all sit back, observe, and play it close to our chest. Any of you hear anything that the rest of us should know, be very careful about making contact. You can call Ed Thomas here—you've all met Ed?--and he'll relay a message to me. Direct contact is just far too risky. All that being said, let's enjoy the evening and get back on with our lives in the morning. Good luck to you all."

Ritch returned to the bar, and turned to Ned.

"Ed, you know Tommy Lee and Heather Locklear are here and have asked me to go to their wedding in Jamaica?"

"Come with me Ed. I want you to check out a room for me."

"Sure. Do I need my test kit for a phone?"

"Just come with me. I've got a little something to take care of and don't think I should be doing it by myself." They walked off together. Ritch spoke candidly with Ned.

"That Heather is one beautiful woman, isn't she?"

"Fine as I've ever seen. I've seen a lot of them. I don't understand what the attraction is to the tattooed drummer, but beauty is in the eye of the beholder."

"He's a nice guy, and women love rock and rollers. I've had a bunch of the bands down here over the years and I'm always surprised to see the most beautiful women on the arm of somebody who looks like a carnival worker, but plays in a band. I'm surprised still."

They came to a heavy metal door with several padlocks. Ritch opened each lock and pushed open the heavy door. The room was dark and smelled odd, like a printing company storage area. Ritch turned on the light and walked to a four-foot square pallet covered by a tarp. He pulled back the tarp.

"Ed, this is what it's all about, here and everywhere else on the planet."

Ned stared at the largest stack of $100 dollar bills he'd ever seen: Four-foot square, two feet high, low guess: Five, maybe, ten million dollars.

"Jesus, Leigh. I didn't know there was that much money in the world. Aren't you nervous storing it here?"

"Sure, that's why I've made arrangements for it to be moved to an extremely safe location tonight."

"Where can you store it that's safer than a bank?"

"I have a very special place. One no one will ever find except me. I want you to watch over the door here while I get a vehicle. I'm going to lock it back up while you keep watch around the corner. No one gets near the place."

"I'll be right here."

"Fine, back in ten with a truck."

Over the next hour, Ritch loaded the back of a covered truck with stacks of money. Ned never got an inkling where the money was headed. He knew from the bureau, that Kalish's banking deal ended with his arrest. Ritch must have felt disaster looming and was securing his future in another place. Ned watched and listened for any hint of where all the money was headed. It never happened. The money and Ritch disappeared, never to be spoken of it again.

The Caymans authorities hadn't been notified of Ned's presence on the island. This was a fact of great concern to the Bureau, and Ned in particular. The Caymans resented the heavy-handed treatment they often received from the U.S. when they tried to crack down on offshore banking interests. A large number of the local bureaucrats were padding their wallets with the overflow of these illegal operations. They didn't want to see the gravy train end and hated the U.S. telling them what to do. The Bureau had made contact only with Scotland Yard and Ned was given a name to call in London in case of an emergency. No police in the Caymans had any knowledge of his presence there. Ned continued to worry he'd be discovered and drowned in the Caribbean. He continued his covert activities, reporting when he could to the home office. Time was growing short to make a play against Ritch. The politics of it would be difficult as the locals loved him and the government officials enjoyed his company. They wouldn't lightly turn on him.

It was, therefore, quite surprising when early one morning, the local authorities showed up at Leigh Ritch's home to conduct a search for drugs.

A complaint that Leigh was using coke had been made. He opened his home up to whatever search they wished, confident his residence was clean. The police captain marched straight to an upstairs bathroom and found an ounce of coke, tightly wrapped, and hidden up under the sink, taped to the bottom, totally concealed from view.

Since the coke was found so fast in such an obscure location, only one conclusion could be made: Ritch had been set up. To say he was indignant was a mild understatement.

"You know I'm being framed here, don't you? You come into my house, I offer you total cooperation, and you go immediately to the bathroom and miraculously find a package of coke the size of a cat's turd. How convenient. What you are getting out of this, Captain?"

"Mr. Ritch, I don't appreciate your inference or your tone. We get tips constantly. Many have pointed your way and we have never taken one step towards you in spite of this. To be accused of setting you up is very disappointing. I'm sure after you've had time to collect your thoughts, you won't feel that way. We are Islanders like you, and it personally troubles me to have to arrest you. But, the law is the law. You'll have to come with me to the station."

"Sure, friend. I'll be glad to."

Ritch called for Bertley to make a call.

"My attorney's number is on the auto dialer in the den. Bertley, tell him to meet me at the station and be prepared to make my bail."

"Yes sir, Mr. Ritch. Right now."

Leigh Ritch was booked and released after posting a ten thousand dollar bond. He was also ordered to not leave the Caymans for any reason without the permission of the court. In a business such as his, many people could find reasons to frame him. The word on the island was that someone was jealous of Ritch and wanted to cause him problems.

Though the offense wasn't enough to ruin his life, it was far too close to his true occupation. From that point on, Ritch made sure that anyone and everyone associated with him knew that no drugs of any sort would be tolerated in his home, his club, or on their person when associating with him. Violation would be considered a direct threat and treated as such.

The arrest did, however, create a small impediment for Ritch. He would have to ask local courts for permission to leave the island, post additional bond, and divulge his destination. His island had become a holding cell.

- CHAPTER SIXTEEN -
PLAYING THE BEST HAND

February 1985 – Onslow Beach – Camp Lejeune, North Carolina

A squad of Marine Corps guards with M16 rifles stood watch over a small trailer used as a beach house for families of military personnel at Camp Lejeune Marine Corps Base in mid-winter. A government sedan and several Jeeps were parked outside. The beach and other nearby trailers were deserted.

Inside, Doug McCullough and Terry Peters interrogated Steve Kalish, who seemed at ease with his interrogators. Over the past several months, they had earned his respect and trust.

"Steve, the time for your gut check is here," Doug said. "The government is very interested in your dealings with General Noriega, the Panamanian banks, and their government in general. By your own admission, you have first-hand knowledge of collusion between drug dealers and Noriega. This information and your willingness to swear to it under oath could be your salvation.

"You're looking at twenty-to-life right now. What if I told you the U.S. Attorney's Office is willing to offer you a term of no more than seven years with possibly less for good behavior and time you've already served? You could possibly be out in three, maybe even two years."

"That wouldn't help a dead man very much," Kalish replied.

"There's the Federal Witness Protection Program," Doug said. "It works. We can keep you and Denise safe. I'm telling you, Steve, this is your only hope. You're safer dealing with us than you are with any of the people you have in the past. You can start over."

"That all sounds wonderful," Kalish said. "Of course, I'll be broke, a convicted felon, and hiding out the rest of my life."

"It doesn't have to be that way. We'll help you restructure your life. Granted, it won't be in a mansion in Panama, and there won't be any private jets or Ferraris, but I don't have any of those things and I'm a happy guy. You have a wonderful woman who's stuck with you through all this. Isn't that relationship worth saving, even if you couldn't salvage anything else?"

"What would I have to do?"

"Testify before a number of grand juries, maybe even to a senator or congressman investigating the Panama situation. You'd have to answer all questions truthfully and to the fullest of your knowledge. If they find you're holding back or intentionally misleading them, then all deals are off.

"We would lose interest in you. Your value to the government would be zero, and the states of Florida, Louisiana, Texas, and Michigan can take their turns with you. You'd still be a very big deal to them. So what's it gonna be?"

"You have to have my answer right now, today?"

"Today, yes. And, to help you make the right decision, I've brought along some professional help."

"Another government psychiatrist to make certain I'm not nuts?"

"Nope, someone far more proficient at getting the truth out of you than that."

Doug opened the door to the trailer and Denise Kalish entered. To Steve Kalish, she was more beautiful than he had ever seen her. He wasn't alone in his assessment. Every man in the place, including the guards couldn't take their eyes off her. She was one of the most naturally lovely women any of them had ever seen.

"Hey, handsome. How are they treating you?"

Kalish rushed over to her. No one in the room made any effort to come between them. He embraced her and kissed her like a man starved for air that only she could provide him. She was now all that was good in his life. He would do whatever it took to hold on to her.

"Baby, you need to cooperate with them. It's our only hope of being together. I'll wait for you, but I can't wait fifty years. You help them and maybe in two years, we can start over. I trust them."

The scene touched Doug McCullough and Terry Peters. Doug walked over to Kalish and put his hand on his shoulder.

"Steve, you and your better half here need to come to a decision. Tell you what I'm going to do. To help you talk in private, we're going to leave you alone, completely alone, except for guards outside, for two hours. You will be left alone a full two hours. You talk about it, and anything else that will help you decide. You understand me?"

He smiled at the couple as he made the offer. It may have been the turning point in the investigation. The two government agents heard clothes hit the floor before the door closed behind them.

*****

Bal Harbor Apartments – Tampa

Ned had been assigned the duty of meeting with buyers in Tampa. With Kalish in prison and Ritch's travel restrictions, someone else had to deal with the buyers. Ritch didn't want this meeting to occur in the Caymans or anywhere near his base of operations. Ned was his best option. Shine would accompany him to furnish background muscle while Ned interviewed buyers. Many were from Texas; their cowboy boots and Stetsons made them stick out like bikers at a beach party.

"Gentlemen, it's been a pleasure. Mr. Ritch appreciates your business and Shine and myself will look forward to meeting with you again in the near future. I'll see to it that your package gets to Leigh this afternoon, as we will be heading back to the islands. Anything else I can do for you?"

The older of two men spoke. Both were couriers who took the risk of buying and selling drugs for the smallest piece of the action.

"Yeah, Ed. How about mentioning me to Mr. Ritch? I've been wanting to do a small deal of my own, maybe ten, fifteen grand. Could you put in a word for me with him? I understand you're his eyes and ears."

"I'll certainly tell him what a pleasure it was to work with you, but I can't offer you any hope for purchases of that size. It costs Mr. Ritch that much to fly Shine and me over here for a week on the jet and put us up. Two hundred grand is pretty much the bottom end of where he does business. You put that much together and give us a call. We'll be glad to listen."

Ned didn't give them the chance to interject. He needed them out the door.

"Well, you fellas have a great day and we'll see that your product arrives in Texas the first of next week."

The two men left the room. Shine walked over to Ed and handed him a beer.

"Damn, Ned, you're one cool son of a bitch. You should get an Academy Award. These poor bastards begging for your help and you're sitting here filming them all the time. They'll be going up the river before too long, thanks to you."

"And you, Shine."

"Yeah, and me. I gotta tell you, though, this is more fun than running stress tests and hauling around other people's money. I get a real kick out of it. Not only can

I not go to prison for it, it's keeping me out of the joint. How do you beat that?"

"It is a high, I'll admit. You watch the door and slow down on the booze while I go next door to check on the surveillance team."

"Right on, Ned. Be right here, slowing down on the booze."

"You really need to, Shine. You're killing yourself with that shit. Plus, I don't like working with you when you're drunk. I'll be right back."

Ned walked to the room next door where two agents had audio and video taping equipment to capture the buys going on in the next room. Over the past two months, they had captured at least two dozen transactions on film. The sting operation was a huge success. It had already exceeded the grandest expectations of all agents involved. Ned tapped three times, twice on the door.

"Coming. All right, Ned. That was fabulous, man."

"You getting it all?"

"Like *Gone With the Wind*. A modern classic. You're getting good at milking these poor saps. They're hanging themselves hoping to get in your good graces and get you to speak to Ritch for them. You enjoy it, don't you?"

"I've been doing this a long time. These guys are milquetoast compared to dealing with Hell's Angels. Bikers can spot a fake a mile away. You've got to be good to get them believing in you."

"So, when's the next customer showing up?"

"Four. About two hours and that's it for this week."

"Four? Damn. The game comes on at three. That's all right, Bobby can run the machines while I watch the game and I'll keep 'em running so he can. Bobby, can't you quit smoking that cigar while we're holed up in this little room? Your smoke is killing me."

"Friggin' wimp, Marty. Cigar smoke is good for you. Makes a man out of you."

"Ned, tell him to put the damn thing out. I can't breathe in here."

"It is pretty bad, Bobby. Can't you give it a rest?"

"I'll take a break. Can't believe you guys are such friggin' wimps. Shine don't mind it. Loves a good cigar and a bottle of Jack."

"He loves 'em too much. I'll be glad when I'm through with him. What a whack job."

"I'm ready to go home, too. What have we done, maybe fifty of these buys? The walls have so many holes in 'em from bugs; it's getting to be like Swiss cheese. I'm glad the Bureau decided to rent these rooms full time till we're finished. I'm so tired of drilling holes, planting ears in the walls, and then having to fill them up. I'm not a painter; I'm an audio expert."

"I'm about ready to see this wrap up myself. Feel like we may be pushing our luck. Okay, you guys hold it down and I'll go babysit Shine till the last mark shows up."

At 4 p.m., the last of the couriers arrived. They were from Louisiana and didn't have the polish of the pair before them, but they had bought from Ritch before and they had access to a lot of money.

"Welcome, come on in, fellas. How was your flight?"

"We drove. Bernie don't like flying, so we drove up in the truck. Damn air's out in it. Hotter than hell."

"Well the air's on in here. Sit down and cool off. I understand you're looking for a larger than usual shipment this time."

"That's right. Pierre wants to buy a hundred bales. Can you handle that much?"

"We handle that much all the time. Pure Colombian, the finest grass. Your boss has been pleased with all the past product hasn't he?"

"Damn right. He's made a fucking killing with it. He said to check with you about it just the same, though. He understood Kalish is in the joint and he thought it might be slowing you all down."

"Kalish is not in for anything that had to do with us and he'll probably be out quickly from what I'm hearing. It's not affecting our ability to get product or conduct business. You've got the cash with you?"

"Right here in my bag. Hey man, what the hell is all that noise next door? Sounds like a party going on. I can barely hear you."

"Must be some guys watching a game on the TV. A lot of fishermen stay here and drink when they come off the boat. They sure are making a racket." Ned hedged with the best of them, but made a mental note to take it out on the agents' asses when he had the chance. They had no business making his job harder.

"And damn, it stinks. What are they doing, burning trash?"

"I think it's a cigar, that's what it smells like to me."

"That's one foul smelling piece of shit."

"What did you say?" The sound from the TV next door was so loud they couldn't hear each other.

"I said it stinks in here. Let's get this over with."

"I'll call the office. They can shut them up."

Ned went to the phone and called the desk clerk.

"I'm sorry to bother you, but would you please call the folks in Room 245 and tell them that Mr. Thomas, next door, said they're disturbing his rest? They're making a lot of racket and the walls here are very thin. Thanks."

The phone could be heard ringing above the racket in the surveillance room. A few seconds later, things quieted down. Ned and the others finished their business and he saw them to the door. He immediately went next door.

"What in hell were you doing over here? You almost blew the whole deal!"

"Sorry, Ned. The Giants scored with less than a minute to go. They might get into the playoffs, man. It was wild."

"I can't believe you guys. It's like trying to conduct a sting operation in an amusement park."

"Sorry, man. We got a little out of control there."

"I'll say. We're done for this trip. I'm going to take Shine's drunken ass back to the Caymans. That should be interesting."

*****

Private Jet Terminal – Tampa Airport

"Sorry, Ed, the Lear isn't available. I knew you were going back today, but Dave didn't see it in the book. He was filling in for me while I was at lunch, and he had the opportunity to lease it out for three days. It's a big-ticket rental and he really didn't know. I'll be glad to get you tickets on the next available commercial flight. Would you be all right with that?"

"I'm fine with it. I just hope Clinton is sober enough to not embarrass me for the one-millionth time. You check on the flight while I check on him."

"Yes, Sir."

Ned went out to the rental car only to find Shine missing. He went back into the private aircraft terminal and heard Shine's unmistakable voice singing off key in the men's room. He walked in behind him.

"Shine, what the hell are you doing in here? We have to hurry and catch a commercial flight over at the main terminal."

"Commercial? I don't like to fly commercial. Where's my Lear?"

"Leigh Ritch's Lear is not available, it's gone. We're flying commercial. You need to sober up and not draw any attention to us on the plane. You don't have any liquor on you do you?"

"Absolutely not, or should I say, Absolut not? Absolut...get it?"

"Yeah, I get it. Stand still."

Ned quickly frisked Shine's jacket, patting him down. He immediately found a liquor bottle in the front inside pocket of the jacket. He removed it and dumped it in the sink.

"Shine, you're just plain nuts. You have anything else on you?"

Shine's refusal to comment could only mean one thing. Ned searched him again.

"A gun? A fucking gun? Are you crazy, Shine? Are you trying to get arrested? You want to blow the entire operation and wind up in prison for the rest of your life? You've got to get serious. Don't ever do this again. This is the last time I'm warning you. I'm beginning to feel like a character in a Three Stooges movie. Damn! Let's go."

Shine muttered under his breath.

"They don't frisk me when I fly on my Lear."

As they left the restroom, the manager of the jet leasing service informed them that they were booked on a commercial flight leaving Tampa in thirty minutes. They had just enough time to return the rental car and make the flight, if they hurried.

*****

Aboard 727 – Bound for Grand Cayman

Ned and Shine just barely made the flight. Not only was short notice a factor, but Shine was also stumbling drunk. Ned took a window seat and Shine sat on the aisle, dead center in the almost full plane. He was feeling no pain. Out of nowhere, he started telling jokes to everyone around him. At first, they weren't too filthy.

"There was these two nuns. Both of them had bad habits."

After three or four jokes, the other passengers couldn't decide if they were part of a hidden camera television show or whether Shine was a traveling comedian. He truly could tell a joke, and the more the crowd cheered him on, the worse he got. He quickly ran out of semi-clean jokes and started to tell stories bad enough to embarrass a sailor. Finally, the flight attendant, noticeably gay, approached him.

"Please, Sir, there are small children on the plane and you are very loud. Could I bring you something to drink?"

"Could you what? I'm sorry, buddy, but I'm straight. Say have you heard the one about the two queers and the anteater?"

"Please, Sir, you need to behave and not disturb the other passengers. I'll go get you a drink. How about that?"

"Sure, pal. I want a shot of whiskey. My old buddy Ned, here, he took my bottle before I got on this plane. I'm starting to feel dry."

"Okay, Sir. I'll go and get you one drink if you'll be quiet."

"Deal, pal. Say, what kind of lipstick are you wearing?"

The flight attendant, beside himself over how to handle Shine, left to go get him a watered down drink. While he was in the plane's galley, Shine decided it was time to get up from his seat and tell more jokes. The group was egging him on and though he was loud and obnoxious, he was funny. Just as the flight attendant returned with the drink, Shine stumbled and fell between another passenger's legs and the seat in front of him. The flight attendant handed the drink to a female flight attendant who was rushing to help and then proceeded to bend down to give Shine a hand. Shine was more than the flight attendant could move, and after getting him about a foot off the floor, they both fell back down with the flight attendant now on top of him.

Shine, sensing an opportune moment to get the biggest laugh yet at the expense of the flight attendant, starting screaming. "Stop him, somebody stop him. He's trying to put it up my butt. Somebody grab him quick. Oh boy, he's got me now."

As rude and cruel as he was to the flight attendant, the other passengers laughed hysterically. Ned, ashamed to admit Shine was with him, yanked him to his feet, shoved him in a window seat, then sat on the aisle to prevent a repeat performance. Within minutes, Shine was out like a light, dead drunk.

- CHAPTER SEVENTEEN -
ALL THE KING'S HORSES

Grand Cayman – Leigh Ritch's Office

"Ed, I hate to ask you to turn around and go right back to Florida, but I've got a few jobs that need taking care of and you're the only guy I want to do it."

"No problem, Leigh. What's up? Does Shine have to go back with me? I swear to God, he's the most trying son of a bitch I've ever spent time with. It's like herding bees with a switch."

"Just you, Ed. I want you to make a few deliveries for me."

"Product?"

"No, we're not touching anything ourselves and positively not here on the island. I've now got the local authorities looking over my shoulder. Whoever planted that half-ounce under the sink doesn't have a clue what they've done. They were assuming that the local cops might think I was a user and try to catch me with a joint in my glove compartment. But the scrutiny's the same as if they knew what we were really into here. It's a bitch to work around."

"And now, Heather and Tommy Lee want to get married in Jamaica so I'll have to post a ten grand cash bond just to leave to attend the wedding. It's not the money, it's just a pain in the ass to get treated like a common criminal."

"There's nothing common about you, Leigh. If they only knew. You want me to deliver money, then? With Kalish out of the loop, how are you making deposits in Panama?"

"Cruise ships, Ed. They stop here, and while they bring tourists to the island, I use them like mail ships to make deposits in Panama. I've got contacts with the cruise lines who are only too willing to help out for some street money."

"Very smart, Leigh, Damn smart. So who will I be delivering the cash to?"

"I need to the pay the guy in Tampa who furnishes all the women. He runs an escort service and sees to it that we get nothing but the finest women. We need to take him a couple big ones."

"Two grand?"

"Two hundred grand."

Ned was momentarily stunned. "That's a lot of pussy."

"You get what you pay for in this world. Am I right?"

"I guess so. Jeez, two hundred grand. I'm in the wrong business. Anything else?"

"I've got a bag of green for Doc McGhee. And finally, I want you to carry a nice package of cash to Kalish's attorney. Steve needs to know we're still trying to help him. I've not been able to get a call through to him or get a report back. His lawyer told me yesterday they had moved him somewhere for a few days of interrogation and didn't bother telling him where they were going. That doesn't sound good."

"You're right, it sure doesn't. What are you doing to protect yourself from all this? It could come back on you and Vogel, couldn't it? I mean, if Kalish talked."

"I don't think he will talk. We always swore to each other that no matter what we heard through the grapevine, whatever the press might say, we'd never give each other up. He just wouldn't do it. I'm confident."

"Well, that's good to know. It'll help us all sleep better. So. You're going to Heather's wedding in Jamaica, huh? Bet that'll be some affair."

"I couldn't miss it. I promised her I'd be there, and I'm going to be there."

"One thing, Leigh. While I'm in the States this time, I think I'll take a week or so and go visit my family in Detroit. My mother isn't doing well and I'll feel guilty as hell if anything happened to her and I hadn't seen her for a long time."

"You go. My folks have always been an inspiration to me. You should go see her. Take two weeks if you want. But try to hold it to two, as you will be missed here. I've put a lot of faith in you, and I just like having you around, keeping an eye on things for me. Grab a couple grand out of the cash box in the club. Enjoy the break. Buy your mother something nice."

"Don't worry, I'll be back before two weeks are over. Well, I guess I'll turn in. Shine literally wore my ass out today."

*****

May 1986 – Federal Building, Detroit FBI Headquarters

Planning for the arrest of Vogel and Ritch entered final stages. All agencies involved in the investigation met, and Ned Timmons presented an account of his surveillance. His undercover work in Detroit, the Caymans, and Florida produced enough documented information to convict everyone involved from the top down.

"I know Ritch is going to attend the wedding of Heather Locklear and Tommy Lee in Jamaica," Timmons said. "His friendship with them is important to him, and he's already posted bond with the Grand Cayman courts so he can leave the island to attend the wedding in Jamaica."

"Ned, we aren't getting any cooperation from the authorities in Grand Cayman, and now they're implying we might have set Ritch up for the small possession charge. We're not going to be able to arrest him there."

That wasn't news to Ned. "Even the police love Leigh. He's a very likeable, smart guy. Hell, I like him, too, even though I know his business. They don't want to deal with that reality on the island. We need to let him make the flight to Jamaica and pick him up at the airport there when he arrives. What do the authorities there say? Are they willing to assist?"

A guy near the back whose name Ned didn't know, piped up. "They seem to be willing to do just about anything we want. He's not Jamaican. A little goodwill gesture that costs them virtually nothing is a good opportunity for them. They get Brownie points with DEA and we get a rich, white guy from the Caymans. Why wouldn't they?"

Doug McCullough offered an overview of the arrest plan.

"We'll have two groups of agents waiting for a proceed signal. Leigh Ritch won't be allowed to disembark in Jamaica. He'll be forced to board a commercial plane for New York.

"We'll have agents on the plane to make sure he doesn't drop off into a wheel well or something and another group will be waiting at JFK for the plane to land. We'll make the arrest there. That way, there can be no jurisdiction problems involved. Jamaica considers him an undesirable alien and will put him on the plane without U.S. intervention. Our involvement won't occur till he's on the ground in New York.

"Soon as the plane touches down, which will be late at night, we'll have a team waiting to arrest Ritch, and another SWAT team in place in Detroit outside Vogel's home. Hopefully, these arrests will be quick and without violence."

Ned interjected with his personal observations. "I'm comfortable that Ritch won't offer any resistance, but Vogel's home is a bunker, loaded with weapons. He tends to be aggressive, so hope for the best, but be prepared for the worst."

*****

May 23, 1986 – Airport, Kingston, Jamaica

In festive spirits, bound for the Hollywood couple's wedding, Leigh Ritch deplaned in Jamaica and walked across the tarmac to the arrival gate where local police stopped him.

"What's the problem, Officer?"

"Sorry, Mr. Ritch. Unfortunately, our government has decided that you may not gain entry into our country."

"Why not? I've been here many times. I'm not a criminal. I'm not wanted anywhere for a crime. I'm just visiting to attend a wedding and I'll be gone in two days. What's the problem with letting me just attend a wedding?"

"Again, I am sorry, Sir. These are not matters that I have any control of whatsoever. I have instructions from my superiors that you must leave the country immediately."

"How do you propose I do that? I arrived on a commercial airline and it's not going back to Grand Cayman. What should I do, just pick any plane and hitch a ride wherever in hell it's going?"

"There's no reason to be angry with me, Sir. I have no control over any of this. I just have my instructions to not allow you access to Jamaica. You must board the plane loading right now for New York."

Ritch was immediately alarmed. "I'm not going to the States. I'll go on whatever plane or airline here that's going anywhere else."

The officer attempted to cajole him. "You will like New York, Mr. Ritch. I've been there. It's very big, an interesting city."

"I'm not going." Ritch stated firmly

"Yes, Sir. You must. You can either accompany us voluntarily, or we will arrest you and place you on the plane. It's your call, Sir." All attempts at a friendly settlement were gone from the officer's voice.

Ritch was working overtime not to show any of the panic he was feeling. His righteous indignation routine was hard to keep in place. He had a very bad feeling about this. "No, it's obviously not my call. As a matter of fact, I'm very suspicious about whose call it is. You won't let me board any other plane except the one bound for New York City?"

"That's correct, Sir."

"Okay, if I must, I must. I promise you that Jamaica will regret this. My company invests a lot of money here. That will come to an end, I assure you."

Escorted to the New York plane, Ritch boarded and took a seat by himself, unaware FBI agents were already on board.

He knew of no pending charges against him in the States, but with the Reo brothers and Kalish in prison, he began to wonder if maybe the worst had occurred: Had he been implicated by the testimony of one of them? It was a long, worrisome flight.

As he deplaned at JFK, Ritch tried to mix with other disembarking passengers and make his way unnoticed through the terminal, but the moment he was inside, he knew that was impossible. Two uniformed New York City cops funneled all passengers single file through a narrow passage, checking each passenger. They were flanked by three FBI agents in suits that seemed to stick out like cactus in a snow bank. He knew where this was headed.

"Mr. Ritch, I'm Agent Owens with the Federal Bureau of Investigation. You're being arrested for suspicion of trafficking in narcotics and conspiracy to accomplish the same. I'll read you your rights and then you will be taken downtown for booking."

"Well, this all comes as quite a surprise. The Jamaican touch was very nice. A real inventive piece of police work."

"I'm sure you, of all people, would appreciate the planning involved in an operation of this sort."

"Let me state, for the record, I don't have a clue what these charges are about. I'm in the real estate business in the Caymans. I've never sold nor even used narcotics of any sort. You have been misinformed."

"Save it for the judge, as they say. I don't write warrants, Mr. Ritch, I arrest people. I'd be willing to bet the charges are based on more than just a hunch. Shall we go?"

*****

Simultaneously, in Detroit

Ned Timmons and FBI agents lay face down in two-foot high meadow of grass outside Michael Vogel's home. In darkness, the men tried to maintain complete silence to not tip off their prey. Ned whispered to the agent beside him in the grass.

"Did you read that article in the paper this week about boxer Tommy Hearns getting scratched by one of his pet cougars he lets run loose in this area?"

"You're shitting me."

"Nope. In the paper and on TV. Full grown cougars. I heard they found two cows all chewed up yesterday."

"You're kidding, right?"

"Swear to God. Found 'em less than a mile from here."

"You mean, there could be hungry lions watching us right now?"

"Yup. Shhhh. We're getting too loud."

After thirty more minutes of silence and swatting black flies who found eight men a tasty treat, everyone heard it at once: A shrill primal scream, unmistakably a cat; a very large cat.

"My god, Ned. Did you hear that?"

"I'm sure we all did. You do have a gun?"

"Yeah, and I'm cocking it right now."

For the next hour, eight agents lay motionless in the grass, waiting for the go-ahead. Every time the wind rustled the grass, they saw 400-pound cats creeping up on them, ready to tear out their throats. Minutes seemed like days.

Three cat screams later, word finally came. The team moved in on Vogel's house and kicked open the front door. A stunned Vogel put up no resistance. The arrests of the three were complete. The fallout would be more than anyone could know at the moment.

*****

United States Attorney's Office – New Bern, North Carolina

A phone call from Washington D.C. ended the jurisdiction fight between U.S. Attorneys in favor of the Eastern District of North Carolina.

"We just got the go ahead," Doug McCullough told Terry Peters. "We'll be handling the prosecution of Ritch, Vogel and Kalish right here.

"The folks in charge agree that the importation here trumps all the conspiracy charges. With Ned's testimony and everyone willing to flip for a deal of some kind, there's no telling how many indictments we'll wind up with. This case will be going on for quite a while."

"What are we up to right now for a head count?"

"Best I can tell, we're already pushing 100 and there are still a lot of names we haven't researched yet.

I'll bet somewhere over a 125, maybe 130 indictments before we're done."

"Damn, this will be full-time for a while."

"That's right, but remember, Terry, you're talking history here. This'll more than likely be the largest drug bust ever in the country. If Kalish's testimony holds up, and I have every reason to believe it will, there's no telling where this might lead."

"I understand he's been asked to testify before the Senate about Noriega's involvement."

"He'd be wise to let 'em hear it all. They can wave their magic wand, and years will disappear from his prison time."

"And with that great looking wife he's got, I know he's wanting to get out as quickly as possible. She seems to be willing to work with him till he's out. It's surprising, with her father being ex-Secret Service, that she'd put up with all this."

"Always the preacher's kids that get in the most trouble."

"Guess you're right. You know, though, Kalish is such a well-spoken, personable guy. It's hard to believe he's one of the biggest dope dealers ever caught. You just can't tell, can you? Could be anybody's next-door neighbor."

"Yeah, I enjoyed talking to him a lot more than any of the staff at the U.S. Attorney's office in Tampa. Talk about hostile." Both men laughed.

"They'll be smarting over this a long time. How about you and me going down to the diner for a burger? There are a lot of details to go over and to tell you the truth, a big, ole juicy cheeseburger would hit the spot for me."

"You and me both."

EPILOGUE

The arrests and prosecutions of Stephen Kalish, Leigh Ritch, and Michael Vogel broke up one of the largest drug smuggling rings ever discovered in the United States. The analysis and follow-up of the defendants' testimonies resulted in the successful prosecution of more than 130 persons. Others involved were not arrested due to lack of evidence.

All three principals gave depositions that were determined to be complete and truthful. Their testimonies resulted in plea agreements and far shorter sentences than they might have otherwise received. The U.S. Government wanted their testimony to support the invasion of Panama and the arrest of Manuel Noriega. Stephen Kalish gave forthright and compelling testimony before the Senate Committee investigating drug running and money laundering in Panama.

On Feb. 5, 1988, Manuel Noriega was indicted in Miami and Tampa on charges of drug trafficking. On Dec. 20, 1989, "Operation Just Cause", also known as the Invasion of Panama, began. U.S. forces took control of Panama in one week. General Noriega took refuge in a church and was serenaded by loudspeakers blaring Van Halen's heavy metal music 24 hours a day until the Vatican complained to President George W. H. Bush about this cruel and unusual form of torture.

Noriega was eventually turned over to the U.S. as a prisoner of war, convicted of the drug and racketeering charges, and sentenced to forty years in a federal prison in Florida.

Noriega served his sentence at the Federal Correction Institution in Miami, in an apartment-style cell nicknamed "the presidential suite" which includes two rooms, a television, a telephone, and exercise bike.

Epilogue

A model prisoner, who claims to have found God, Noriega was extradited to Paris where he had been convicted in absentia for money laundering. He eventually returned to Panama where he is now under house arrest because his lawyers contend that under Geneva Conventions of War, Noriega, a U.S. prisoner of war, must be returned to Panama upon his release from prison.

Noriega faces a twenty-year prison sentence there, where he was convicted in absentia for the 1985 murder and beheading of a political opponent.

Based on their confessions and willingness to testify about the dealings of their organizations, Ritch, Vogel, and Kalish received favorable sentencing. None of the three served more than seven years, despite the possibility of life behind bars.

Stephen Kalish spent almost seven years in jail. He was a model prisoner who soon gained trustee status. Ned Timmons recalls visiting him in Florida, and seeing him in the warden's office enjoying a gourmet meal from a local restaurant.

Upon release, Kalish declined the government offer for Federal Witness Protection Program. The general belief regarding his decision was that he must have deposited considerable money under his name and a change of identity would have eliminated the possibility of ever retrieving it. He had already signed over all visible funds and income to the government for restitution.

Upon release, Kalish returned to Panama before settling in Southern California where he became a successful businessman.

Stephen Kalish is not listed on the U.S. Bureau of Prisons website as a federal prisoner, perhaps because he was allowed to serve some of his sentence at a county jail in Florida. He was released about the same time as Leigh Ritch and Michael Vogel, both of whom were released in the mid-1990s. Kalish wasn't required to forfeit his condominium in Panama City along with its contents, although he did forfeit millions of dollars to the U.S. Government.

Michael Vogel had all his wealth confiscated, and served a seven-year prison sentence. An alcoholic, he lives in the Detroit area where, sources indicate, he is a vendor of sex toys. There are no known pictures of Vogel.

Leigh Ritch served his time and returned to the Cayman Islands where he is involved in real estate development. The large pallet of money Ned Timmons saw was never found nor forfeited to authorities.

Doc McGhee never served any time. He paid a fine and was ordered to organize anti-drug tours by several of his bands, mainly Bon Jovi, touting the evils of drugs to youth in the U.S. and overseas. It is said that the band and the plane were under the continual influence of drugs during the entire tour.

Heather Locklear and Tommy Lee were never implicated in any way with the organization.

Terry Peters, now retired from the FBI, lives near Wilmington, North Carolina, where he operates a private investigations firm.

Ned Timmons retired from police work and is president of LSS Consulting, an investigations firm with offices in Detroit and Grand Cayman.

Doug McCullough is a judge on the North Carolina Court of Appeals, and lives in Atlantic Beach.

APPENDIX 1

June 13, 2001

Government Entities Informant Practices
Congressman Dan Burton
2185 Rayburn HOB
Washington, D.C. 20515

Dear Mr. Chairman,
Our office conducts investigative research concerning governmental and individual misconduct in Medical Malpractice and RICO cases. We would like to bring to your attention our findings in specific cases as well as our ongoing investigation concerning Government Entities Informant Practices.

We recognize where there is ignorance on a subject. The subject area in question would most likely remain unfettered and continue as "untouchable" as the Federal Witness Security Program has remained. However, while recognizing humans are not unerring, we must also enlighten our ignorance in problem areas, by researching and correcting them. Specifically, when it is in the name of justice, and individual lives have been remarkably altered in a negative fashion. Errors in the program have resulted in decades of incarceration, irreversible mental health damage, loss of finances and assets, loss of family members while incarcerated, very basic medical needs denied, and in some extreme cases, loss of life, all due to the unrelenting use of informants for what we label as "suspect" purposes.

Is there a financial benefit to the arresting and prosecuting agencies, or individuals involved in these cases, that outweighs the law and one's life regardless of the cost? In our ongoing independent research, we have recognized a distinguished pattern that seems to

Appendix 1

favor those informants that have the greatest income and assets to lose through forfeiture procedures. However, on the contrary, it would be the gain of income and assets to those involved in the criminal procedures. Moreover, when the income and assets are in copious amounts such as that in the case of Stephen Kalish, an informant that was given a deal that would allow him to serve a drastically reduced eight year prison term and retain $20 Million from his past criminal drug enterprise, the government gains a great deal. The government lost nothing in this case and gained $3 Million, a Yacht, a Ferrari, and additional assets, this goes without mentioning the numerous others additional forfeited criminal income and assets that was rendered to the government because of Kalish's testimony as an informant. This alone displays how lucrative just one case can be for the government and certainly suggests a titanic driving force regardless of whom it hurts.

Appendix 1

Appendix 1

Bobby M.

Bobby M. With Drugs

Appendix 1

Adams Creek

Bundle of Cash

Appendix 1

Doug McCullough, Federal Prosecutor; Ned Timmons, FBI Special Agent; Terry Peters, Special Investigator

Stephen Kalish

Appendix 1

Doc Mcghee

Leigh Ritch

Appendix 1

Cape Lookout

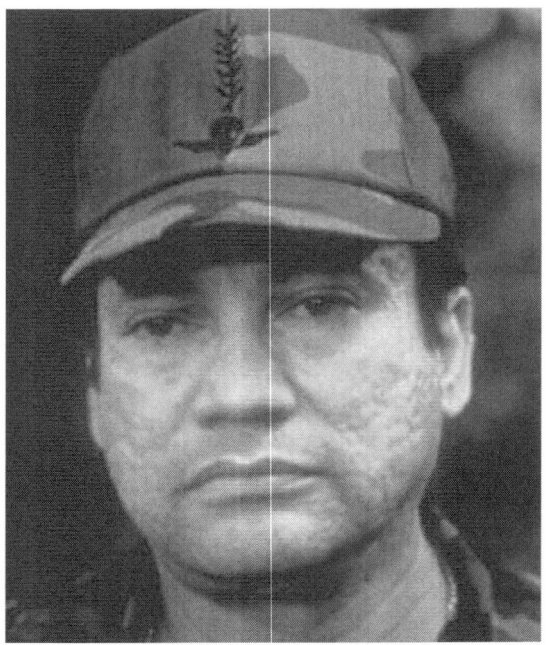

General Noriega

Appendix 1

Arrest of Manuel Noriega, 1990

Returning to the Scene

APPENDIX 2

S. Hrg. 100-654

DRUGS AND MONEY LAUNDERING IN PANAMA

HEARING
BEFORE THE
PERMANENT SUBCOMMITTEE ON INVESTIGATIONS
OF THE
COMMITTEE ON GOVERNMENTAL AFFAIRS UNITED STATES SENATE

ONE HUNDREDTH CONGRESS

SECOND SESSION

JANUARY 28, 1988

Printed for the use of the Committee on Governmental Affairs

U.S. GOVERNMENT PRINTING OFFICE
85-064　　WASHINGTON : 1988

For sale by the Superintendent of Documents, Congressional Sales Office
U.S. Government Printing Office, Washington, DC 20402

Appendix 2

OPENING STATEMENT OF SENATOR ROTH
Senator ROTH:
January 28, 1988

Thank you, Mr. Chairman. Thank you for your cooperation in this effort. The world's attention has recently, of course, been focused on Panama. The reports from Panama include allegations of corruption, bribery, and even murder. As a result, there has been continued unrest in Panama. Disgruntled Panamanian citizens took to the streets, the military-dominated government attempted to stifle dissent, and the U.S. Embassy was even attacked.

Panama is, of course, vitally important to the United States, in part because of the Panama Canal, in part because of the close ties between the Panamanian people and the people of the United States. But here today we focus on a problem of equal significance to the security interests of the United States, the role played by Panamanian officials in facilitating the narcotics pipeline. To put it bluntly, Panamanian officials, including the most powerful one in the country, General Manuel Antonio Noriega, are being charged with making lots of money by helping drug smugglers and money launderers ply their trade. Any such practices must stop.

Today we will hear, under oath, from an admitted drug smuggler, Stephen Kalish, who lived in Panama under the name Skip Brown and will state that he directly paid General Noriega for the privilege of using Panama not only as a safe repository for his money but as a base of operations for his smuggling activities. I must say, any such role played by General Noriega or any other Panamanian officials would be nothing short of outrageous. It has been no secret that for some years

Appendix 2

now, Panama has provided a safe and secret haven for the world's wealthiest narcotics traffickers. Easy creation of secret corporations and strict bank secrecy laws guarantee protection and anonymity to money launderers. Panama is close to the United States and uses the American dollar, which avoids the inconvenience of exchanging currency. Frankly, I wish we could convince Japan to do the same.

As the staff discovered in the course of an 18-month investigation, which included a staff trip to Panama, we have learned that because of these facts, the Panamanian banking system has been flooded with American dollars. Consider that between 1982 and 1987, Panamanian banks had a surplus of over $3.8 billion in American dollars to return to the United States Federal Reserve. Where is the money coming from? As we will hear from a representative of the Customs Service, in a recent U.S. Customs' operation known as *Buckstop*, over $16 million American dollars illegally bound for Panama was seized at three locations in only 6 months. If that is what we came up with in random seizures in just 6 months, you can imagine what slipped through.

There are, in fact, very few drug money laundering operations that do not involve Panama in some way. I expect that Panamanian officials will dismiss the testimony we will hear today as the fabrications of a narcotics trafficker out to save his own skin. If that is the case, if Mr. Kalish made all this up, then how did he come by several Panamanian passports, one of which bears diplomatic credentials? Why did Mr. Kalish's wife receive a handwritten note from General Noriega welcoming her to Panama? Mr. Kalish is, after all, an admitted drug smuggler. That was his business before he went to Panama and his business while he lived in Panama. How is it that Mr. Kalish received an

Appendix 2

irrevocable letter of credit from the National Bank of Panama for $1,995,000 to finance the purchase of a helicopter for the Panama Defense Forces? Clearly, we have evidence of drug-related corruption extending to the highest levels in Panama. We must confront this corruption and take measures to abolish it if we are serious about winning the war against drugs.

This Subcommittee, under both my past chairmanship and now under our distinguished chairman, Senator Nunn, has repeatedly attempted to highlight the indispensable role that money laundering plays in enabling the international drug trade to flourish. Back in 1982, we alerted the Congress to the role played by off-shore banking institutions to hide drug profits. While some progress has been made in the intervening years, it seems perfectly clear that a number of countries have not gotten the message. We are involved in a war on the international drug trade, and in this war there can be no neutral bystanders. Our national security interests are just as directly threatened by the dope dealing and money laundering authorized or tolerated by public officials in Panama as our interests would be threatened by the closing of the Panama Canal. The best hope to eliminate these illegal activities is to ensure that a stable, democratic government exists in Panama, one that observes the law, not violates it. Congress has authorized the imposition of sanctions on those countries that will not help us, but the Executive Branch has not yet chosen to impose the anti-drug sanctions against any country. Although, as Senator Nunn has properly stated, the Administration froze U.S. aid after the attack on the U.S. Embassy, and Congress imposed additional sanctions in the omnibus spending bill. Moreover, last year, our distinguished chairman and I proposed a bill, which is now law, to tighten standards for defining "full

Appendix 2

cooperation" by other countries in the fight against the international drug trade and to add sanctions against those countries which refuse to cooperate. We may need some more backbone in the Executive Branch to see that those sanctions are implemented. I want to strongly commend my good friend and colleague, the chairman, Senator Nunn, for holding these hearings. He has been a leader in Congress in the fight against drug trafficking. As I previously stated. Senator Nunn and I have worked together on legislation to strengthen sanctions against foreign countries facilitating the drug trade. His staff has been most helpful in this investigation. I particularly want to commend Eleanor Hill and her staff for their assistance. As the chairman has properly pointed out, it has been a real joint effort. I look forward to continuing to work with Senator Nunn on this vital issue.

*****

Senator NUNN: Mr. Kalish, do you want to introduce your lawyer?

Mr. KALISH: Yes.

Senator NUNN: This is my attorney, Samuel Buffone.

Senator NUNN: Senator Trible, would you like to make an opening statement?

Senator TRIBLE: Mr. Chairman, I have no opening statement. I look forward to hearing from the witnesses. Thank you.

Senator NUNN: Mr. Kalish, we swear-in all witnesses before this Subcommittee. So, if you will stand and hold up your right hand and take the oath. Do you swear that the testimony you give before this Subcommittee will be the truth, the whole truth, and nothing but the truth, so help you God?

Mr. KALISH: I do.

Appendix 2

Senator NUNN: Thank you. Let me get the name of the counsel again, please.

Mr. BUFFONE: Yes, Senator. My name is Samuel Buffone.

Senator NUNN: Could you give us your address?

Mr. BUFFONE: 1607 New Hampshire Avenue NW. My law firm is Asbill, Junkin, Myers and Buffone. That is in Washington, D.C., Senator.

Senator NUNN: Mr. Buffone, you are not going to be testifying, but will be advising your client. Is that correct?

Mr. BUFFONE: That is correct.

Senator NUNN: Mr. Buffone, if we pose any questions that you would like to discuss with your client, you will have the right to do so prior to his answer.

Mr. BUFFONE: Yes, Senator.

Senator NUNN: Do you have any procedural questions?

Mr. BUFFONE: No, I do not, Senator NUNN:

Senator NUNN: Thank you. I will ask Senator Roth to take the lead at this point. Senator Roth, you will be officially presiding, but I will be here most of the time to work with you.

Senator ROTH: Thank you, Mr. Chairman. Mr. Kalish, before you start your testimony, you are under oath and you understand the penalties for not speaking the truth before this Subcommittee. Is that correct?

Mr. KALISH: Yes, sir, I do.

Senator ROTH: Mr. Kalish, would you please proceed, then, with your statement?

Appendix 2

TESTIMONY OF STEPHEN MICHAEL KALISH, CONVICTED NARCOTICS SMUGGLER

Mr. KALISH: Thank you, Senator. My name is Stephen Michael Kalish. I am a convicted marijuana smuggler, and have been incarcerated for the past 43 months. While I have been involved in marijuana smuggling for most of my adult life, the level of my illegal conduct significantly increased in the summer of 1983. At that time, I was instrumental in the importation of 250,000 pounds of marijuana. In the past, the problems of buying the marijuana, arranging transport, off-loading and final distribution were successfully dealt with by my organization. However, the sheer volume of cash generated in 1983 soon overwhelmed our organization. As the marijuana payments came in from our distributors, we stored the cash in Tampa, Florida. The currency filled entire rooms. Although we were sending out millions of dollars to our Colombian suppliers, at one point we had in excess of $35,000,000 in Tampa. We used money counting machines but had to stop any counting because we could not keep up with the volume.

This experience made me realize that dealing with the cash from larger importations was a serious problem. I began to devote my attention to establishing secure methods of removing this cash from the United States, and banking it abroad. In addition to the proceeds of our recent importation, I was far along in the planning of larger operations. I planned a 1,000,000-pound importation, and had already purchased the marijuana in Colombia. This load was to be carried by ocean-going tug and barge up the Mississippi River. A second 400,000-pound

Appendix 2

importation was planned using a containerized cargo vessel we had purchased. I anticipated that these operations would produce $300 million. Accordingly, I began to seek out banking havens in earnest. We had worked in the Cayman Islands in the past, but found it unacceptable for sums of this magnitude. I was aware of changing relations between the United States and the Cayman Islands, and feared a loss of bank secrecy. The Cayman banks were simply not capable of dealing with this volume of money. After looking into European and Caribbean havens, my attention was drawn to Panama. Its reputation as a large-scale banking center was well known. I arranged through two intermediaries to visit the country for a trial run. I was told to bring at least $2 million as a show of my seriousness. I placed $2.3 to $2.5 million in a suitcase and traveled to Panama on a private jet. On September 22, 1983, my chartered Lear jet was met by a limousine at the Omar Torrijos Airport in Panama City. My luggage was not searched at Customs. I was driven to the offices of Cesar Rodriguez. He had impressive offices on two floors in the Bank of Boston building in downtown Panama. Rodriguez had surprising resources. I met with lawyers, bankers and government officials on my first visit to Cesar's office. I purchased shell corporations from him and immediately set up accounts and deposited most of the money I had brought with me. When I explained that I had millions of dollars to bank and invest in Panama, he offered me an entire package of corporate, banking and investment services and even armored car delivery of my moneys from Omar Torrijos Airport. Rodriguez took me to dinner with his partner, Enrique Pretel, who was also described as having close ties to the Panamanian government. Over dinner, I expressed interest in bringing into Panama $100 million. I did not want to disclose at this point my plan to bring in three

Appendix 2

times that amount. I also mentioned my concerns over safety and security. During my initial meetings at Rodriguez's office, a Panamanian official was present. He informed Rodriguez that the Drug Enforcement Administration had notified G-2, the intelligence arm of the Panamanian military, that my plane was under surveillance upon departure from the United States. I was advised to send the plane back to the United States, which I did.

Rodriguez and Pretel were extremely interested in doing business. To impress upon me the level of their influence in Panama, they informed me that General Noriega, Panama's military ruler, was their partner. They quickly proved that this was not idle talk. The next day, I was taken to General Noriega's private home. I had been instructed to bring a gift for the General large enough to show how serious I was about doing business in Panama. I placed $300,000 cash in my briefcase. During a casual discussion with the General that lasted approximately 30 minutes, I discussed my desire to live in Panama and to invest my moneys there. I made it clear at that time that it was my intention to bring extremely large sums of cash to Panama. As the meeting broke up, I left the briefcase in his office and began to exit the room. General Noriega called me back and told me that I had left my briefcase. I told him that it was for him, and he smiled.

That night, I was invited to a party with the General at the Panama Canal offices. He was extremely friendly, and he told me to continue to deal with Rodriguez and Pretel and that he would do whatever he could to assist me. He also thanked me for the briefcase.

Throughout the next 10 months, I used Panama as the base of my operations, first leasing a condominium and then buying a home in the San Francisco area of

Appendix 2

Panama City, in close proximity to General Noriega's home. My relationship with General Noriega became closer until he became a full-scale co-conspirator in my drug operations. I transported nearly all of my money to Panama. My jet was given special treatment at Omar Torrijos Airport on all of my trips to Panama. I taxied to the Air Force base at a corner of the airport so that my arrivals and departures would not be observed. I became a full partner in Rodriguez, Pretel and Noriega's business, Servicios Touristicos. Two hundred thousand dollars of my $400,000 payment for 25 percent of the business was for Noriega, who was indeed our partner in all of our deals. My partners had several lucrative contracts with the government of Panama, and the Forces of Defense. Pretel and Rodriguez owned aircraft which flew military personnel in Panama.

As a favor to the General, I financed and arranged the purchase of an executive helicopter and a 727/100 jet aircraft. In late 1983, Noriega discussed with me his desire to purchase a Boeing 727 jet aircraft. I negotiated the price for $2.2 million. I made the initial deposit of $500,000 and assisted in financing the balance. Noriega later agreed to use the plane for our money laundering operations. We planned to fly planeloads of money out of Washington, D.C. under diplomatic cover. I also purchased an executive helicopter for Noriega. I provided long-term financing secured by a government guarantee.

My partner in the United States and I had purchased a Lear jet 35 which I made available to Noriega. In fact, he told me he borrowed the jet to fly to Washington to meet with President Reagan in November of 1983. Our relationship was not one-sided. Noriega provided me with military protection and favorable treatment while I was living in Panama. I was issued three Panamanian passports, one being a Panamanian diplomatic passport.

During my time in Panama, I was brought ever more into Noriega's confidence. He discussed with me his concerns over the upcoming elections of Nicholas Barletta, who was running for President. It was his plan to use his share of our money laundering and drug smuggling proceeds to assist in the financing of this election. In the spring of 1984, events brought me closer to General Noriega. Prior to that time, I decided to attempt an importation into a United States commercial port. Since any direct shipment of marijuana from Colombia would be scrutinized, I arranged for transshipment through Panama, and obtained customs seals by large payoffs to Panamanian officials. For a fixed fee, Noriega personally approved of this operation. A series of events led General Noriega to ask me to postpone this operation. A large amount of ether, a necessary commodity in the production of cocaine, was seized in Colon, Panama. An operating cocaine lab was discovered in the remote Panamanian jungle. One thousand kilograms of cocaine was seized in Miami from a Panamanian cargo plane. General Noriega asked me to contact my sources in Colombia and find out what was going on. I learned from my sources in the Medellin Cartel that a $5 million bribe had been paid to Panamanian officials to protect their operations in Panama. A high-ranking Panamanian official, Colonel Melo, had been bribed. Melo was behind the cocaine lab and ether shipments; he was intending to assassinate Noriega while he was in Europe and seize control of Panama. I passed word of this to Noriega, and Melo, his associates, and the Colombians were arrested immediately. These arrests angered the Colombians, and I was caught in the middle. I arranged for the release of these Colombians

Appendix 2

and established my ability to facilitate their business in Panama. The Cartel was looking for a way to continue to launder $50 to $100 million a month produced from its west coast U.S. cocaine operations. My links to Panama made laundering of this volume of money possible. The General embraced the scheme for his percentage, and I began to negotiate with the Medellin Cartel to ship and launder vast amounts of cocaine profits. After these events, Noriega dealt directly with me and asked that I cut out Pretel and Rodriguez. Noriega was always extremely concerned about the discovery of Panamanian involvement in drug trafficking.

On February 16, 1984, my future wife and I visited Noriega at his ranch in the interior of Panama. He ordered flowers for my wife and left her a note that I believe you have seen. His real purpose for inviting me was not social. He had previously agreed to a $4 million fee, $1 million up front for facilitating and assisting in the transshipment of marijuana through Panama that I had planned. He, however, wanted additional assurances that the U.S. end was covered and that Panama's role was insulated. I also guaranteed that all of the proceeds would come back to Panama.

My involvement in Panama ended abruptly with my arrest in Tampa on July 26, 1984. I have been incarcerated ever since. Senators, if you have any questions, I would be happy to answer them.

Senator ROTH: First, Mr. Chairman, I do submit for the record, the Minority Staff Statement summarizing our investigation, and a number of documents for the record, some of which are under seal.

Senator NUNN: Without objection, they will be admitted to the record.

Senator ROTH: Mr. Kalish, let me ask you the most obvious question first. What direct payments did you

Appendix 2

make to General Noriega for the smuggling of drugs or the laundering of drug money?

Mr. KALISH: Senator Roth, there were several occasions where I paid Noriega money. For drug shipments, I personally paid General Noriega $250,000 as partial payment on the $1 million fee for the transshipment of the containers through Panama. I also paid General Noriega $300,000 upon my first meeting with him in his home in Panama City. There were several occasions when General Noriega received kickbacks from different transactions that I was involved in with the government. One in particular was the purchase of the executive helicopter I bought for General Noriega. The helicopter was valued at $1.65 million. However, I was issued a letter of credit for $1,995,000. There was $350,000 that was paid in kickbacks. Noriega received 1/3 of that. There were several other payments to General Noriega involving loans that I made to the government, and other contracts that I had with the government. There was a $500,000 payment that I made at the request of General Noriega for the purchase of the 727/100 aircraft. There was also $200,000 cash that he received upon the purchase of 25 percent of the company Servicios Touristicos.

Senator ROTH: So these are a series of payments that you personally know went to Noriega?

Mr. KALISH: Yes, sir. These are payments that I was personally present at while they were paid. Senator, I spent millions of dollars in Panama trying to bring myself closer to General Noriega. Some were direct payments from my drug shipments, but others were to better my relations with the man: in the purchase of the executive helicopter; in the purchase of the 727/100 aircraft. I made available to General Noriega, and in terms of dollars it could be considered several hundred thousand dollars, the use of my Lear jet, which he used

Appendix 2

quite extensively on flights to Washington, D.C.; to New York City; to Las Vegas; on numerous flights. I also made several flights at his request for several other officials that traveled to and from Panama. I also presented Noriega with several gifts. During Christmas I gave the general and his wife jewelry valued at $25,000 to $30,000. At Noriega's birthday party, I provided him with collector items: a rifle and two pistols which were valued at $20,000 to $25,000.

Senator ROTH: Now, let me go back to these direct payments. Did you keep a record of those payments?

Mr. KALISH: Yes, sir, I did.

Senator ROTH: Is this your record of these payments, or a Photostat of those records?

Mr. KALISH: Yes, sir. What I would like to explain is I was in the business of not creating a paper trail. However, these documents were found in my property just recently. Those indicate payments to General Noriega. There's a $300,000 notation, which is the gift that I gave to "Tony"; gave to General Noriega at his home.

Senator ROTH: What does the word "Tony" mean?

Mr. KALISH: The General's name is General Manuel Antonio Noriega. His close friends refer to him as "Tony", and I also referred to him as Tony.

Senator ROTH: So wherever "Tony" appears here, that indicates your accounting records show that you made a payment to him?

Mr. KALISH: Yes, sir, it does.

Senator ROTH: Now, let me ask you: How do we know you did not make this record up after you were seized?

Mr. KALISH: Senator, I was arrested in July of 1984. I have been incarcerated ever since. Pursuant to a plea bargain agreement with the United States Government, I forfeited several pieces of my property. I

Appendix 2

owned a home in Panama City and shipped to the United States Customs in the United States all of my property out of my Panamanian home. These documents were discovered in a file cabinet. I have not had access to these documents since my arrest.

Senator ROTH: Let us again look over at this document. As I understand it, that $1,995,000 was a loan to purchase the helicopter; is that correct? [See Exhibit I on p. 49.]

Mr. KALISH: Yes, sir. An executive jet helicopter.

Senator ROTH: Now, would you explain how that transaction worked?

Mr. KALISH: Sir, I was asked by General Noriega to assist in the purchase of a helicopter. The Forces of Defense related to me that their budget would not allow for the purchase of a helicopter, especially for $2 million. I agreed to do so. I paid $1,995,000 in Noriega's behalf to Enrique Pretel, Cesar Rodriguez, and the helicopter company in Dallas, Texas. I was promised repayment of these moneys, and to guarantee that promise, Noriega instructed the National Bank of Panama to issue an irrevocable letter of credit to my company being Servicios Exclusivos de Panama.

Senator ROTH: Now, can you see this blown-up document here?

Mr. KALISH: Yes, sir.

Senator ROTH: What does that represent?

Mr. KALISH: That is a copy of the irrevocable letter of credit from the National Bank of Panama.

Senator ROTH: What is the National Bank of Panama?

Mr. KALISH: It is the central bank in the country of Panama.

Senator ROTH: For the government?

Mr. KALISH: Yes, sir, for the government.

Appendix 2

Senator ROTH: And this is an irrevocable letter of credit doing what?

Mr. KALISH: This guarantees that if the Forces of Defense ever default in their monthly payments to me, I can present this letter of credit to the National Bank of Panama, and it will be paid in full for $1,995,000.

Senator ROTH: In other words, you made $1,995,000 available for a helicopter that I think you said cost $1,695,000.

Mr. KALISH: Yes, sir. That is correct.

Senator ROTH: In return, as a guarantee, the Defense Forces, through the bank, issued this letter of credit which guaranteed you payment is that correct?

Mr. KALISH: Yes, sir, that is.

Senator ROTH: Are they still paying you for this helicopter?

Mr. KALISH: Yes, sir, they are.

Senator ROTH: When was the last payment received?

Mr. KALISH: The Forces of Defense have continued to pay me for the past 4 years on this contract that I have with them for the helicopter. I received a check from the Forces of Defense just recently, several days ago.

Senator ROTH: The last payment was made several days ago. So the indebtedness is continuing to be acknowledged?

Mr. KALISH: Yes, sir. And these payments, I might add, are transferred to the U.S. Customs Service and have been. It is part of my plea bargain agreement with the United States Government that I forfeit these checks.

Senator ROTH: Now, these payments being made by the Panama Defense Forces include the total amount, the full $1.9 million, is that correct?

Mr. KALISH: Yes, sir, that is correct.

Appendix 2

Senator ROTH: And that includes $300,000 kickback, of which you received $100,000 and General Noriega received $100,000, is that correct?

Mr. KALISH: Yes, sir, that is correct.

Senator ROTH: So, in effect, the Defense Forces were making a kickback, according to your testimony, to Noriega.

Mr. KALISH: Yes, sir, that is correct. And in every business agreement I had with General Noriega in Panama, this was the standard operating procedure.

Senator ROTH: In other words, you are saying that no transaction, no landing, no activity involving your drug activities in Panama could be conducted without making some kind of a payment to the General?

Mr. KALISH: Yes, sir. That is essentially correct. Not all moneys were paid to the General. I paid moneys to several other officials in the Panamanian Defense Forces. I paid money to several different majors that were in the Defense Forces. However, General Noriega was certainly aware of these payments. For example, my landing in Omar Torrijos Airport. There was always money exchanged with one of the military officials at the airport just as consideration on my part. Certainly not expected, and certainly not necessary.

Senator ROTH: How much were these payments?

Mr. KALISH: Several hundred dollars upon each landing.

Senator ROTH: Why don't you explain that operation?

Mr. KALISH: Yes, sir. At Omar Torrijos Airport, the Panamanian Air Force has a base of operations at the far corner of it. To avoid being observed by whatever U.S. officials were in Panama at the time, we would taxi directly to the Air Force base, which would allow us to disembark from the aircraft without being observed by anyone. We could take whatever luggage

Appendix 2

and whatever equipment we were bringing to Panama, and place it directly into our vehicles, and exit from the military side of the airport.

Senator ROTH: Your activity involved, as you have already indicated, not only the General, but a number of others in the Panama Defense Forces. Can you go into a little detail how widespread this activity was in the military and among other officials of the Panamanian government, to your personal knowledge?

Mr. KALISH: Yes, sir. I had met several high-ranking military officials. I knew Colonel Purcel, who was head of the Air Force in Panama. I had met Colonel Justinez, who is in charge of G-4, the accounting department in the military. I was associated with a Major Perez, who was stationed in Panama City. I was associated with a Major Fundora, who was also stationed in Panama City.

There are several others that I cannot recall at the moment. I always felt that it was in my best interest to become friends with as many of these officials as I could. Cesar Rodriguez was very close to all of these individuals, and most of these military personnel I met in the presence of Cesar Rodriguez. I just felt it was prudent for me to maintain good relations with these people.

Senator ROTH: Now, let me make sure I understand what you are saying. I ask you to be very careful. You mentioned a number of individual names, at least two colonels and a major. Are you saying from your personal knowledge, that you know that they had knowledge or were involved in drug activities?

Mr. KALISH: I did not have personal communications with Colonel Purcel or Colonel Justinez in regards to my drug activities in Panama.

Senator ROTH: Did they have knowledge, say, of General Noriega's activities?

Appendix 2

Mr. KALISH: It would be impossible for them not to have knowledge of my activities. They observed my comings and goings between the country of Colombia and Panama. They observed me carrying heavy suitcases from my aircraft on several occasions.

Senator ROTH: Let me go back to the note you referred to in your testimony. Who is Denise, and what was the occasion for her receiving the note that you mentioned in your testimony? Here is the note here.

Mr. KALISH: Yes, sir. Denise is my wife. She was my girlfriend at the time. I had been invited to the interior of Panama, to General Noriega's ranch. I flew my wife in from Los Angeles, California, and she came to the ranch. Unbeknownst to me, General Noriega had prepared a bouquet of flowers and written this note for my wife.

Senator ROTH: Now, how do we know that this note was not written by somebody else?

Mr. KALISH: Well, at the time, there were four people at the ranch: myself, my future wife, General Noriega, and his girlfriend.

Senator ROTH: The question I am asking is: How do we know that you did not make up the note, write the note yourself?

Mr. KALISH: The note was discovered in a search of a vehicle in Tampa, Florida. After my arrest in July of 1984, the FBI searched my belongings and discovered this note in one of my wallets.

Senator ROTH: Would you read into the record what the note says?

Mr. KALISH: Yes, sir. "Miss Denise, welcome to Panama. Your friend, General Noriega, 18 February 1984, Panama."

Mr. BUFFONE: Senator Roth, I think Mr. Kalish has something to add to that last response.

Appendix 2

Mr. KALISH: Yes. There were five individuals at the ranch that I referred to earlier.
Senator ROTH: Instead of the four?
Mr. KALISH: Yes, cooking while we were there.
Senator ROTH: At this time, I would like to yield to the distinguished chairman, Senator Nunn
Senator NUNN: Thank you very much, Senator Roth. Recapping for a moment, Mr. Kalish, is it your testimony you personally told General Noriega that you were engaged in drug trafficking?
Mr. KALISH: Yes, sir, it is.
Senator NUNN: Is it your testimony that you told him you were engaged in illegal drug trafficking?
Mr. KALISH; Yes, sir, it is.
Senator NUNN: No doubt that he knew that.
Mr. KALISH: No question in my mind.
Senator NUNN: Did you tell General Noriega that the monies you planned to invest in Panama were the profits of your illegal drug activities?
Mr. KALISH: Yes, sir. Specifically, I told him they were profits from my marijuana smuggling activities.
Senator NUNN: Was anyone else present besides you and General Noriega when you had these conversations?
Mr. KALISH: Yes, Senator. Enrique Pretel was present on a number of occasions, as well as Cesar Rodriguez.
Senator NUNN: Now, what has happened to those two individuals?
Mr. KALISH: Cesar Rodriguez was murdered in Medellin, Colombia. Enrique Pretel is currently living in Panama City.
Senator NUNN: So, one of those people is still alive, and in Panama City.
Mr. KALISH: Yes, sir, that is correct.

Appendix 2

Senator NUNN: Is it your testimony you personally delivered payments of money to General Noriega in exchange for his assistance with your illegal drug activities in Panama?

Mr. KALISH: Yes, sir, that is correct.

Senator NUNN: In fact, you did that on several occasions.

Mr. KALISH: Yes, sir. Several.

Senator NUNN: In addition, your testimony, according to the chart on the stand to your right, is that it was over $4 million in either money or gifts in kind that you delivered to General Noriega?

Mr. KALISH: Mr. Senator, I am not sure what the exact total is. But, yes, it was millions of dollars.

Senator NUNN: It was millions of dollars. Now, when you went to Panama the first time, did you have contact with Mr. Rodriguez?

Mr. KALISH: That is correct.

Senator NUNN: And, shortly thereafter, did you have contact with General Noriega?

Mr. KALISH: Yes, sir. The very next day.

Senator NUNN: The very next day. Is it unusual in the drug business to go to a country and go right up the ladder, and meet with the top leader?

Mr. KALISH: Yes, sir. I was quite surprised at this. When I was told that I would be meeting General Noriega, I had no idea who General Noriega was. It had to be explained to me that he was actually the military ruler of Panama.

Senator NUNN: Was he also the President of Panama at that time?

Mr. KALISH: I am not certain. I do not believe so.

Senator NUNN: During the course of your drug activities, did you pay off individuals in the United States?

Appendix 2

Mr. KALISH: No, sir, I did not. I was associated with a Teamster official in Detroit, Michigan, who was to pay a U.S. Customs official in New York City.

Senator NUNN: Can you tell us about that? Who was that, what was the amount, and so forth?

Mr. BUFFONE: Senator Nunn, Mr. Kalish is involved in several ongoing grand jury investigations that may well lead to indictments. I have advised Mr. Kalish that, unless you instruct him to the contrary, it would be well to not name certain individuals that we believe are under investigation, but to identify them generically for you.

Senator NUNN: All right. Could you give us the generic information, then?

Mr. KALISH: Yes, sir. There was an individual in the Detroit, Michigan, area associated with the Teamsters' Union that provided us with the vehicles we used in the transporting of our marijuana. We had decided to attempt an importation into the United States, into a U.S. commercial port using containers on a cargo ship. The individual in Detroit, Michigan, reported to me that he had a source in the U.S. Customs Service that would permit the entering of these containers into the United States. I paid this gentleman in Detroit approximately $825,000 for payments to his Customs source, as well as payments for the vehicles I was going to need for this operation.

Senator NUNN: Did you ever have personal contact with the Customs source?

Mr. KALISH: No, sir, I did not.

Senator NUNN: Was the name of the Customs source ever revealed to you?

Mr. KALISH: It was not.

Senator NUNN: You do not know the name?

Mr. KALISH: No, sir, I do not.

Appendix 2

Senator NUNN: Do you know if, in fact, that money was delivered to a Customs agent?

Mr. KALISH: No, sir, I do not.

Senator NUNN: So, all you know at this stage is that you delivered the money to an individual in Detroit, who said that he was going to turn it over to an individual in the Customs Service, is that right?

Mr. KALISH: Yes, sir.

Senator NUNN: Or more?

Mr. KALISH: One individual in the Customs Service who would be on duty at the time the containers arrived into the port of New York.

Senator NUNN: You do not personally know whether that ever occurred?

Mr. KALISH: No, sir, I do not.

Senator NUNN: As far as you know, that individual could have been keeping the money and just telling you a lie?

Mr. KALISH: Yes, sir. That is possible.

Mr. BUFFONE: Senator Nunn, with your indulgence.

[Pause.]

Mr. BUFFONE: Thank you, Senator.

Senator NUNN: How about other individuals in the United States or any other State or local Government? Did you on any occasion involve such individuals in payoffs?

Mr. KALISH: No, sir, not in the United States.

Senator NUNN: You mentioned in your testimony, that you were planning to send a large marijuana shipment up the Mississippi River on a barge. Is that right?

Mr. KALISH: That is correct, Senator.

Senator NUNN: Did you, in fact, carryout that operation?

Appendix 2

Mr. KALISH: No sir. I was arrested prior to the actual importation.

Senator NUNN: Were you involved in marijuana exclusively, or did you import other drugs?

Mr. KALISH: No, sir. I was associated with one shipment of cocaine from Colombia into the United States. That was a 1,000 kilogram importation into the State of Louisiana. The shipment was with some individuals in Medellin, Colombia. I had a peripheral role in the affair, although I was instrumental in making the introductions.

Senator NUNN: That was on one or two occasions?

Mr. KALISH: One actual importation, Senator.

Senator NUNN: Would you give us an estimate of how many shipments of marijuana you brought into the United States?

Mr. KALISH: Fifteen, 20 large shipments of marijuana.

Senator NUNN: Would you give us an estimate of the amount of money you derived from such illegal narcotic activity over your career?

Mr. KALISH: Approximately $20, $25 million.

Senator NUNN: Were you the top man in your organization, or was somebody above you?

Mr. KALISH: Upon my arrest in 1984, I was the top man in my organization. Prior to that, there were other individuals who had seniority in the organization, who certainly had more money than I had, and had certainly been more successful in the business than I was.

Senator NUNN: What was the situation? Had they retired and you had taken over?

Mr. KALISH: There were disagreements, as there usually are in these types of organizations. There were arguments over the profits that were realized from different importations. Our particular organization consisted of three separate groups, which came together in late 1981. There was a group of individuals from the Detroit, Michigan, area who were responsible for the distribution of the marijuana. There was a group of individuals from Texas who I was associated with, who specialized primarily in the off-loading and the logistics of the actual importation. Then there was the Leigh Ritch group from the Tampa, Florida, area who maintained the contacts with the Cayman Islands, the Colombians, and also assisted in the distribution of the marijuana.

Senator NUNN: In effect, by the time you were arrested, you were in charge of all three groups?

Mr. KALISH: Yes, sir, that is correct.

Senator NUNN: How many people were involved in each group?

Mr. KALISH: Approximately 50 to 60 people in each group. At the time of my arrest, there were approximately 180 people working for the organization.

Senator NUNN: Before you were the head man, how many people were above you in the organization?

Mr. KALISH: Two.

Senator NUNN: Have you given their names to Federal officials?

Mr. KALISH: Yes, sir, I have.

Senator NUNN: You have cooperated fully on that?

Mr. KALISH: Yes, sir, I have.

Senator NUNN: I will refrain from asking additional questions regarding those individuals, since I understand there are pending investigations on that subject. You have had a lot of experience in narcotics trafficking. Were you also a user?

Mr. KALISH: Yes, sir. I used marijuana daily for many years.

Senator NUNN: Do you consider your use of marijuana to have been addictive or simply a habit?

Appendix 2

Mr. KALISH: It was simply a habit, Senator.
Senator NUNN: Do you consider marijuana addictive?
Mr. KALISH: No, sir, I do not.
Senator NUNN: Do you consider it harmful?
Mr. KALISH: Yes, sir, I do.
Senator NUNN: In what way?
Mr. KALISH: Senator, I believe that any drug can be harmful; in particular, marijuana causes the individual to lack the drive he needs to accomplish his goals in life. I think the biggest harm that comes from the use of marijuana is the use of the drug by younger children in our country today. I have been incarcerated for 43 months now, and for the last 19 months I have served this time in the county jails across the United States. In these county jails, I see people that come directly from the street that have destroyed their lives from the use of drugs. Although it may not be specifically marijuana, marijuana has certainly led to their downfall. I feel a great deal of remorse and responsibility for my crimes. I have done my best, and this is one step, in repaying my debt to society. I think that the drug problem is a serious problem in this country, and I have many thoughts on how to deal with it.
Senator NUNN: Well, that is the next question. Since you have observed U.S. law enforcement efforts from the other side of the fence, what do you think of them?
Mr. KALISH: Well, I think that you have made great steps in the right direction over the past couple of years, with the legislation that has been passed.
Senator NUNN: Which legislation in particular?
Mr. KALISH: I think that the Anti-Drug Abuse Act of 1986 will begin to show significant results in the very near future.

Appendix 2

Senator NUNN: Because of what features, penalties?

Mr. KALISH: Because of the increased moneys allocated to the U.S. Customs Service, to the Drug Enforcement Administration, and the increased penalties. I believe that you must trace the money, Senator. The money is the reason that we all become involved in this business. I believe that if you could eliminate Panama as a secure banking haven for people involved in the drug business, I think that you would take away one of their major tools that assists them in their importation of drugs into the United States. I believe the problem of drugs in this country, Senator, is a result of the demand for these drugs in the United States. I believe that as long as there is a demand in this country for marijuana, for cocaine, and for other drugs, there will always be these Colombians and these Americans that are willing to supply those drugs. The monies are just too great.

Senator NUNN: Are you saying that one of the primary focuses of governmental efforts in combating drugs should be to try to get the demand down and educate the American people?

Mr. KALISH: Absolutely, Senator. I believe that sound drug awareness programs are the key to stopping the drug problem in this country. It's very important that the children of this country realize the dangers that they're facing, and realize that drugs will eventually destroy their lives.

Senator NUNN: Did you realize this while you were selling drugs?

Mr. KALISH: No, sir, I didn't. As I said, I was involved in drug trafficking at a very high level. I was insulated from the events surrounding me. I did not see what was happening to people in this country. When I

Appendix 2

was arrested in 1984, the problems weren't nearly as severe as they are today.

Senator NUNN: You think the drug problem has gotten worse?

Mr. KALISH: Yes, sir, much worse.

Senator NUNN: Is it worse for marijuana, cocaine or heroin, or all three? For which drugs have we seen an increase in usage?

Mr. KALISH: Specifically cocaine, Senator. Specifically crack cocaine.

Senator NUNN: What do you consider to be the most dangerous drugs now being used widely?

Mr. KALISH: Cocaine.

Senator NUNN: Why?

Mr. KALISH: Because it is destroying an entire generation of youth in this country.

Senator NUNN: Thank you, Senator Roth?

Senator ROTH: Could I just ask one quick question based on what Senator Nunn has just elicited from you? Is it true that if we could stop money laundering, that would be a major blow in the drug trafficking?

Mr. KALISH: Absolutely, Senator. Without the accessibility of the banks, and the ability for us to use these banks to launder these monies back for the purchase of our equipment in our operations, back for the purchase of our homes and our jets, it would cripple us terribly.

Senator NUNN: Senator Roth, maybe we better take a brief recess now. We've got a vote on, so let's take about a 10-minute recess.

[Recess.]

Senator NUNN: We will come to order. Senator Roth?

Senator ROTH: Thank you, Mr. Chairman. Mr. Kalish, now you have testified that during your first

Appendix 2

meeting with Noriega, you made it very clear that you had lots of money. Did you say how much?

Mr. BUFFONE: Mr. Roth, with your indulgence, Mr. Kalish would like to amplify one of his answers that he gave as you were leaving for the vote, if we could come back to that question?

Senator ROTH: Yes, that would be fine.

Mr. KALISH: I would like to address the issue briefly on your question of how to help interdict the drugs flowing into the United States. I failed to mention that we as drug smugglers always knew that we outnumbered the U.S. authorities. I believe that the U.S. Customs Service and the Drug Enforcement Administration can never, at their level of agents in the field today, stop us from our drug trafficking. I also wanted to clarify the issue of my organization. The organization I was associated with was directed by three individuals. Certainly, Michael Vogel and Leigh Ritch, who were my partners in the organization, exerted at least as much authority over our operations as I did.

Senator ROTH: Let me go to your first comment, because it's a matter that concerns me, that is, how do we get enough agents and other personnel to effectively attack the drug problem. Now, you've talked in your own specific case of huge amounts of money. But that's merely a small pebble, isn't it, of the total amount available to those involved in drug smuggling? Is there any way that government, even if it spent billions, would begin to meet the kind of resources available to the drug smuggling people?

Mr. KALISH: Senator, I believe that if they directed their efforts in different areas; for instance, in the tracing of wire transfers into the United States; I know that there are hundreds of thousands of wire transfers, but there aren't hundreds of thousands of wire transfers

Appendix 2

from the country of Panama; I believe that if there were more agents in the field to investigate the cases that are before them, they would be able to successfully prosecute more cases. It is just impossible and I have realized this since I have begun to cooperate with the authorities that there just are not enough agents to investigate all the leads, even the leads that I have given the authorities.

Senator ROTH: I would like to go back to a question that I raised previously and that is, money laundering. Do you believe that the money laundering operations is an area that would be good to concentrate on in order to effectively cripple drug smuggling?

Mr. KALISH: Yes, sir, absolutely. If you take the profit out of the drug trade, there won't be those to follow in my footsteps.

Senator ROTH: Let me go back to my earlier question of your first meeting with Noriega. Did you have a well... skip that for a moment, because I think those questions were asked by the Chairman...did you have a fixed arrangement as far as money is concerned with Noriega? If so, what was it?

Mr. KALISH: Yes, sir, in regards to the transshipment of the containers of marijuana through Panama, the agreement was: $4 million, to be paid for the transshipment; $1 million in advance, $3 million upon the completion of the operation. In addition, all the proceeds from this operation would be returned to Panama, and these proceeds would be laundered through the Panamanian banks.

Senator ROTH: Now, you were told to bring at least $2 million for your first meeting in Panama. Who so instructed you?

Mr. KALISH: I was instructed by an individual in the South Florida area who is currently assisting this investigation. Senator, I don't know if I should mention this individual's name at this time.

Senator ROTH: Well, we won't insist on that. But let me go back to this. How much did you actually pay Noriega of the promised $4 million, or where he asked $4 million?

Mr. KALISH: Yes, sir. I paid General Noriega $250,000 as the first payment of the $1 million payment that I had agreed to pay General Noriega, Cesar Rodriguez, and Enrique Pretel, for their assistance in Panama.

Senator ROTH: Now, I understand you deposited $2 million of your money in a bank in Panama on your first visit there. The clerk will show you a deposit slip dated September 23rd. Is that where you put the money?

Mr. KALISH: Yes, sir, that's correct.

Senator ROTH: You mentioned that during your time in Panama, you acquired three passports. How difficult were three passports to come by, particularly the diplomatic one?

Mr. KALISH: They were no trouble at all, Senator. I acquired each of the passports at different times.

Senator ROTH: Why was it no trouble at all? Isn't it normally pretty difficult to get several passports?

Mr. KALISH: Yes, sir, it is, but not when the military ruler of the country is authorizing you to receive these passports.

Senator ROTH: So you're saying that Noriega played a role? What was his role in this?

Mr. KALISH: He approved of the passports. I specifically spoke to General Noriega in regards to the diplomatic passport. I told him that I was concerned that I wanted to be an accredited diplomat at some point while I was living in Panama. And prior to the purchase

Appendix 2

of this passport, I wanted to know that it would be authentic.

Senator ROTH: How much did you pay for the passports?

Mr. KALISH: Excuse me, Senator?

Senator ROTH: Did you pay anything for the passports?

Mr. KALISH: Yes, sir, I did. For the first passport I obtained, I paid $25,000. For the diplomatic passport that I obtained, I paid $60,000.

Senator ROTH: Who did you pay the sums to?

Mr. KALISH: To Cesar Rodriguez.

Senator ROTH: Now, we have a document here of your accounting sheets which show a $60,000 payment listed as passport. The clerk, I think, has given you a copy. Does that reflect your payment for the diplomatic passport?

Mr. KALISH: Yes, sir, that reflects the payment I made to Cesar Rodriguez for the diplomatic passport.

Senator ROTH: When were these sheets made and how were they obtained by the U.S. authorities?

Mr. KALISH: As I testified to earlier, Senator, these sheets were found in the shipment that was made to United States Customs pursuant to my plea bargain agreement. I had an entire container of furniture and office equipment, filing cabinets, and so forth delivered to the United States. U.S. Customs received this container and found these documents.

Senator ROTH: What was the need for the passports?

Mr. KALISH: Senator, I was always looking for new forms of identification. I had initially approached Cesar Rodriguez in an effort to obtain a passport in the assumed name of Frank William Brown. I was travelling extensively in Columbia and several other countries that required a passport for travel. I did not

Appendix 2

wish to travel under my own name. I did not have a passport in my own name. Therefore, I acquired the Panamanian passport.

Senator ROTH: Now, I'd like to turn for a moment to the Lear jet that you and your partner purchased in the United States. Was this Lear jet registered as N39292?

Mr. KALISH: Yes, sir, that's correct.

Senator ROTH: Now, we have a Department of Transportation document which shows Lear jet N39292 as being owned by Personal Jet Management Leasing, Inc. Is that one of your companies?

Mr. KALISH: No, sir, the company belongs to an individual in Ft. Lauderdale. The company was created upon my direction for the purchase of this aircraft.

Senator ROTH: Why did you have the company set up by this individual? What was the purpose of that?

Mr. KALISH: The purpose of it was to hide the money that actually purchased the aircraft. We wanted to insulate ourselves from any possible forfeiture to the United States Government of this aircraft if in fact they ever realized that it was owned by drug smugglers. There were attorneys hired in the Cayman Islands that negotiated with attorneys in the Florida area. They incorporated an additional company in the Cayman Islands named Jet Finance. Jet Finance became the lien holder of this aircraft, although it was owned and operated by Personal Jet Management & Leasing; the actual lien holder was Jet Finance of the Cayman Islands. Later on, I incorporated an additional company in Panama called Jet Finance of Panama, and had the lien transferred to the Panamanian corporation.

Senator ROTH: So all three of these corporations were actually involved? I think we have documents referring to them, but they were all involved in your operation?

Appendix 2

Mr. KALISH: Yes, sir, they are. I used all these corporations in an effort to conceal the true ownership of the aircraft.

Senator ROTH: Was there any other reason for setting them up in this way?

Mr. KALISH: To prevent the U.S. authorities from seizing the jet at any time.

Senator ROTH: Now, you also said you bought airplanes for Noriega. Why would he need you to buy airplanes for him? Why didn't he just buy them himself with government funds?

Mr. KALISH: Senator, Panama is a very small country, and the Forces for Defense have a very limited budget. Noriega knew that I had millions of dollars in Panama that I was willing to invest, and he knew that I would be favorable toward investing these monies at a high rate of return. He approached me in regards to the 727/100 jet aircraft. He approached me and asked if I would negotiate with a company in Panama City, which I did.

Senator ROTH: Now, what planes did you actually buy or help finance for him?

Mr. KALISH: As I just stated, the 727/100 aircraft. I made a $500,000 down payment on this aircraft. I believe there's a check reflecting that payment. I also assisted in obtaining the financing for this aircraft from the company in Panama City. I also purchased an executive helicopter for General Noriega with my own funds, as the letter of credit reflects. My cash outlay was $1,995,000, although I immediately recovered $100,000. I also gave to the General, after my arrest, a helicopter that had been seized at the cocaine lab in the Panamanian jungle. Due to my assistance in that particular affair, the Medellin Cartel had given to me an Aero Commander 1000, valued at $1 million. They also gave me the helicopter that the Panamanian

Government had seized. And they also gave me a substantial amount of cash. The cash came from the monies that I recovered from the bribes to Colonel Melo and other businessmen in Panama City.

Senator ROTH: Were any kickbacks involved in these transactions?

Mr. KALISH: Yes, sir, in all of the transactions, as I've said. In particular, on the 727/100 aircraft, after I made the $500,000 down-payment, I was given the bill of sale and title to a Panamanian turboprop aircraft, a Lockheed Electra. I was given this aircraft. I was told to sell the aircraft in Ft. Lauderdale, and take the proceeds of this aircraft and repay my $500,000 deposit, and divide the rest of the monies with General Noriega and myself.

Senator ROTH: Now, we have a document here showing payment from your account to Aeronautics and Astronautics for $500,000. Is this related to the purchase of the first 727?

Mr. KALISH: Yes, sir, that's a check I wrote on my personal account.

Senator ROTH: Was there a kickback involved in that, and from whom?

Mr. KALISH: Actually, the kickback was, I was given title to a Lockheed Electra aircraft valued at $1 million.

Senator ROTH: We have a document here showing a sale of a Lockheed Electra by the Panama Defense Forces to a Personal Jet Management Leasing, Inc. Is this the same Lockheed Electra you were given in return for purchasing a plane for Noriega?

Mr. KALISH: Yes, sir, it is.

Senator ROTH: I want to make certain the record is clear on this. The chart shows a copy of the irrevocable letter of credit dated December 21st, 1983, from the National Bank of Panama, made out to Exclusive

Service of Panama, to Anglicize it. What is your relationship to this company?

Mr. KALISH: Senator, I incorporated Servicios Exclusivos de Panama myself in Panama. I am sole owner of that corporation, and I hold all shares in that corporation. I believe the shares are presently in the custody of the United States Government.

Senator ROTH: All right, let me again ask you, how did you come by this letter of credit? Would you explain that carefully?

Mr. KALISH: I asked for some type of guarantee.

Senator ROTH: You asked who?

Mr. KALISH: I discussed with General Noriega and Enrique Pretel that, the fact that I would like some sort of guarantee that the forces of defense would continue to make these payments, regardless of whether I was in Panama or not. I discussed it with my banker. My banker instructed me to request an irrevocable letter of credit. Noriega agreed to the terms and instructed the chairman of the National Bank of Panama to issue me an irrevocable letter of credit for that amount.

Senator ROTH: Now, am I correct in my understanding that the payments have continued to be made to you, but not through the letter of credit? You haven't had to draw on that?

Mr. KALISH: No, sir, I haven't had to draw on the letter of credit. The Forces of Defense have continued to make these payments.

Senator ROTH: As you said, they have recently made a payment, which of course was seized by the U.S. Customs.

Mr. KALISH: Senator, these funds are not actually seized. The way this works, the Forces of Defense deliver to my bank in Panama a check each month. The value's determined through a number of ways. I in turn

Appendix 2

take this check and wire it to a U.S. Customs account in the United States.

Senator ROTH: What is the sum of these checks?

Mr. KALISH: At the present they're approximately $36,000 a month.

Senator ROTH: And as I asked you earlier, the payback includes the $300,000? That was the sum of the kickback?

Mr. KALISH: Yes, sir, that's correct.

Senator ROTH: You also mentioned that Noriega used your Lear jet on occasion. Why did he want to use your Lear jet rather than his own in flying to Washington?

Mr. KALISH: Senator, the Lear that I owned and operated was a late model Lear jet. We had spent in excess of $150,000 just in redoing the interior of the aircraft. It was, quite frankly, a very beautiful aircraft. Noriega had nothing like this at his disposal. And I felt it would be prudent to offer this jet to Noriega for his use. He also knew that we kept excellent maintenance records on this aircraft, and he could feel safe flying in it.

Senator ROTH: Now, we have as Exhibit 8 a flight log and Mr. Chairman. I would ask that all these Exhibits, one through nine, be included as part of the record.

Senator NUNN: Without objection, they will be so included.

Senator ROTH: Mr. Kalish, these flight logs show a flight of N39292 from Panama to several destinations, including Washington, D.C. Is that the flight you referred to in your testimony?

Mr. KALISH: Yes, sir, it is.

Senator ROTH: What did Noriega tell you about his alleged meeting with President Reagan?

Appendix 2

Mr. KALISH: Upon General Noriega's return to Omar Torrijos Airport, I was invited to wait for Noriega in the receiving line. He stopped at the receiving line and informed me that he had discussed with President Reagan two issues: One was the fact that the United States wanted Panama to open up its bank for U.S. scrutiny. The second issue was the President wanted Noriega to assist in fighting the communists in Nicaragua. Noriega assured me that he would never open up the banks in Panama.

Senator ROTH: Now, you have no personal knowledge; you're merely repeating what you were told, is that correct?

Mr. KALISH: Yes, sir, I'm merely repeating what General Noriega told me in Panama.

Senator ROTH: Now, you say you paid off Panamanian officials in order to obtain custom seals. Whom did you actually pay?

Mr. KALISH: I paid the head of Aduana, which is Customs in Panama, $180,000 for customs seals for the containers.

Senator ROTH: I'm going to ask one more question, then I think maybe Senator Sasser has some questions he'd like to ask. Did you file customs currency reporting forms before you made that first trip?

Mr. KALISH: No, sir, I never filed customs currency forms.

Senator ROTH: Why not?

Mr. KALISH: Because I was transporting illegal funds, and they would be seized.

Senator NUNN: Senator Sasser?

Senator SASSER: Thank you, Senator Roth Thank you, Mr. Chairman. Mr. Chairman, I have a statement which I would like to have inserted in the record at this point.

Appendix 2

Senator NUNN: Without objection.

Senator SASSER: Mr. Kalish, the airplane that General Noriega flew to Washington, the Lear jet I think you characterized it as a Lear 35, is that correct?

Mr. KALISH: Yes, sir.

Senator SASSER: This is the Lear jet that you had spent so much money refurbishing the interior on. Was this the same Lear that you originally went to Panama in? And that the DEA reported to Panamanian intelligence that you had landed?

Mr. KALISH: No, sir, it was not.

Senator SASSER: So it was a different aircraft?

Mr. KALISH: Yes, sir, it was.

Senator SASSER: To your knowledge, had the Drug Enforcement Agency fingered this Lear 35, so to speak that is, identified it with you?

Mr. KALISH: How did I control the what, Senator? No, sir, they did not.

Senator SASSER: Now, let me just ask you a few questions about money in the operation. I assume that you got involved in the drug trade for the money; is that correct?

Mr. KALISH: Yes, sir, that's correct.

Senator SASSER: And you were amassing so much currency that, according to your statement, it was filling rooms in Tampa?

Mr. KALISH: Yes, sir, that's correct.

Senator SASSER: And so the medium of exchange was currency of course, and it was counted in Tampa. When did you transport the currency to Tampa?

Mr. KALISH: Tampa was a staging area for the transshipment of the monies to the banking havens that we were using. At that time, we were using the Cayman Islands. We encountered several problems over the shipments of such large amounts of money. We, at one particular bank, delivered $12 million in $20 bills

Appendix 2

and the head offices in Nassau refused to accept any more small bills from us. In addition, the Colombians had their own resources for shipping their monies abroad. I was instructed to pay them approximately $25 million in Miami. And therefore, Tampa was a staging area for the shipments of these monies to Miami.

Senator SASSER: Did you bank any of this money in the United States?

Mr. KALISH: No, sir, we did not.

Senator SASSER: In other words, you had no contact, no intercourse, with banking facilities here in the United States of America with regard to the cash that you derived from the sale of drugs?

Mr. KALISH: Senator, it was our decision not to associate with any banks in the United States. The reason being, the monies were too available for forfeiture and seizure by the United States Government. We preferred to ship our monies overseas to where the United States authorities would not have access to it.

Senator SASSER: And so you would transport this money in cash?

Mr. KALISH: Yes, sir, we would; in suitcases; in cartons; different ways.

Senator SASSER: Just as a matter of curiosity, you said that in Tampa rooms were filling up with currency and you were counting the money with money-counting machines but still you couldn't keep track of it. Who counted the money? Employees?

Mr. KALISH: Yes, sir, people that worked for me. It was a very difficult job. It required the wearing of surgical mask and gloves because of the lead content in the monies. It was such a difficult job that we could not count all the money. And we finally stopped counting the money and let the banks count the money upon delivery in the countries that we were laundering our money through.

Appendix 2

Senator SASSER: Well, how did you control theft on the part of the money counters, just as a matter of curiosity?

Mr. KALISH: How did I control the what, Senator?

Senator SASSER: In other words, did the money counters themselves take a slice out of the money?

Mr. KALISH: Yes, sir, you're absolutely correct. There's not a great many people that I would place with $35 million and feel comfortable. However...

Senator SASSER: In cash.

Mr. KALISH: In fact. However, the individuals that were responsible for counting this money were well connected with the organization. They had been friends of mine since high school. And I trusted them implicitly.

Senator SASSER: But even if these friends leaked off $50,000 or $100,000, you hardly would have missed it with the currency that was coming through there, would you?

Mr. KALISH: I wouldn't have missed it.

Senator SASSER: Let me, also as a matter of interest, Mr. Kalish, how did you get into this business of selling marijuana?

Mr. KALISH: Senator; that might take hours for me to explain. It began at a very early age.

Senator SASSER: In high school?

Mr. KALISH: Yes, sir, early high school.

Senator SASSER: Were you a user of marijuana in high school?

Mr. KALISH: Yes, sir, I was.

Senator SASSER: And then did you procure marijuana to sell to your fellow students in high school?

Mr. KALISH: Yes, sir, I did.

Senator SASSER: Was that the beginning of your trading and trafficking in drugs, selling marijuana to fellow students?

Appendix 2

Mr. KALISH: Yes, sir, that's correct.

Senator SASSER: Did you set up a ring in high school, then, for procuring and selling marijuana?

Mr. KALISH: No, sir, I did not. It was not nearly that extensive. At the time I was in high school, I was living on my own and supporting myself; and there was not a ring as such. It was simply selling small amounts of marijuana to feed myself, and support myself while I went through school.

Senator SASSER: But apparently when you branched out and got into it in a big way, you took some of your high school associates with you?

Mr. KALISH: Yes, sir, many of them.

Senator SASSER: How did you entice them to do the business? Did it take much enticement?

Mr. KALISH: No, sir, it did not. They all felt the way I did. All of our friends used marijuana. We had never seen any adverse effects from using that marijuana. They were just as interested in earning the large amounts of money from trafficking in the drug as I was.

Senator SASSER: Did you see anything wrong at that time in trading and trafficking in marijuana?

Mr. KALISH: No, sir, not at that time. But there was a point in my life when I realized.

Senator SASSER: And what brought you to that realization? Was it being arrested and incarcerated?

Mr. KALISH: No, sir, it was when I began dealing with a group of smugglers from the Miami area. They were extremely violent people. They were motivated strictly by greed. They had a very low value for human life. And I realized that whatever social redeeming value I thought my business had at the time, it was just a fantasy of my own, and I was incorrect in assuming such things. But I was so involved and so committed at

Appendix 2

that point, I was never able to extract myself from the business.

Shortly thereafter, I was arrested for a very large amount of marijuana. I played a very insignificant role in the organization at this time. I was simply an off-loader. I assisted in the unloading of the marijuana. However, I was portrayed as somebody much more significant. I depended on this organization to provide me with my attorneys' fees, to pretty much care for me. And therefore, I was obligated to continue to work for this organization.

Senator NUNN: Senator Sasser, would you yield for just a moment?

Senator SASSER: Yes, I'd be glad to.

Senator NUNN: I thought a few minutes ago, Mr. Kalish, you said that when you were arrested you were the top man in the whole organization and you had 180 people working for you.

Mr. KALISH: Senator, this is an arrest in 1978-1979, excuse me, in December. My arrest in Tampa was in July of 1984.

Senator NUNN: Oh, so at that time you were the head man?

Mr. KALISH: Yes, sir.

Senator NUNN: With Senator Sasser you were referring to a 1978 arrest?

Mr. KALISH: Yes, sir, this is an earlier time in my life. I was arrested several times for drug importations.

Senator NUNN: Thank you.

Senator SASSER: Mr. Kalish, after you were arrested for the first or second time, did it occur to you that you ought to get out of this business?

Mr. KALISH: Yes, sir, I considered it. However, I never had the courage or the resolve to do so.

Senator SASSER: You say you never had the courage. Were you afraid to get out of the business?

Appendix 2

Mr. KALISH: Not necessarily afraid. I wasn't in fear for my life at that point. I just did not know what I would do. I expected a lengthy incarceration if I didn't have the best attorneys that money could provide. And I just didn't get out of the business.

Senator SASSER: All right. Well, now, what do you think is going to happen to you now, Mr. Kalish, when and if you ever get out of the penitentiary? Is the life expectancy pretty short for those who talk about what goes on in the drug trafficking business?

Mr. KALISH: Yes, sir, by my testifying here today, I place my wife and my family and myself in great jeopardy. I'm fully aware of that. But I have to start making my amends to society for the crimes I've committed. I expect to spend a great deal of time in prison, Senator. I have many more years to spend in prison. And believe me, spending time in prison as a cooperating witness is certainly the hardest time you can spend in prison. But I have plans for my future. I have a wonderful wife and a very nice family. And I expect to live a long life.

Senator SASSER: Now, let me take you back if I may to the occasion when you chartered a tow boat, a barge, to move a massive quantity of marijuana up the Mississippi. How far did you get with that scheme?

Mr. KALISH: First of all, Senator, I did not charter it. I actually purchased a barge in Louisiana, a fuel barge, an ocean-going fuel barge. I purchased an ocean-going tug, also. I purchased one million pounds of marijuana in Baranquilla, Colombia. The marijuana was actually delivered to Baranquilla.

Senator SASSER: Did you have any problem purchasing that marijuana?

Mr. KALISH: Yes, sir.

Senator SASSER: Because of the quantity?

Appendix 2

Mr. KALISH: Because of the size of the operation in Baranquilla there. That's quite a large amount of marijuana, although the Colombian that I was associated with there in Baranquilla was well known for being able to deliver such large shipments. In this operation, part of the marijuana was indeed loaded on this barge. The off-load sites, the sites where we were actually going to unload the marijuana, had already been arranged. The operation was literally hours away from beginning at the time of my arrest in Tampa in July 1984.

Mr. BUFFONE: Senator, I might add that much of that is the subject of ongoing grand jury investigation.

Senator SASSER: Well, counselor, let me proceed as far as I can. And if I start treading on thin ice here, you'll admonish us and we'll draw back. Mr. Kalish, what was the destination of this marijuana you were moving up the Mississippi or intended to move?

Mr. KALISH: The State of Missouri, Senator, not far from the St. Louis area.

Senator SASSER: And was that to be a distribution point for other areas in the country?

Mr. KALISH: Yes.

Senator SASSER: That's simply the point of unloading?

Mr. KALISH: Yes, sir. Primarily the northeast United States, the major cities. New York, Chicago, Detroit. Although there was a large part of it going to the West Coast.

Senator SASSER: How far did you get with this scheme?

Mr. KALISH: As I said a moment ago, the marijuana was being loaded on to the barge at the time of my arrest.

Senator SASSER: In Colombia.

Appendix 2

Mr. KALISH: In Colombia. After my arrest, I instructed, actually requested that my partners not continue in the operation, because I realized that we had been under continual surveillance by the FBI and Drug Enforcement Administration and I thought they would be taking a great risk if they pursued this operation.

Senator SASSER: Now, in the latter stages of your career, you also got involved in the cocaine business; is that correct?

Mr. KALISH: Yes, sir.

Senator SASSER: And the principal source of supply for the cocaine was also Colombia?

Mr. KALISH: Yes, sir. The marijuana came from Baranquilla, Colombia. The Medellin Cartel, which is a city in Medellin, Colombia, were the people primarily responsible for the cocaine that I was associated with.

Senator SASSER: Were there any two countries involved in the trading and trafficking and drugs that you're aware of other than Colombia and Panama?

Mr. KALISH: Senator, there's officials in many, many countries involved in the trafficking of drugs; or I should say, the facilitating of the trafficking of drugs. Senator, at one time, and I can name several countries, Jamaica, the Bahamas, Mexico, Honduras, Belize, Panama, Colombia, all those countries were, had officials that we were connected to at one time or another, accepting our monies for the landing of aircraft, safe harbors of ships, transshipment of monies.

Senator SASSER: There have been some allegations that some in the Sandanista government in Nicaragua are involved in dealing the drug trade. Do you have any personal knowledge as to whether or not that's true?

Mr. KALISH: Yes, sir, I was told by an individual associated with the Medellin Cartel that they had set up

Appendix 2

the largest cocaine manufacturing lab in the world in Nicaragua.

Senator SASSER: And where was that cocaine manufacturing plant in Nicaragua, do you know?

Mr. KALISH: No, sir, I don't. I don't have firsthand knowledge of it.

Senator SASSER: Did you hear any accusations the so-called contra forces being involved in the distribution or manufacture of drugs at all?

Mr. KALISH: No, sir, I did not.

Senator SASSER: And when did you hear these allegations about Nicaraguans?

Mr. KALISH: I heard them as a result of the assistance I provided the Colombians in recovering the bribes that they had paid for the safety and protection in operating their cocaine lab in Panama. I secured the release of some of their equipment; the release of several Colombians in custody; and developed a close association with these people. And after a brief period of time they informed me it was their feeling that setting up the cocaine lab in Nicaragua was a terrible idea, and that was how I came to hear that information.

Senator SASSER: They said setting up a cocaine lab in Nicaragua was a terrible idea?

Mr. KALISH: Yes, sir. They felt that Nicaragua was under intense scrutiny by the United States, and they felt that it was not a good idea to manufacture cocaine in a country that's in such turmoil.

Senator SASSER: Did the Colombians feel that they could do business with the present government of Nicaragua?

Mr. KALISH: Senator, all I can say is I was not told...

Senator SASSER: To your knowledge, just what you know of your own knowledge.

Appendix 2

Mr. KALISH: Yes, sir, certain officials in that government.

Senator SASSER: Did they name any of those officials?

Mr. KALISH: No, sir, not of my own personal knowledge, I cannot say.

Senator SASSER: I have no further questions.

Senator ROTH: Okay, thank you.

Senator SASSER: I have just a very few additional questions. In answer to the Chairman, you said you headed your organization when you were arrested the final time. What was your relationship with the Colombia groups that supply the marijuana? You were not a part of a family in any way, were you?

Mr. KALISH: No, sir, I was not. Initially, my partner, Leigh Ritch, was connected to a particular individual in Colombia. This gentleman headed up his organization. I was introduced to the Colombian through my partner, Leigh Ritch. The Panamanian aspect of our organization was my primary concern, and I had most of my dealings with the Panamanians. However, in the United States my partner in Detroit headed up the U.S. end of the operation.

Senator ROTH: Let me ask you this question. Back when you first went down to Panama, you had a bundle of money. Why somewhere along the line didn't you just decide to keep that cash you had and quit the whole thing? Why didn't you take all this cash and retire?

Mr. KALISH: Senator, I was a fugitive from the United States at the time. At that time I did not expect to live a very long life, and there was literally nothing that I could involve myself in aside from marijuana trafficking that would provide me with the safety and security that I needed.

Senator ROTH: Was one of the reasons that Panama was key because of their bank secrecy laws? Was that a critical factor in making that a haven?

Mr. KALISH: Yes, sir, it was, in addition to the fact that the military government of Panama would assist us in our operations, and have been assisting people like me for years. In my dealings with the individual in Baranquilla, Colombia, he had informed me that he himself had paid monies to General Noriega in the early 1980s for his assistance.

Senator ROTH: Let me ask you the question another way. If Panama did away with its secrecy in banking laws that enabled dummy corporations to be created quickly as well as maintain the secrecy of deposits, would that be a major blow to the laundering of money in Panama?

Mr. KALISH: There's no question about it, Senator.

Senator ROTH: That's all the questions I have, Mr. Chairman.

Senator NUNN: Mr. Kalish, how did you bring marijuana into this country? What was the usual method—boat, plane?

Mr. KALISH: Senator, I've imported marijuana through the use of airplanes, trucks, by boat. The larger importations were accomplished by the use of different seagoing vessels. In one particular importation in Louisiana, we used an ocean-going tug and barge. On numerous occasions we used fishing vessels, whether they be shrimp vessels or some other sort of vessel. Sometimes we used offshore supply vessels that are used to service the drilling rigs off the coast of the United States. Probably several other kinds also.

Senator NUNN: Were you operating when Federal authorities were conducting an intensive effort around the Miami-South Florida area?

Appendix 2

Mr. KALISH: Yes, sir, we were. One time I was actually at the airport when I believe our Vice President had flown into Miami.

Senator NUNN: Were you involved in narcotics at that time?

Mr. KALISH: Yes, sir, I was, quite extensively.

Senator NUNN: How about that trip? Were you involved at the airport in a smuggling operation?

Mr. KALISH: I didn't have drugs on me at that particular time, although I was certainly actively engaged in importation.

Senator NUNN: What effect did the Federal crackdown in South Florida have on your operation?

Mr. KALISH: Well, I was arrested in July 1984.

Senator NUNN: So, you were among those caught in that operation?

Mr. KALISH: Yes, sir, I would think so.

Senator NUNN: Did you shift any of your operations elsewhere during that time, or did you continue to import drugs into South Florida?

Mr. KALISH: We never actually imported drugs into South Florida. We were aware of the major concentration of agents and effort in South Florida. Therefore, we certainly never considered actually importing drugs into South Florida. We always used remote rural areas, Louisiana, Mississippi, North Carolina, and South Carolina.

Senator NUNN: That implies airplanes, right?

Mr. KALISH: Airplanes and seagoing vessels. They all have coastlines, extensive coastlines.

Senator NUNN: Did most drug smugglers shift elsewhere when Federal authorities conducted intensive operations such as the one on South Florida?

Mr. KALISH: Absolutely. Whenever there was a concentration of personnel in an area there was a shift.

Appendix 2

Senator NUNN: In your operations, did you use sophisticated technology—radios, computers, fast planes, that kind of thing?

Mr. KALISH: Yes, sir, we had the best that money could buy, the best electronics, the best detection equipment.

Senator NUNN: Tell us a little bit about that.

Mr. KALISH: Well, all our vessels were equipped with satellite navigation. We had the finest radio equipment we could buy. We had the best scanners we could buy. We monitored all the police frequencies quite extensively. I believe the FBI just began to scramble their calls just recently. Prior to that they didn't have the money, I believe, to scramble their radio traffic.

Senator NUNN: So you were intercepting FBI and other law enforcement communications?

Mr. KALISH: Yes, sir. We spent months setting up our security nets in an area that we were attempting an importation in. We literally knew all movements.

Senator NUNN: All movements by law enforcement?

Mr. KALISH: Yes, sir.

Senator NUNN: How about the Coast Guard?

Mr. KALISH: We were not primarily concerned with Coast Guard, although we watched their stations. We were not concerned with Coast Guard interdicting our vessels.

Senator NUNN: Why?

Mr. KALISH: Because we had taken steps to screen ourselves from the Coast Guard, with refrigeration equipment installed on our fishing vessels to prevent the infrared photographic detection from their over-flights. We always fit into a profile that would not, that would not raise any eyebrows.

Appendix 2

Senator NUNN: Did you study profiles developed by Federal law enforcement agencies?

Mr. KALISH: Oh, I didn't study it. But I had been informed of it.

Senator NUNN: In terms of both Federal and State drug interdiction efforts, you're basically saying that your equipment and so forth were more sophisticated than that possessed by the law enforcement people who were trying to apprehend you. Is that right?

Mr. KALISH: I don't know that it's more sophisticated. It's just that there were so many more of us, and so few of them. It was just impossible, given the manpower and the resources that they had available at that time, for them to stop us.

Senator NUNN: Regarding Federal law enforcement efforts against narcotics trafficking, do you believe that additional resources are essential?

Mr. KALISH: Yes, sir, I do.

Senator NUNN: Are we going to get a real payoff on those additional resources, or is it just a never-ending spiral? Can we really succeed in stopping or greatly reducing the flow of drug traffic by interdiction?

Mr. KALISH: I think you have already begun to greatly reduce the introduction of marijuana into this country. I can't say that in regards to the cocaine coming into this country today.

Senator NUNN: Is that because marijuana comes in such large bulk shipments, and so forth?

Mr. KALISH: Yes, sir, it's much more difficult to transport and much easier to detect. As far as the never-ending funding for law enforcement, I believe that if the monies are directed in the proper ways, I think that you will have a great deal of success. However, as I stated earlier, I am a firm believer that the education programs and the rehabilitation centers are the most important tool in deterring drug use in this country.

Appendix 2

Senator NUNN: What's your age?
Mr. KALISH: 35 years old.
Senator NUNN: Do you have children?
Mr. KALISH: No, sir, I do not.
Senator NUNN: How old were you when you started using marijuana?
Mr. KALISH: 15 years old.
Senator NUNN: Did you ever use cocaine?
Mr. KALISH: Yes, sir, I did.
Senator NUNN: What age were you then?
Mr. KALISH: 19, 20 years old.
Senator NUNN: Do you have any message you'd like to give to the young people of America?
Mr. KALISH: Yes, sir, I do. I think they need to think before they use these drugs. I think they need to realize, at least try to understand how damaging these drugs can be, and what can happen to them if they use these drugs. The trouble is, Senator, children don't realize what they're doing when they use these drugs. And after they've become enmeshed in the entire drug scene, they're so deep that they can't extract themselves from it.
Senator NUNN: Is that basically the pattern of your life?
Mr. KALISH: Yes, sir, it is.

AUTHOR'S NOTES

While serving as a federal prosecutor, I realized the Kalish-Ritch-Vogel smuggling organization was unique, as it had achieved not only financial success, but had also impacted our Government's foreign policy. I believe this case goes well beyond the story of how the conspirators were arrested. Over the years, I held onto a variety of reports by federal or state agents, correspondence, and articles on facets of the case, as I knew that this story should be told.

When Les Pendleton and I put this manuscript together, we decided to tell the story through dialogue, even though we were not present for the conversations described. While we may not know the exact words spoken, we do know what happened, thus the speakers must have said something similar to the words we attribute to them. In many instances, we have a report or transcript that quotes the speakers, and in those instances, we have used the words set out on the report or transcript.

As this is a work of non-fiction, the reader has the right to know the source material utilized to support each chapter. That information is set forth in the following notations.

CHAPTER NOTES

Chapter One – Abandoned Lady
Documented by DEA Report of Investigation (DEA-A) by Special Agent Edward R. Hinchman dated 7/12/82. Copy in author's possession.

Chapter Two – Federal Eyes
Detailed information regarding the items seized, comes from N.C. State Bureau of Investigation Report by Special Agent Fred McKinney dated 8/5/82 and 8/6/82 - copy in author's possession.

Chapter Three – The Three Meet
The meeting described in this chapter is detailed in interviews by the FBI with witnesses George Sharer and Clinton Anderson. Copies of the Reports of Investigation (FBI 302) are in the author's possession.

Chapter Four – Early Confidence and Easy Money
Interviews with numerous witnesses, principally Sharer and Anderson mentioned above, document the events set forth in this chapter. These events are also described by Steven Kalish in his own interviews. Additionally, a Detroit newspaper series summarizes all of these events. Again, copies are in the author's possession.

Chapter Five – Second Swing
The main smuggling events are recounted by several witnesses, including those listed above. Doc McGhee's participation is described in an article from 6/91 edition of GQ entitled "The Outlaw Past of Doc McGhee" by Fred Goodman.

Chapter Six – The Green, Green Grass

Chapter Seven – Unleashing the *Bulldog*

Chapter Eight – Connecting the Dots
The same source information described earlier (Anderson, Kalish, Sharer interviews) summarize the events described in these chapters.

Chapter Nine – Bank of Noriega

Chapter Ten – General Ecstatic

Chapter Eleven – In Love in Panama
Kalish himself describes most of these events in his statements to the FBI as well as in his testimony to the U.S. Senate set out in the Appendix. Kalish testified in great detail about those events during Noriega's Miami trial.

Chapter Twelve – Nothing Good Lasts Forever
Clinton Anderson, when interviewed by the FBI, describes the events surrounding his being shot by Larry Garcia and his decision to become a cooperating witness. FBI Special Agent Ned Timmons also describes recruiting Anderson in his report. Copies of these reports are in the author's possession.

Chapter Thirteen – Infiltration
Reports by FBI Special Agent Ned Timmons, including some transcripts of taped conversations, document the undercover investigation conducted on Grand Cayman. Summaries of the tapes and some of the reports are in the author's possession. Interviews with Timmons fill in gaps not covered by the reports.

Chapter Fourteen – Like Ducks on a Pond

Kalish and Anderson interviews, plus Timmons's investigative reports provide the details set out in this chapter. The jurisdiction battles between the various federal prosecution districts were personally participated in by the author and described in this and subsequent chapters. While the author participated in these inter-departmental "turf wars", some correspondence in the author's possession corroborates these events.

Chapter Fifteen – Grabbing the Marbles

Events where the author participated personally are documented by letters in the author's possession, newspaper articles and various investigative reports.

Chapter Sixteen – Playing the Best Hand

Kalish's decision to become a government witness is described in FBI reports and interviews, Noriega's trial testimony, and FBI Senate Hearing testimony. Special Agent Timmons's reports document his continued contact with Leigh Ritch.

Chapter Seventeen – All the King's Horses

FBI arrest reports and summaries describe the arrests of both Ritch and Vogel. The Detroit Free Press article also describes all of the main events, including the arrests.

Certain events that occurred cannot be explained by the author. For instance, when Kalish's lawyers first informed the prosecutors from Tampa and North Carolina that Kalish might have information regarding Noriega, why did Tampa rebuff his offer of cooperation with a plea proposal that provided for punishment that gave him no consideration for his cooperation? Was this an attempt to suppress his information in an effort to allow the CIA to continue using Noriega as a source on Castro?

As a military intelligence officer, the author attended a then-classified briefing on Latin America conducted by a CIA regional analyst. After the briefing, I approached the speaker and asked the CIA briefer if the Agency had information that Noriega was involved with drug trafficking.

The briefer replied that some Panamanians and Columbians had made such allegations for purely political reasons, but the CIA had no reason to believe that was the case. This was well after Kalish had been interviewed by the FBI. Did they not know of Kalish's information or were they ignoring it?

The CIA's utilization of Noriega as a source is beyond the scope of the author's ability to observe. Yet there were strange, abnormal actions taken regarding Kalish's allegations. His allegations would not have been followed up on, absent the Camp Lejeune interviews described herein.

Eventually, due to President Reagan's forthright stance, Noriega was eventually indicted and later prosecuted. While the author was not on the trial team (the case was tried in Miami), the information developed as described here was a key part of the government's case, and contributed to his conviction.